RESEARCHING HISTORICAL
SCREEN AUDIENCES

RESEARCHING HISTORICAL
SCREEN AUDIENCES

Edited by Kate Egan, Martin Ian Smith
and Jamie Terrill

EDINBURGH
University Press

Edinburgh University Press is one of the leading university presses in the UK. We publish academic books and journals in our selected subject areas across the humanities and social sciences, combining cutting-edge scholarship with high editorial and production values to produce academic works of lasting importance. For more information visit our website: edinburghuniversitypress.com

© editorial matter and organisation Kate Egan, Martin Ian Smith and Jamie Terrill, 2022
© the chapters their several authors, 2022

Edinburgh University Press Ltd
The Tun – Holyrood Road
12 (2f) Jackson's Entry
Edinburgh EH8 8PJ

Typeset in 10/12.5 pt Sabon
by IDSUK (DataConnection) Ltd

A CIP record for this book is available from the British Library

ISBN 978 1 4744 7781 9 (hardback)
ISBN 978 1 4744 7783 3 (webready PDF)
ISBN 978 1 4744 7784 0 (epub)

The right of Kate Egan, Martin Ian Smith and Jamie Terrill to be identified as editors of this work been asserted in accordance with the Copyright, Designs and Patents Act 1988 and the Copyright and Related Rights Regulations 2003 (SI No. 2498).

CONTENTS

List of Figures vii
Acknowledgements ix
Notes on Contributors x

Introduction 1
Kate Egan, Martin Ian Smith and Jamie Terrill

PART I BEING CREATIVE IN HISTORICAL AUDIENCE RESEARCH: RE-EVALUATING THE FIELD

1. Audience as Palimpsest, or the Structures of Cinematic Feeling: On Historical Film Audience Research and Cinema's Imaginative Power 17
   Daniel Biltereyst

2. From Cinema Culture to Cinema Memory: A Conceptual and Methodological Trajectory 34
   Annette Kuhn

3. Constructing Cinema Audience Histories: Methodological Choices and Challenges 49
   Karina Aveyard

PART II RECONSIDERING NATIONAL AND TRANSNATIONAL CINEMAGOING HISTORIES

4. Cinemas and Cinema Audiences in the 'Third Space' in Warsaw, 1908–1939 65
   Karina Pryt

CONTENTS

5. German Films in Brazil: Immigration, Associations and National Film Culture 86
   Wolfgang Fuhrmann

6. Emotional Communities in the Cinema: Tracing Emotion in Mass Observation Cinema Records, 1937–1950 102
   James Jones

PART III   SHAPING AUDIENCE EXPECTATIONS: CINEMA MANAGERS AND MARKETING STRATEGIES

7. 'Make Your Public Curious': Cinema Management, Film Advertising and Audience Taste in England, c. 1920–c. 1960 123
   Robert James

8. Harry Sanders: Remembering a Life in Cinema Management 146
   Robert Shail

9. *The Yellow Teddybears*: Exploitation as Education 166
   Adrian Smith

PART IV   HOME VIEWING CONTEXTS AND AUDIENCE MEMORIES

10. Archives, Sources and Memories for a History of Early Italian TV Audiences 185
    Damiano Garofalo and Cecilia Penati

11. *The Exorcist* in the Home: Remembering Parental Regulation 203
    Martin Ian Smith

12. Childhood Memories of Horror Films in the Home: Questions, Patterns and Contexts 223
    Kate Egan

Index 239

FIGURES

1.1	Cover of the German movie magazine *Illustrierte Film-Kurier* with Richard Tauber	24
1.2, 1.3	Stills from a Dutch promotional newsreel about the screening of the German feature film *Never Trust a Woman*	25
1.4	Advertising for the Amsterdam premiere of *Never Trust a Woman*	26
4.1	Layer of spatial information visualising location and categorisation of cinemas on a city plan of Warsaw for 1911	73
4.2	Thematic map using census data to visualise the ethnic context of cinema dispersion created for 1911	75
4.3	Layer of spatial information visualising location and categorisation of cinemas according to their size created on a plan of Warsaw for 1922	77
4.4	Layer of spatial information visualising location and categorisation of cinemas according to their size created on a plan of Warsaw for 1936	77
4.5	Thematic map using census data to visualise the ethnic contexts of the cinema dispersion created for 1922	79
4.6	Thematic map using census data to visualise the ethnic contexts of the cinema dispersion created for 1936	79
5.1	Exhibition of the L.D.L.-Film Service at the annual school festivity of the Olinda School in 1936	92

FIGURES

8.1	The Prime Minister is not available	150
8.2	Sanders's art deco programme design for The Lido, Islington	152
8.3	A typical promotional 'wheeze' designed by Harry Sanders for *The Letter*	153
8.4	Sanders campaigns (successfully) to keep the Granada open on Sundays	154
8.5	Typical notebook designs for a publicity campaign	155
8.6	One of Harry Sanders's characteristically inventive playbills	159
9.1	Displays at the premiere of *The Yellow Teddybears*	176
9.2	Dancers dressed as schoolgirls at the premiere of *The Yellow Teddybears*	177

ACKNOWLEDGEMENTS

We would like to thank everyone at Edinburgh University Press, particularly Gillian Leslie, Richard Strachan and Eddie Clark, for their guidance and investment in this book project. In addition, many thanks to the Department of Theatre, Film and Television Studies, Aberystwyth University for their funding support for the Researching Past Cinema Audiences conference, and to all delegates who attended the conference for making it such an enjoyable and intellectually stimulating event. In particular, we would like to thank Martin Barker, Daniel Biltereyst, Sue Harper and Annette Kuhn for their support and encouragement. Kate would also like to thank Jamie Sexton for his feedback, and Tim Noble for his support. Martin would like to thank his wife, Jo, and little Cora for their unwavering enthusiasm and for putting up with lots of one-way conversations about a scary film neither of them enjoys. Jamie would like to specially thank Emily Ham for her support and encouragement, and the 'Cinema Memory and the Digital Archive' team for their guidance.

NOTES ON CONTRIBUTORS

Karina Aveyard is an Associate Professor in the School of Art, Media and American Studies at the University of East Anglia, UK. She is the author of the *Historical Dictionary of Australian and New Zealand Cinema* (2018) and *The Lure of the Big Screen: Cinema in Rural Australia and the United Kingdom* (2015), and co-editor of *Watching Films: New Perspectives on Movie-Going, Exhibition and Reception* (2013) and *New Patterns in Global Television Formats* (2016).

Daniel Biltereyst is Professor in Film and Media History and director of the Cinema and Media Studies research centre (CIMS) at Ghent University, Belgium. Besides exploring new approaches to historical media and cinema cultures, he is engaged in work on film and screen culture as sites of censorship, controversy, public debate and audience engagement. His recent publications include *The Routledge Companion to New Cinema History* (2019, with Richard Maltby and Philippe Meers), *Mapping Movie Magazines: Digitization, Periodicals and Cinema History* (2020, with Lies Van de Vijver) and a monograph on film control and censorship in Belgium (2020).

Kate Egan is senior lecturer in film and media at Northumbria University, UK. She is the author of *Trash or Treasure?: Censorship and the Changing Meanings of the Video Nasties* (2007), *Cultographies: The Evil Dead* (2011) and (with Martin Barker, Tom Phillips and Sarah Ralph) *Alien Audiences* (2016).

She is also the co-editor of *Cult Film Stardom* (with Sarah Thomas, 2012) and *And Now for Something Completely Different: Critical Approaches to Monty Python* (with Jeffrey Weinstock, Edinburgh University Press, 2020). She is currently working in collaboration with Jamie Terrill on practice-based research focused on the Dirt in the Gate cinema events and their audiences at the Shelley Theatre, Bournemouth, and planning and developing further research on audience memories of horror film and television.

Wolfgang Fuhrmann holds a PhD in Film Studies and is an Associate Researcher, Department of Film Studies, University of Zurich, Switzerland. His research interests included transnational film history, Latin American cinema and German colonial cinema. He is author of *Imperial Projections: Screening the German Colonies* (2015) and is guest editor (together with Marius Kuhn, Zurich) of 'Transnationales Kino', *Montage AV* 28(1) (2019); and has also authored 'Cinema Nacional, para quem? Associações, Recepção e Transnacionalismo', *História: Debates e Tendências* 16(2) (2016), 328–41. He has held teaching positions in Germany, Switzerland and the Americas. He is currently living in Bogotá, Colombia.

Damiano Garofalo is an Assistant Professor in Film and Television Studies at Sapienza University of Rome, Italy, where he teaches Cinema History and Television History. After having obtained his PhD in Cultural Studies at the University of Padua, he was a post-doctoral researcher at the Catholic University of Milan, where he worked at Ce.R.T.A. – Centro di Ricerca Sulla Televisione e gli Audiovisivi (Centre for Media and Television Studies). In 2019 he was also hosted as a Visiting Scholar at The Ohio State University. He has published two books: *Political Audiences: A Reception History of Early Italian Television* (2016) and *Storia sociale della televisione in Italia* (2018).

Robert James is a Senior Lecturer in History at the University of Portsmouth, UK. His research interests centre on British society's leisure habits in the late nineteenth to mid-twentieth centuries. He is author of *Popular Culture and Working-Class Taste in Britain 1930–39: A Round of Cheap Diversions?* (2010), and co-editor (with Roy Vallis) of *Hollywood and the World* (2014) and (with Brad Beaven and Karl Bell) of *Port Towns and Urban Cultures: International Histories of the Waterfront, c. 1850–2000* (2016). He has also published widely on film censorship, cinemagoing and popular taste, and public libraries and reading habits in Britain in the twentieth century. He is a founder member of the Port Towns and Urban Cultures research group, and is currently investigating the civic role of cinema managers in British port towns in the first half of the twentieth century.

NOTES ON CONTRIBUTORS

James Jones graduated with a PhD in History from the University of Sussex in 2019. His research focuses on the roles that emotion and space played in historical cinemagoing. His recent work includes '"These Intimate Little Places": Cinema-Going and Public Emotion in Bolton, 1930–1954', *Cultural and Social History* 16(4) (2019), 451–66.

Annette Kuhn is Professor and Research Fellow in Film Studies at Queen Mary University of London, UK, and a Fellow of the British Academy. Publications include *Family Secrets: Acts of Memory and Imagination* (2002), *An Everyday Magic: Cinema and Cultural Memory* (2002), *Little Madnesses: Winnicott, Transitional Phenomena and Cultural Experience* (2013) and (with Guy Westwell) *Oxford Dictionary of Film Studies* (2012; 2nd edn, 2020). She was Director of the ESRC project 'Cinema Culture in 1930s Britain' and is currently Co-Investigator of the AHRC-funded project 'Cinema Memory and the Digital Archive'.

Cecilia Penati teaches 'Languages of Radio and Television' at Università Cattolica del Sacro Cuore, Milan, Italy. At the same university, she is senior researcher at Ce.R.T.A. – Centro di Ricerca Sulla Televisione e gli Audiovisivi (Centre for Media and Television Studies). At IULM University of Milan she teaches Media for Arts. She has written the books *Il focolare elettronico. Televisione italiana delle origini e culture di visione* (2013), *La TV delle donne. Brand, programmi e pubblici* (with Anna Sfardini, 2015) and *La nuova fabbrica dei sogni. Miti e riti della serialità televisiva americana* (2016).

Karina Pryt graduated from the 19th high school in Warsaw, Poland, and studied modern history and German literature at the Albert-Ludwigs-University in Freiburg im Breisgau, Germany. Her doctorate in history on cultural diplomatic relations between Germany and Poland in the 1930s (Befohlene Freundschaft. Die Deutsch-Polnischen Kulturbeziehungen 1934–1939, Osnabrück, 2010) triggered her interest in both the incorporation of film in politics and the economic and social history of cinema. Currently, she is working at the Institute for Theater, Film and Media Studies at the Goethe University in Frankfurt am Main, Germany. Funded by the German Research Foundation (DFG), she is examining the local cinema culture in Warsaw 1895/6–1939 from a transnational perspective utilising a variety of sources in different languages (Polish, Yiddish, Russian and German). She is also dealing with the adaptation of the geographic information system QGIS to historical research.

Robert Shail is Professor of Film and Director of Research in the Leeds School of Arts at Leeds Beckett University, UK, where he leads the REF submission in film, music and performing arts. He is widely published on post-war British cinema with a focus on directors, stardom and masculinity. More recently he has focused on popular culture for children including cinema and comic books; his Leverhulme-funded study of the Children's Film Foundation was published by Palgrave/BFI.

Adrian Smith has research interests in independent distribution and exhibition during the 1960s, and also writes extensively from archival material relating to debates around censorship. He is a regular contributor to film magazines and writes booklet essays for Blu-ray releases.

Martin Ian Smith completed his PhD at Northumbria University, UK, and has published on censorship, experimental film and audience research in *Film International*, *Participations* and *Journal of British Cinema and Television*.

Jamie Terrill is a Research Associate at Lancaster University, UK, where he currently works on the AHRC-funded project 'Cinema Memory and the Digital Archive: 1930s Britain and Beyond'. His recently completed PhD explored the history of cinemagoing in rural Wales, a topic on which he has published. His wider research interests include approaches to film historiography, rural cultures and the visual culture of extreme sports subcultures.

INTRODUCTION

Kate Egan, Martin Ian Smith and Jamie Terrill

Since Robert Allen and Douglas Gomery's 1985 call for a revision of film historiography, the study of historical audiences has flourished; not just in terms of the quantity of work, but also in the breadth of methods, approaches and the variety of audiences under consideration. Equally, in the spirit of Allen and Gomery, scholars interested in the experiences, memories and tastes of historical audiences have sought to continually reassess their approaches and foci. This has ensured a responsive discipline that seeks to escape and reject the static trappings of the *old* that has required the New Film History (see James Chapman, Mark Glancy and Sue Harper, 2007). It is perhaps fitting, then, that the New Film History, a term first popularised by Thomas Elsaesser (1986) as a means of defining Allen and Gomery's call for revision, has since been assessed and responded to by those whose research has moved beyond a textual focus, and instead foregrounds audience experience and the cinema as a social space of exhibition. Such scholars may consider themselves to be part of the New Cinema History, with the use of the word *cinema* quite purposefully juxtaposed with the arguably more text-centric approaches of the New Film History. Building upon the New Film History's revisionist approaches, a key understanding of what defines the New Cinema History is, as Richard Maltby (2011) argues, a desire to represent the history of audiences 'from below'. This is not to say, however, that the study of cinema audiences to this point had been entirely formed of institutional studies removed from lived day-to-day experiences, the use of primary source testimony or competing archival evidence.

Indeed, the seeds of the New Cinema History can be found even before publication of Allen and Gomery's *Film History*, with Jeffrey Richards's *The Age of the Dream Palace* (1984) using textual analysis alongside archival data to investigate the experience of cinemagoing in 1930s Britain, particularly for working-class audiences. As Daniel Biltereyst also observes in his chapter in this collection, the roots of screen audience studies can be traced to a number of pre-World War II sociological studies of cinemagoers, which made fledgling observations on audience habits, perceptions and tastes within differing contexts. Further to this, Annette Kuhn's major 'Cinema Culture in 1930s Britain' study (CCINTB) (1994–7) drew heavily from sociological approaches, and indeed was quite tellingly awarded funding from the Economic and Social Research Council (ESRC), rather than the more typical Arts and Humanities Research Council (AHRC) funding received by film and cinema researchers. Kuhn's work thus blurred the boundaries between disciplines, inspired by oral history methods and approaches that had a driving force within postmodern sociology and anthropology in assessing day-to-day experience, such as those employed by Stanley Cohen (1972) in his study of the Mod and Rocker subcultures in 1960s Britain. Sociology is not the only discipline to influence audience historians; both Kuhn and Jackie Stacey (1994) incorporated elements of oral history, linguistics and psychoanalysis to test and unpack not just *what* participants said but *how* memory narratives of past cinemagoing were formed through discourse and subconscious processes. The importance of these works in revising approaches to the study of historical audiences was pivotal, with Daniel Biltereyst noting in a 2018 keynote – which has been adapted as his chapter within this collection – that Kuhn's work in particular was 'more or less the start of a big part of the field we're in'.

Since the 1980s and early 1990s and the work of Stacey and Kuhn, the study of historical audiences has flourished, and with it so have the methods and approaches that can be implemented, a continually evolving and modifying toolset driven by inspiration from ongoing scholarship and advancements in modern computing and networking technology. Striking quite a different approach from the largely qualitative norm of the field, John Sedgwick's (2000, 2006) POPSTAT methodology drew upon mathematics and quantitative data analysis to create an index for historical film popularity, deriving measures of audience taste and preference from these findings. Building on this work, Petr Szczepanik (2012: 167) devised a simplified version of POPSTAT, putting more weight on the length of a film's run in the cinema and allowing for a modification of Sedgwick's approach to be used in areas where less variety of data is available. Elsewhere, some historical audience scholars have incorporated the rapid developments of late twentieth- and early twenty-first-century computing and networking. This has ranged from the use of internet-hosted surveys to garner a large number of global perspectives (Egan 2020) or to permit access to niche or minority audience groups who would otherwise be difficult to engage (Stokes et al. 2021), to the utilisation of geographic information systems (GIS) to explore and visualise the spatial nuances of cinemagoing and exhibition (Klenotic 2011; Ercole et al. 2017; Caughie et al. 2018).

More recently, the implementation of creative methodologies has emerged as a means of further engaging audiences in the process of historical research. Sarah Neely, for example, has collected and encouraged creative writing prose from past cinemagoers to 'promote the role of the imagination in relation to memory and the cinema-going experience' (2020: 43), a more 'suggestive' than strictly empirical approach in comparison to the methodologies discussed thus far, which allows for an active consideration and acknowledgement of the fallibility of memory narratives. This creative methodology also chimes with the recent push, certainly within British academia, to better engage and impact the public with our research. Such a push and ability for researchers to engage with the wider public has been furthered by the same networking and technological developments that have allowed for the employment of online ethnographic data collection. Greater bandwidth, access to smart devices and improvements in interactive web design in recent years have introduced online digital archives, allowing data to be available more readily to both scholars and the public, and also the data to be easily searchable and managed either by keywords or through filters. Recent studies such as 'In Search of Italian Cinema Audiences in the 1940s and 1950s: Gender, Genre and National Identity' (2013–16) have made many of their findings and outputs – including video interviews and GIS mapping data – freely available on a bespoke website, allowing anyone access to what would have previously sat in physical archives with only snippets and interpretations of the extant data published. Making full use of the breakdown of contact boundaries that the internet can provide, a spin-off project, 'CineRicordi', was created to crowdsource digital artefacts directly from Italian audiences. This spin-off resulted in a website of the same name, where some 300 crowdsourced archival documents can be found, along with the option to submit one's own memories, images or video as digital donations (Treveri Gennari and Culhane 2019). Elsewhere, and chiming with the revisionist themes discussed thus far, the previously existing archive of interviews, letters, memorabilia and other documents collected by Kuhn during the CCINTB project is now being digitised and made available freely online for the first time as part of 'Cinema Memory and the Digital Archive' (2019–22), some twenty-five years after the initial data gathering. This project also seeks to actively engage with the wider public, through a series of workshops and events that utilise the archival data, along with creative outputs inspired by the archive and created through artist residencies.

Revisionism does not just apply to methods; as we as a field reassess and hold ourselves accountable in the avoidance of becoming static, new topics and areas of investigation are uncovered and existing gaps in knowledge are rightly identified and become subject to a call for study. In recent years, this has included rural and small nation audiences (Thissen and Zimmermann 2016; Treveri Gennari et al. 2018); memories of cinemagoing within periods of war (Farmer 2019); the role of cinema staff as a mediator between the cinemagoing experience and the screen (Balogh 2017; Terrill 2019); reassessing the contexts and audience responses to films at both their original release and in subsequent viewing (Stokes 2007; Barker 2016); and the appraisal of contexts and experiences of home viewing or non-cinematic media audiences (Ruiz et al. 2020; Alcott 2019), to name just a few examples. It is through the investigation of fresh audience contexts which perhaps makes this edited collection most valuable, which is by design.

This book was first conceived at the Researching Past Cinema Audiences conference held at Aberystwyth University in the spring of 2018. Here, audience scholars from across the world met for three days to present their historical audience focused research. At the conference, whilst methods were a point of discussion in many papers, it was striking how many of the presentations identified gaps in existing knowledge to which their research aimed to make vital contributions. As is the way with conferences, some of the papers were reflecting on work that was near its conclusion or had already been completed, whilst others were in the formative or middle stages of their study. Over the course of the three days, it became apparent that there was potential for two different avenues of publication for the important work being shared: one with a relatively short period of turnaround, ideal for the studies which were ready to share their findings, and the other this collection, with its longer period of gestation and thus allowance for further data to be uncovered and arguments to be tied together. The former took the shape of a themed section within the May 2019 issue of *Participations*, which, as we noted in this themed section's introductory article, had a particular focus, across the section's articles, on the 'creativity and flexibility' of sources employed, along with 'the ways in which these sources are analysed, interpreted and (frequently) combined' to answer key questions pertaining to historical audiences (Egan et al. 2019: 681).

Being Creative in Historical Audience Research: Re-evaluating the Field

Whilst – as was the case with our *Participations* themed section – a wide range of sources and methodologies are utilised and tested throughout the following chapters, it is especially the aim of this edited collection to showcase historical screen audience studies in an array of different periods, settings and contexts. Indeed, in doing so this collection of essays reinforces what has been outlined here in relation to revisionism and holding ourselves (as a field) accountable, with the scholars within this collection identifying gaps to be addressed and modifications to be made to existing knowledge and approaches. Such overt engagement with the reappraisal of current methods and foci within the discipline is a key element of the first part of this edited collection: 'Being Creative in Historical Audience Research: Re-evaluating the Field'. Opening this part, appropriately as an adaptation of his keynote from the conference that conceived this collection, is Daniel Biltereyst's chapter, which assesses the current state of the field of New Cinema History. Here, Biltereyst argues that there is much work yet to be done within the field, particularly in relation to the role of the film text within cinematic experiences, the imaginary power of film on/for audiences and the impact of this on their view of the world outside of the cinema. To exemplify his arguments, he offers a case study of the German talkie *Never Trust a Woman* (1929/30) and assesses the popularity of the film within the Netherlands and Belgium, despite its negative reviews. Reflecting upon the film's working-class *mise en scène* compared with the 'high culture' aura of the film's star, Richard Tauber, Biltereyst highlights the value of considering 'lived experiences', even if assumed rather than empirically gathered, where the temptation may be to rely on statistical, economic or press data. Through this, and akin to Treveri Gennari and Culhane (2019), Biltereyst here raises the notion that New Cinema historians have arguably strayed too far from consideration of the film text within their arguments and approaches.

In the opening of his chapter, Daniel Biltereyst notes the importance of Annette Kuhn's 'Cinema Culture in 1930s Britain' (CCINTB) project and its vital role in moving audience historiography towards the researching of the experience of film and cinemagoing. In her chapter 'From Cinema Culture to Cinema Memory: A Conceptual and Methodological Trajectory', Kuhn provides new insight on the process and methodologies that led to the unexpected finding of a specifically cinema-related subtype of cultural memory – dubbed 'cinema memory' – within her participants' recollections. Kuhn's meta-analysis of CCINTB's research and arguments provides a valuable lesson for researchers in trusting their findings, even if they differ from an expected hypothesis or current norms of the field, a sentiment that echoes Allen and Gomery's calls for historiographical revisionism. Kuhn also presents three distinctive modes of cinema memory, providing examples from the CCINTB dataset that feature recollections pertaining to the text; those situated within contexts of an informant's life events; and, importantly, memories concerning the activity of cinemagoing. In doing so, Kuhn provides compelling evidence of the process of distilling raw remembrance narrative and discursive data into cinema memory, which, in turn, illustrates the validity of cinema audience historiography shifting its emphasis from cultural history to cultural memory.

Karina Aveyard's 'Constructing Cinema Audience Histories: Methodological Choices and Challenges', the final chapter in this section, continues the theme of assessing one's own – or the field's – methods by exploring how cinema audience histories can be located, constructed and understood. Focusing upon her own work on post-World War II histories of volunteer-led community cinema in the United Kingdom, Aveyard reflects upon the methodological challenges of her study, most notably balancing a combination of historical and contemporary sources as a means to identify patterns of 'continuity and interconnection' across differing temporal contexts. Similar to both Biltereyst's and Kuhn's respective discussions of meta-analysis of methods and approaches, Aveyard explores the role of the researcher within historical audience research and the extent to which ideological perspective can inform the 'objects and outcomes of critical research'. The chapter then sees Aveyard challenge her own approaches and influence on her research, as well as providing detail of the types of issues researchers will face when uncovering archival data, along with reconciling that researchers will never be able to immerse themselves within history as they can with the present. Whilst Aveyard was able to observe the reactions, perceptions and experiences of contemporary community audiences and volunteers first-hand, archival and oral testimony sources and her interpretations of these had to be the guiding evidence for comparable historical experiences. As has been previously suggested by Sarah Street (2000), acknowledging the limitations and contexts of one's sources is a valuable step in making us accountable in our exploration of the past. Similarly, Barbara Klinger has called upon film historians to consider an 'histoire totale', total history, by collecting and comparing as many competing sources as possible. Beyond these meta considerations, Aveyard's chapter provides valuable detail about the history and contemporary contexts of community cinema and the cultural and social importance of such schemes to their local communities. She also importantly critically assesses the politics and nature of volunteer work within such community enterprises, maintaining that whilst her research found no evidence of misuse or negativity from volunteers, it is important for researchers to ask questions of this model else scholarship risks becoming complicit in any potential exploitation.

Reconsidering National and Transnational Cinemagoing Histories

The second part of this collection illustrates the fundamental benefits of collating and considering a wide range of sources when investigating historical audiences, particularly in scenarios where conducting a fresh ethnographic study is not possible or even preferable. As well as demonstrating the value of employing other sources within historical audience research, each chapter here questions, through these methods, conceived notions or assumptions about national contexts of cinemagoing history in their respective locales.

Karina Pryt's chapter, 'Cinemas and Cinema Audiences in the "Third Space" in Warsaw, 1908–1939', primarily utilises GIS mapping to examine the cinema and audience topography of Warsaw, Poland prior to World War II. The war devastated the left bank of Warsaw, with Pryt noting that this saw the destruction of most cinemas and theatres, including most primary source data pertaining to them, and, sadly, almost the entire Jewish population of the city. As she notes, this population constituted the majority of the region's film production and distribution personnel, resulting in Warsaw losing its status as the capital of Poland's film industry. Such a degree of loss presents difficulties for a researcher interested in exploring audiences, with Pryt noting, in a complement to Aveyard's arguments, that it requires 'archaeological precision and critical academic self-reflection' to suitably uncover and identify findings. Thus, whilst also drawing upon existing scholarship within Warsaw and Jewish studies, Pryt uses datasets from 1911, 1922 and 1936 to inform her mapping practices and aid the identification of patterns and changes within this lost cinemagoing and audience topography. Similar to Sedwick's POPSTAT, Pryt uses this data to make informed interpretations about the popularity of certain venues to differing demographics of the city, drawing on matters of cinema quality, class, religion and language and, of course, the impact of the rapidly changing and turbulent cultural backdrop of the period.

In contrast to Pryt's use of GIS data to establish topographic patterns of social cinemagoing, Wolfgang Fuhrmann's 'German Films in Brazil: Immigration, Associations and National Film Culture' uses primary source archival documents, including financial reports and written correspondence, to overturn the assumption that German Cultural Films shown in Brazil during the 1930s were purely aimed at and consumed by the German immigrant population, not least as Nazi propaganda. Rather, he argues, German Cultural Films – and the educational associations that organised their screening – can be seen as part of a 'dynamic' wider Brazilian film culture of that period, with audiences consisting of Germans and Brazilians. Analogous to Biltereyst's arguments, and indeed to those of Treveri Gennari and Culhane (2019), Fuhrmann here demonstrates the value of exploring the role and importance of specific film texts – and their content – within social cinema and historical audience studies.

As with the previous two chapters, James Jones's 'Emotional Communities in the Cinema: Tracing Emotion in Mass Observation Cinema Records, 1937–1950' seeks to aid our understanding of specific audience communities. Though, unlike the more easily definable audience groups discussed by Pryt and Furhmann, Jones employs Mass Observation documentation to explore 'emotional communities' formed by British audiences. To achieve this, whilst also demonstrating the revisionist need for scholars to draw on research from outside film and television studies, James draws upon theories from the field of emotions' history, highlighting the link between personal and collective emotion and culture. Importantly, James also tests and questions the validity and strength of Mass Observation data in assessing the experience of cinemagoing emotion. Indeed, beyond being a fascinating study that highlights the nuances of cultural emotion in post-war Britain and the role of cinema as a space of emotional community against a 'stiff-upper-lip' backdrop, James's work also shows how a frequently used dataset such as the Mass Observation records can be approached in a revisionist manner to extract new findings and arguments.

Shaping Audience Expectations: Cinema Managers and Marketing Strategies

Since the birth of cinema, there have been those who have sought to measure and assess the success of films and even cinemas themselves, with the ultimate goal of garnering a better understanding of audience tastes and demands. Films, and therefore cinemas, rely on marketing to entice audiences into the auditorium, as illustrated most recently through the triangulation methods of *Italian Cinema Audiences* (Treveri Gennari et al. 2020). This part therefore makes key contributions to existing work through detailed exploration of case studies which provide new perspectives on the impact of cinema management and film marketing strategies on audience and public perception of both films and venues. The first two chapters consider different perspectives in relation to one key cinema manager, Harry Sanders. Robert James's chapter '"Make Your Public Curious": Cinema Management, Film Advertising and Audience Taste in England, c. 1920–c. 1960' situates the practices of Harry Sanders, who managed a number of cinemas across Britain between 1913 and 1963, against those of his contemporaries and the changing backdrop of cinema exhibition through his career. James outlines a number of marketing tactics used by Sanders and others, illustrating the proactive nature of these managers and their work in response to the rapidly changing societal and cultural contexts of early to mid-twentieth-century Britain. Overall, James's work stresses the overlooked nature of the cinema manager within film and cinema historiography, with his findings on the nuanced relationship between managers, audiences, films and marketing strongly illustrating the potential for further study on cinema management and staff, as key facilitators and often invisible linchpins of the cinemagoing experience in key periods of its history. Indeed, important first steps have been made in the development of such scholarship, including Jon Burrows's 'The Projection Project' (AHRC funded, 2014–18) and Eva Balogh's (2017) work concerning usherettes.

Complementing James's framing of Sanders against his contemporaries, Robert Shail's 'Harry Sanders: Remembering a Life in Cinema Management' then provides a micro-history of Sanders's career. Akin to James's work, Shail employs archival records contained within the Harry Sanders Archive. Yet, whilst James combines materials from this collection with a wider range of sources to paint a macro view of twentieth-century cinema management and marketing decisions across Britain, Shail considers the archive as a whole in order to piece together a 'mosaic' of Sanders's career and management practices across the various cinemas where he worked. Through his piecing together of items from this archive, including marketing materials, trade publications and newspapers, along with Sanders's notebooks and diaries, Shail's research complements but also goes beyond existing scholarship on box office data and cinema ledgers to consider what we can learn about past cinemagoing experiences from examining, in depth, the personal archive of a key individual who marketed and managed them. Amongst discussion of marketing stunts and schemes that Sanders employed to attract audiences, the role of the cinema manager as an entertainer and spectacle in their own right emerges from Shail's work here, as does the important work managers engaged in as civic figures whose relationship and familiarity with the local community was arguably more extensive and effective than more official figures like local councillors. Whilst both Shail's and James's chapters may not engage with audience tastes or practices as directly as other works within this collection, their studies of cinema management shed invaluable new light on how the cinemagoing experience was anticipated and shaped before the audience even stepped into the auditorium.

Shifting from a focus on the management of cinemas to the management of film marketing, Adrian Smith's '*The Yellow Teddybears*: Exploitation as Education' employs competing evidence – including interviews, censorship records, newspaper articles and other archival materials – to explore the exploitative/educational duality of the production, promotion and reception of British film *The Yellow Teddybears* (1963). By combining new interviews with archival data, Smith identifies and investigates historical traces of the educational events surrounding the film and its promotion in the UK in the 1960s,which, for Smith, were informed by what he terms a 'sex/altruism binary', the origins of which can be found in traditions of exploitation cinema marketing in the US. Akin to Biltereyst's arguments in Chapter 1, Smith's work illustrates the continued value, in historical audience research, of exploring specific case study films in order to identify 'the competing voices involved in a particular film's public signification' (Klinger 1997: 110) and, consequently, to foreground the ways in which these competing discourses shaped the expectations and responses of past audiences in particular cinematic contexts.

Home Viewing Contexts and Audience Memories

Thus far, the book's chapters have largely concerned audiences within contexts of cinemas and cinemagoing. Yet, we have quite purposefully used *screen* in the title of this collection rather than *cinema* – this is an issue that will clearly continue to become more prominent, not least as the dichotomy of viewing portals as being either a cinema screen or a television set (broadly speaking) continues to be challenged by a myriad of viewing devices and potential spaces of spectatorship. We would argue that there is, consequently, a need to more consistently and profitably draw consideration of home viewing and television audiences into the paradigms and cultural contexts of New Cinema historiography, not least as the line between film and television continues, post-home video, to increasingly blur through streaming platform distribution and escalating production values and runtimes. There is a pressing need, therefore, to consider audiences and their non-theatrical viewership through the same or equivalent approaches, concepts, methods and sociocultural foci that are employed to explore past cinemagoing. Annette Kuhn's chapter in this collection notes that a shift from cultural history to cultural memory approaches benefited our understanding of past cinema audiences; a revisionist approach to the study of home viewing audiences could also uncover valuable cultural contexts informing a, to date, significantly underexplored form of past audience experience.

Indeed, a key contribution to this nascent area of historical enquiry is Damiano Garofalo and Cecilia Penati's 'Archives, Sources and Memories for a History of Early Italian TV Audiences', which studies the practices, meaning making and cultural contexts of early Italian television audiences, a focus which they argue has been lacking within Italian media studies. The authors note that the study of Italian audiences of other media, particularly cinema, has been relatively well explored, but that the study of the nation's past television audiences has only recently begun to receive attention. Overtly drawing from New Cinema History methodologies, primarily the collection and analysis of empirical oral history and primary source archival materials, the authors examine perceptions and the reception of television from early Italian audiences (from roughly 1954 onwards) situated and informed by contexts such as geographic, religious and economic divides. The authors address a number of such contexts that inform audience perceptions of early television, with the temporal context of post-war Italy and the resultant state of the country's varying economic, political and religious elements being notable aspects of analysis here.

Though television can be read and analysed as a broadcast medium, the physical object of the television set itself has, since the adoption of formats such as VHS and DVD, facilitated a different paradigm of home viewing. Martin Ian Smith's chapter, '*The Exorcist* in the Home: Remembering Parental Regulation', employs a grounded theory approach to explore memories of those who had first encountered the controversial horror film *The Exorcist* (1973) at home as children. In doing so, he identifies a form of censorship that differs from those typically discussed in relation to cinemagoing, where national and civic bodies and cinemas themselves are usually instrumental in deciding and enforcing censorship. In contrast to cinema-specific censorship, Smith examines the role parental regulation played in memories of the censorship and accessibility of childhood home viewing, offering a paradigm of six typical parental regulation categories in relation to *The Exorcist*. Whilst outlining perceptions of film consumption and censorship that are arguably unique to home viewing contexts, Smith also demonstrates the continued value of examining text-specific histories and memories of past audience experiences, a recurrent theme throughout this collection.

Kate Egan's chapter, 'Childhood Memories of Horror Films in the Home: Questions, Patterns and Contexts', provides further exploration of the importance of the home as a venue and context for the viewing of films. But whereas Smith's chapter centres around a single film, eliciting text-specific memories, Egan focuses more broadly on the horror genre, which she identifies as having been dominated, in various ways, by home viewing contexts since the 1970s. Drawing on interviews conducted at the Dirt in the Gate Movies events in Bournemouth (which predominantly focus on the screening of horror films from the 1970s and 1980s), Egan considers the important roles played by past technologies, people, spaces and sensory experiences in respondent memories of horror films in the childhood domestic context and, consequently, the continued meanings and significance of these memories in the present day. Through her findings, and through relating them to key research on childhood and family audiences by David Buckingham in the 1990s, Egan also considers the potential role audience memory research could play in challenging or complicating existing, dominant public conceptions about horror fans and their history of consumption practices.

The chapters in this collection represent a snapshot of the present and future of historical audience studies as we approach forty years since Allen and Gomery's call for a revision of cinema historiography. The wide range of topics, methodologies, geographies and forms of audiences investigated across these chapters illustrates the commitment of scholars within the field of historical audience studies to keep continual development and revisionism as a core tenet. In particular, there is, across the book, a consistent assessing and testing of current approaches to the study of historical audiences, particularly through calls to continue to recognise the significance of film texts in audience histories and their incorporation into our sociocultural approaches; the value of using our existing toolset of methods and approaches in relation to television and home viewing audiences, as well to tertiary aspects of cinema history such as management practices; and the necessity of collecting a wide range of competing evidence as a means of mapping out, fully and with complexity, national and transnational audience histories, particularly those which are informed by complex political circumstances.

BIBLIOGRAPHY

Alcott, Thomas (2019) 'Not Putting Away Childish Things: The Importance of Childhood in the Audience Reception of Professional Wrestling Stars', *Participations* 16(1), 3–29.

Allen, Robert and Douglas Gomery (1985) *Film History: Theory and Practice*. New York: McGraw-Hill

Balogh, Eva (2017) 'Stars in the Aisles: Cinema Usherettes, Identity and Ideology', *Participations* 14(1), 22–48.

Barker, Martin (2016) '"Legolas, He's Cool . . . and He's Hot!" The Meanings and Implications of Audiences' Favorite Characters', in CarrieLynn D. Reinhard and Christopher J. Olson (eds), *Making Sense of Cinema: Empirical Studies into Film Spectators and Spectatorship*. New York: Bloomsbury Academic, pp. 97–118.

Biltereyst, Daniel (2018) 'Audience as Palimpsest. Mapping Historical Film Audience Research'. Keynote given at Researching Past Cinema Audiences: Archives, Memories and Methods conference, Aberystwyth University, UK, 26–28 March 2018.

Caughie, John, Trevor Griffiths and María A. Vélez-Serna (eds) (2018) *Early Cinema in Scotland*. Edinburgh: Edinburgh University Press.

Chapman, James, Mark Glancy and Sue Harper (eds) (2007) *The New Film History: Sources, Methods, Approaches*. Basingstoke: Palgrave Macmillan.

Cohen, Stanley (1972) *Folk Devils and Moral Panics: The Creation of the Mods and Rockers*. London: MacGibbon and Kee.

Egan, Kate (2020) 'Memories of Connecting: Fathers, Daughters and Intergenerational Monty Python Fandom', in Kate Egan and Jeffrey Weinstock (eds), *And Now for Something Completely Different: Critical Approaches to Monty Python*. Edinburgh: Edinburgh University Press, pp. 207–25.

Egan, Kate, Martin Ian Smith and Jamie Terrill (2019) 'Introduction to Themed Section: Researching Past Cinema Audiences', *Participations* 16(1), 680–6.

Elsaesser, T. (1986) 'The New Film History', *Sight and Sound* 55(4), 246–51.

Ercole, Pierluigi, Daniela Treveri Gennari and Catherine O'Rawe (2017) 'Mapping Cinema Memories: Emotional Geographies of Cinemagoing in Rome in the 1950s', *Memory Studies* 10(1), 63–77.

Farmer, Richard (2019) 'The Dying of the Light: The Blackout, Cinemas, and Cinemagoing in Wartime Britain', *Participations* 16(1), 762–77.

Klenotic, Jeffrey (2011) 'Putting Cinema History on the Map: Using GIS to Explore the Spatiality of Cinema', in Richard Maltby, Daniel Biltereyst and Philippe Meers (eds), *Explorations in New Cinema History: Approaches and Case Studies*. Malden, MA: Wiley-Blackwell, pp. 58–84.

Klinger, Barbara (1997) 'Film History Terminable and Interminable: Recovering the Past in Reception Studies', *Screen* 38(2), 107–28.

Maltby, Richard (2011) 'New Cinema Histories', in Richard Maltby, Daniel Biltereyst and Philippe Meers (eds), *Explorations in New Cinema History: Approaches and Case Studies*. Malden, MA: Wiley-Blackwell, pp. 3–41.

Neely, Sarah (2019) '"Reel to Rattling Reel": Telling Stories about Rural Cinema-Going in Scotland', *Participations* 16(1), 778–95.

Neely, Sarah (2020) '"The Story of the Reel that Went for a Swim": Cinema Memory and the History of the Highlands and Islands Film Guild as Narrated through Oral History Interviews and Surrounding Metadata', *Northern Scotland* 11(1), 42–59.

Richards, Jeffrey (1984) *The Age of the Dream Palace: Cinema and Society in the 1930s*. London: I. B. Tauris.

Ruiz, Pollyanna, Tim Snelson, Rebecca Madgin and David Webb (2020) '"Look at What We Made": Communicating Subcultural Value on London's Southbank', *Cultural Studies* 34(3), 392–417.

Sedgwick, John (2000) *Popular Filmgoing in 1930s Britain*. Exeter: University of Exeter Press.

Sedgwick, John (2006) 'Cinemagoing in Portsmouth during the 1930s', *Cinema Journal* 46(1), 52–84.

Stacey, Jackie (1994) *Star Gazing: Hollywood Cinema and Female Spectatorship*. Abingdon and New York: Routledge.

Stokes, Melvyn (2007) '*Gone With the Wind* (1939) and the Lost Cause: A Critical View', in James Chapman, Mark Glancy and Sue Harper (eds), *The New Film History: Sources, Methods, Approaches*. Basingstoke: Palgrave Macmillan, pp. 13–27.

Stokes, Melvyn, Matthew Jones and Emma Pett (2021) *Cinema Memories: A People's History of Cinema-Going in 1960s Britain*. London: Bloomsbury.

Street, Sarah (2000) *British Cinema in Documents*. London: Routledge.

Szczepanik, Petr (2012) 'Hollywood in Disguise', in Daniel Biltereyst, Richard Maltby and Philippe Meers (eds), *Cinema, Audiences and Modernity: New Perspectives in European Cinema History*. London: Routledge, pp. 166–85.

Terrill, Jamie (2019) 'More to the UK than England: Exploring Rural Wales' Cinemagoing History through its Showmen', *Participations* 16(1), 738–61.

Thissen, Judith and Clemens Zimmermann (eds) (2016) *Cinema Beyond the City: Small-Town and Rural Film Culture in Europe*. London: BFI Publishing.

Treveri Gennari, Daniela and Sarah Culhane (2019) 'Crowdsourcing Memories and Artefacts to Reconstruct Italian Cinema History: Micro-histories of Small-Town Exhibition in the 1950s', *Participations* 16(1), 796–823.

Treveri Gennari, Daniela, Danielle Hipkins and Catherine O'Rawe (eds) (2018) *Rural Cinema Exhibition and Audiences in a Global Context*. Cham: Palgrave Macmillan.

Treveri Gennari, Daniela, Catherine O'Rawe, Danielle Hipkins, Silvia Dibeltulo and Sarah Culhane (2020) *Italian Cinema Audiences: Histories and Memories of Cinema-Going in Post-war Italy*. New York: Bloomsbury.

PART I

BEING CREATIVE IN HISTORICAL AUDIENCE RESEARCH: RE-EVALUATING THE FIELD

1. AUDIENCE AS PALIMPSEST, OR THE STRUCTURES OF CINEMATIC FEELING: ON HISTORICAL FILM AUDIENCE RESEARCH AND CINEMA'S IMAGINATIVE POWER

Daniel Biltereyst

Over the last two decades, historical film audience research has become a booming part of film and cinema studies.[1] Twenty years after Annette Kuhn's pioneering work on cinema culture in 1930s Britain (Kuhn 1999a, 1999b, 2002), the time when film scholars thought about audiences as spectators or as mere film-textual constructions seems to have passed. Research on audiences now concentrates on real audiences' experiences of film and cinema in the past. Thereby we could make a distinction between scholarly work on filmic and cinematic experiences. Although it is probably not very productive to draw a hard line between film and cinema,[2] we could argue that filmic experiences refer to audiences' reception of and engagements with films, whereas cinematic ones deal with how audiences are engaged with cinema as a broader social and cultural institution. One of the arguments put forward in this chapter is that it is precisely the latter type of audience cinematic engagement that has recently received a great deal of attention, particularly in relation to the cinemagoers' encounter with the place where movies were consumed and with the overall social experience of cinemagoing.

This chapter argues that much work still needs to be done, particularly in reassessing the connections between filmic and cinematic experiences – or in assessing cinema's imaginative power on, or for, audiences. This chapter on the state of the field will probably raise more questions than it provides answers. Paraphrasing Albert Camus ([1942] 2013), who forced his readers to think about the truly crucial questions in philosophy (in his monumental case, it was the question of suicide, or the judgement whether life is or is not worth living), I dare to raise the (much more humble) question whether film studies – and historical film audience research in particular – has really profoundly investigated key questions on cinema's societal role. One of those questions which really matters in relation to cinema (Maltby 2007) is the one dealing with the (often overwhelming) power of the cinematic experience and of the filmic imagination on real audiences. Next to asking questions about when, where, how and with whom people went to see moving pictures, this chapter argues that it is time to start to understand in more detail how cinema's imaginative power informed, inspired, and maybe even influenced or triggered people to look differently at the world they knew outside the cinema (as a place).

Before turning to these issues, I will start by raising a series of questions on historical audience research as a field, or a subfield. Questions like: is it an emerging field? What are the issues we are investigating, and the questions we are asking ourselves? What are the sources we are using? How do we conceive the filmic and cinematic experience? How have we studied audiences' engagements or relationships with cinema? How has our work changed the understanding of cinema's role in society? Is it safe to say that work on historical film/cinema audiences has shown that cinemagoing was a social activity, that people were active and selective, and that films were not that important at all, that they were only a pretext (in the two meanings of the word: a filmic text and a reason for doing something else)? Does this mean that films were not really important, and that the cinema experience was above all a social practice? Isn't that a bit too easy a summary of what our research brings forward? What about structural issues, and what about differences in cinema experiences, over time, across cultures, gender, class, generations?

Is it a Field?

The first question we should raise, of course, is whether historical film audience research is an emerging (sub)field within film/cinema studies. One observation here is that, undoubtedly, there has been a major change in the last twenty years or so in how we look at cinema audiences of the past. One aspect of this change deals with the variety of disciplinary and methodological perspectives. In the past, research on audiences was intensively inspired by traditions coming from the critical arts, philosophy, literary studies or psychoanalysis that specialised in text-oriented approaches to how film as a text and as an apparatus implied, constructed, addressed or 'interpellated' audiences (Gelly and Roche 2012). Only marginal attention was given to real 'flesh-and-blood' audience experiences. Over the past decades, a broad stream of empirical research on the 'real audience' (Stacey 1994: 54) contributed to the emergence of a field where different traditions, concepts and methodologies of audience research meet (Biltereyst and Meers 2018). Under the New Cinema History umbrella (Maltby et al. 2011; Biltereyst et al. 2019), a wide variety of perspectives, tools and methods are now utilised, which are usually associated with history (oral history), economy (market analysis) and the social sciences (for example, questionnaires, qualitative interviews, participant observation, ethnography). These include those coming from historical demography (for example, Thissen 2019) and sociology (for example, Glen 2019), ethnographic research (for example, Richards 2003; Klien-Thomas 2019), oral history (for example, Jernudd 2013) and memory studies (for example, Kuhn et al. 2017; Treveri Gennari and Dibeltulo 2017). If historical audience research is an emerging field, it is an ever more mature and multidisciplinary one.

Another aspect of the change relates to the variety of levels or dimensions of the cinematic experience which are examined. Rather than only looking at how film texts position audiences as spectators, the field is now open to many other, previously less studied levels of the filmic and cinematic experience. Much attention has been given to studies on different dimensions of exhibition as a place (for example, the geospatial and socio-geographic location of a venue), as a space (the experience of that place, or the imaginary and socially embedded version of the place), and as the precondition of the cinema experience (for example, Forest 2017). The field has also started to investigate issues of architecture and cinema's spatial organisation and of its appeal to audiences (for example, Barefoot 2019). We are using corporate reports, and other institutional recordings and testimonies on the audience coming from the industry. Studies deal with advertising, programming strategies and box office revenues (for example, Sedgwick 2000; Garncarz 2021) as a means to get a grip on audiences' consumerist behaviours, preferences and choices. Researchers examine letters and other traces which deal with popular cinephilia, historical fandom, or fan strategies and practices (for example, Juan 2020). Magazines are also precious sources for understanding the multiple interactions between the film industry and cinemagoers, including the issue of the discursive construction of film fans and cinemagoers (Biltereyst and Van de Vijver 2020). A dominant approach within the field, of course, is oral history and interviewing older cinemagoers on issues of film choice and preference, the practice of cinemagoing, and many more levels of the cinematic experience of the past.

Using Jérôme Bourdon's typology of sources for doing historical audience research, we could say that the field is now also more than ever starting to use a wide variety of traces of the cinematic experience. Although there is a clear preference for 'sources from below' (oral reports and other forms of direct evidence of audiences as witnesses, talking about their own film consumption and cinemagoing experiences), there is a growing interest in using the other categories Bourdon identifies. This includes the usage of 'sources from above', consisting of statistics and data produced by the industry and 'media elites' like production and distribution companies, exhibitor networks, media managers and policy makers. These sources have their own bias, of course, but they are interesting because they are mostly generated in order to gain insight into the audiences that these elites tried to target. A third category of sources, which Bourdon labelled as those 'from the side', refers to sources which do not emanate from the world of cinema itself, but from other social actors whose main function and interest were not to observe cinema audiences. These include texts, testimonies and other traces from non-cinematic actors like, as Bourdon indicates, legal actors or other media reacting upon the arrival of a new medium (for example, newspapers on cinema). In the context of the cinematic experience, we could also think about the world of literature and the arts in general, particularly their references to cinema and 'the cinematic'. We will come back to this underexplored category, but as Bourdon (2015: 15) indicates, these might be an 'extremely rich array of sources', precisely because they allow the researcher to displace attention from cinema, become less cinema-centric, and put the cinematic experience into a broader perspective (Morley 2009).

Is it an Emerging Field?

If historical film audience research is vibrant and expanding in terms of perspectives, traditions, methodologies and sources, and with a broadening attention to the different dimensions of spectatorship and audiences' experiences, one could ask whether it is an emerging field. Maybe this sounds a bit exaggerated, but research on film audiences can be seen as part of a very old research tradition. In fact, work on film audiences is among the oldest and most prolific areas in modern media or communication research. Before World War I, social scientists and psychologists were dealing with cinema's meaning for, and influences on, audiences. In Germany, Emilie Altenloh ([1914] 1977) conducted a class-informed sociological analysis of film audiences in 1911. Using surveys, Altenloh's *Zur Soziologie des Kino* found that there were no differences in the frequencies of cinemagoing between natives and long-time inhabitants of a city like Mannheim on the one hand, and recent migrants and commuters from the country on the other. In 1916, another pioneering work on cinema audiences appeared in the USA by the American-German psychologist Hugo Münsterberg ([1916] 2002). In his *The Photoplay: A Psychological Study*, Münsterberg looked at audiences' attention, memory and imagination, as well as audiences' emotions.

In the interwar years, research on audiences' cinematic and filmic experiences thrived; as Richard deCordova argued, 'audience studies proliferated in the 1920s and 1930s, particularly those focused on children' ([1990] 2002: 159). Besides industry-supported statistical research on audience profiles and cinema attendance, much work was conducted in an academic environment as well as being sponsored by private foundations like the various well-known studies for the Payne Fund. The latter refers to a sophisticated, multi-methodological series of research projects and publications on the impact of cinema and other new communication technologies on American youth (Blumer 1933; Cressey 1938; Jowett et al. 1996). In the 1930s and 1940s, amazing work was done on film audiences, which is still more than just worthwhile reading for film audience researchers today. These include *Middletown: A Study in Modern American Culture* by the American sociologists Robert and Helen Lynd ([1929] 1956), Herbert Blumer's *Movies and Conduct* (1933), Paul Cressey's reflections on his work on youngsters and cinemagoing for the Payne Fund (1938), and *Sociology of Film: Studies and Documents* (1946), a seminal, multi-methodological enquiry on the experience of cinema in the UK by German immigrant and sociologist Jacob-Peter Mayer. This work is well known, but there is much more to be discovered in terms of government-supported audience observations, industry-financed studies of cinema attendance, and lots of other unexplored audience surveys (for example, Wets 1920, a government-sponsored enquiry on film audiences in Belgium). It is also necessary to look beyond the boundaries of film or cinema research and look at historical research on, for example, leisure, labour, migration, class (e.g. Rosenzweig 1983) and gender (Peiss 1986) – work which emphasises the importance of films and cinema in bringing people 'close to the mainstream of [American] society' (Rosenzweig 1983: 221).

A probable answer to the question of where to start with historical film audience research is that we at least need to be aware of this tradition, and even that one of the first things to do is to profoundly map this rich body of work, and to understand and use it as a source. One of the very special peculiarities of the field of historical film/cinema audiences is that we can look back, and that we are even able to use this rich body of research from the past as primary source material now. We can critically reuse, re-examine, reinterpret it. Of course, we need to be critical, to take into account all kinds of bias, and we need to interrogate and be careful in how we deal with this amazingly rich body of research. This work on film audiences is interesting not only for what it tells us about film audiences in the past, but also for understanding institutional discourses on those audiences, on how they were conceived, looked at, studied, and on how these studies were used for whatever purpose.

One advantage of conceiving the field of historical film audience research as being critically part of this old tradition is that we should learn from it in terms of the kinds of knowledge it produced. One critical observation is that, typically, textbooks on media audience research are often reduced to a story about competing paradigms, theories and methodologies, with mainstream traditions like survey and effects research clashing with more interpretative traditions, and vice versa. However, looking back, we can only observe that this proves to be quite unproductive. From a critical realist perspective, we can only see that the use of particular methods, obviously, produced particular kinds of data and knowledge on audiences. It indicates also that a triangulation of methods, approaches, sources, theories and concepts is probably not a bad idea.

Looking at research on historical film audiences from this perspective today, it is interesting to read Paul Cressey's reflections, back in 1938, about how to conceive the 'motion picture experience' (Cressey 1938: 518). In his insightful article on his work on cinema audiences for the Payne Fund Studies, Cressey referred to the abundance of particularistic studies on film audiences, where 'the motion picture experience is studied only segmentally and never in its essential unity' (1938: 518). Cressey's sophisticated study of young boys' cinemagoing practices in New York was not published, partly because it was methodologically innovative and because he resisted a hypodermic needle-type theory of film effect on audiences.[3] In his reflective article for the Payne Fund on film audiences, 'The Motion Picture Experience as Modified by Social Background and Personality', Cressey proposed a broad research agenda as an answer to what he called 'widespread loose thinking' on cinema's impact (1938: 517). Rather than considering cinema as a unilateral social force where patrons are passive agents, Cressey proposed to look at cinema as a series of reciprocal interrelationships, between the screen and the spectator, between screen patterns and social values, between the dark space of the cinema and the community where it was located.

In this programmatic article, Cressey argued that '"going to the movies" is a unified experience involving always a specific film, a specific personality, a specific social situation and a specific time and mood', and he added that therefore we need a 'program of research which does recognize all essential phases of the motion picture experience' (1938: 518). Trying to investigate the 'interaction between imagination and social behaviour', Cressey (1938: 521) argued for a multiplicity of methods and sources, using (in his case) different techniques, such as statistics on film attendance, film preferences, interviews, observations, research on the motion picture theatre's location, advertisements, but also non-cinematic data like healthcare records, data available at public libraries, social data concerning the boys' families, and so on. Reading his work,[4] it is clear that Cressey's extremely multifaceted research agenda is still refreshing today, and is one that has never been fully operationalised.

What is the Cinema Experience?

This brings us to the question of the cinema experience, and of how one can operationalise Cressey's plea for understanding the unified 'motion picture experience'. Within film studies and film theory there is a substantial amount of literature on this issue of the film or cinematic experience, with a great deal of Balkanisation in terms of traditions and paradigms – from phenomenological, cognitive theoretical to more cultural studies oriented approaches. Following Cressey, one could accept that they all say something about it and the fact that the audience cinema experience consists of various layers. In his work, Cressey did not seem to problematise how these interrelate to each other. Work like that produced for the Payne Fund, and Cressey's in particular, indicates that one cannot fully understand or grasp the complexity of film and cinema audiences' experiences unless a multiscopic perspective is used, precisely because audiences are intrinsically multilayered: audiences are real and constructed; they are discursive and material; they are active, passive and everything in-between; they are consumers and citizens; they are massive but also individual, atomised as well as being part of wider social and cultural ensembles.

Understanding historical audiences could be looked at as recognising that 'audience' is a container concept, a sort of a mosaic. Examining audiences involves conceiving them as a palimpsest, or a complex multilayered record consisting of different dimensions where one surface can be partially erased, and then overwritten by another, with yet another on top of it. Doing historical cinema audience research often consists of searching the available sources in order to be able to scratch as much as possible of the different layers or dimensions of the cinematic experience. These dimensions comprise audiences' experiences of the venue as a place and space (for example, going to the cinema, experiencing the venue, other people in there, practices), of how they were attracted by the programme and the film, as well as their experience of the film and everything around it (stars, genres, styles . . .). From this perspective, it seems to be necessary to reintegrate the film as a meaningful text and its appeal to audiences. A pragmatic multiscopic approach not only brings forward levels of audience agency in terms of activity, selection, imagination and joy, but it also includes issues of structure like the industry's strategies to attract and guide particular audiences through programming, advertising and marketing.

Understanding the complexity of the cinematic experience does not only require taking into account both top-down and bottom-up dimensions of it, or reconsidering the good old classical social sciences structure/agency model in relation to cinema audiences (Bilsreyst and Meers 2011). It also needs to seriously take into consideration non-cinematic dimensions like class, gender, race and other social markers. As an illustration, I would like to expand on a case study on the reception of a popular film in Ghent. In the research I have done with colleagues on film programming, popularity and historical audiences in this Belgian city in the 1930s, it turned out that a now completely forgotten German movie, *Never Trust a Woman* (*Ich glaub' nie mehr an eine Frau*, 1929, Max Reichmann), was among the most popular in 1933.[5] The film kept on returning for several years, especially in venues in popular workers' districts. In the first half of the 1930s, the movie was second in Ghent in terms of longevity of exhibition, and was shown at least until 1936.

Figure 1.1 Cover of the German movie magazine *Illustrierte Film-Kurier* with Richard Tauber (no. 1341, December 1930). (Source: Author's collection.)

This completely forgotten German movie was one of the first German talkies, and can be conceived as a sort of a star vehicle, built around the world-famous Austrian tenor Richard Tauber, singing for the first time onscreen in this picture. Although the film is not, or is only briefly, mentioned in most German film historiographical accounts, it turns out that it was a major success, not only in some parts of Germany,[6] but also in Belgium and the Netherlands. In Belgium, Reichmann's feature film with the Austrian tenor was shown with great success in most of the major cities. In the Netherlands, where the movie ran for four years, *Never Trust a Woman* was among the top films of the early 1930s, returning to cities like Amsterdam, Rotterdam, the Hague, Utrecht and Leiden several times.[7] In Amsterdam, the film ran in the most important premiere cinema, Tuschinski (in May 1930), where it became such a hit that the exhibitor made a promotional newsreel which is a real goldmine for scholars interested in the history of film audiences.[8] In the newsreel we see cheerful cinemagoers waiting to get in, and we see them queuing before the venue. People wave at the cameraman, and they sing the songs they have just heard.

The question of why *Never Trust a Woman* failed to be canonised is an interesting one, but falls outside the scope of this chapter. What is more interesting here is to try to understand why a movie like *Never Trust a Woman* (that

Figures 1.2 and 1.3   Stills from a Dutch promotional newsreel about the screening of the German feature film *Never Trust a Woman (Ich glaub' nie mehr an eine Frau*, 1929, Max Reichmann) in the Amsterdam Tuschinski film theatre, shot in May 1930 by the Polygoon agency. (Source: Dutch Sound and Vision Institute.)

received negative reviews in the press) was an evergreen, so why it was so successful, at least in the Netherlands and Belgium (Dibbets 2019). In our attempt to understand why the movie grabbed people's imagination, we tried to use as many sources as possible. One of the findings was that the movie's release was accompanied by a massive advertising campaign, with for instance in Belgium, the use of at least four different stylish posters, one of which focused on a large image of Tauber's head. Much of this promotional material focused upon, or tried to capitalise on Tauber's fame, and on the fact that, for the first time, it was possible to see the world star singing onscreen. This was accompanied by a cross-media campaign (for example, the release of a record with most of Tauber's songs from the movie on it), with merchandising (for example, Tauber cigars), and so on. We could not conduct oral histories, of course, but, next to programming analyses, we could rely upon box office data for one film venue in Deinze near Ghent (Cinema Palace), showing that it was also one of the absolute top films of 1934 at this venue.

Although the film is filed as a lost film, we were lucky enough to see it – which was an eye-opener. Watching the movie, it became clear that, as some of the critics had already indicated, *Never Trust a Woman* was indeed an aesthetically unpretentious film with a rather sentimental, even banal love story. The movie is a low-class drama about an incestuous love affair between a sailor coming back home to Hamburg, and a woman who turns out not only to be a prostitute but also his sister. So, it is a rather melodramatic (and at times hilarious) love story with Richard Tauber playing the role of the sailor's friend. It is probably not interesting to interpret the movie here in terms of its German cultural context; what is interesting, however, is that *Never Trust a Woman* is a sort of a *Dirnenlied* film (a movie with songs about the world of prostitutes), with clear references to low-class settings. The movie openly deals with poverty, exploitation and illicit love affairs, along with the aforementioned provocative content like prostitution and the incestuous love affair. What is intriguing is that, at least in Ghent, the movie was mainly shown in popular film venues in working-class districts. It is important to consider extra-filmic elements in relation to Tauber's star status, with an aura of high culture surrounding the tenor – which audiences could now enjoy through

Figure 1.4   Advertising for the Amsterdam premiere of *Never Trust a Woman* (*Ich glaub' nie mehr an eine Frau*, 1929, Max Reichmann) in the Tuschinski film theatre, published in the newspaper *Algemeen Handelsdagblad*. (Source: Delpher.)

the film. Tauber's public performances in the Netherlands and Belgium were expensive, but through the film people could enjoy another world, yet recognise themselves in the social setting, the characters, themes and events in the movie. They probably enjoyed the mixture of high- and low-class elements, or at least a respectful 'high-culture' treatment of low-class issues.

For film audience researchers, this is all quite speculative because it is impossible to interview the people who originally went to watch the movie, and seemingly enjoyed it. But what this tiny case study on *Never Trust a Woman* seems to indicate is that the film text obviously is important for understanding the interaction between imagination and social behaviour, as Cressey called it (1938: 521), and that we need to fully integrate this into a consideration of the cinematic experience, of course. Cinema's success should then be linked to something less tangible, to a feeling – a certain feeling of belonging to, or a recognition of, something which goes further than the individual. Following Raymond Williams's slippery but productive concept of 'structures of feeling' (1977: 128–35), we could call this dimension the wider cinema experiences, or the structures of cinematic feeling or experiences (ibid.: 132). In case studies like the one on the German movie *Never Trust a Woman*, where we have data on which film played where and for how long, where we have some box office results and information on press coverage, promotion and marketing strategies, and where we have the film, we can start scraping away at layers of real and potential cinematic experiences. The cinema experience then refers to a particular set of lived experiences of films and cinema at a certain time and place, and within particular social formations of class, gender, race.

Another example of how to think about temporary formations, or about structures of cinematic feeling, is to look at *cinematic models* like rural cinema, community cinema, the film society model, and so on. This refers to a particular temporary configuration around a specific venue, a screen, a projector, darkness, with particular types of films and genres, and involving particular viewers, behaviours and enjoyments. Most of the work on historical cinema cultures concentrates on the mainstream theatrical model, the urban or metropolitan film exhibition model which is often presented as the one made or preferred by the industry. It is a variable model with (more or less) precise locations (city centre), films and programmes (for example, new releases), with a particular audience composition (for example, class-mixing), and which promotes a certain mode of filmgoing, and installs a certain 'dispositif' for watching films. There are many other socially and spatially embedded models such as forms of rural film exhibition and cinemagoing (for example, Thissen and Zimmerman 2016; Treveri Gennari et al. 2018).

It is useful to think about other cinematic models as well, precisely because the structure of each model is subject to particular variation in where it is located; in what it offers in terms of films; in how it appeals to particular audiences; in how it employs other spatial strategies; in what is allowed and not in the cinema in terms of practices; in who is attending the cinema, with whom, and how they behave, and so on. Although I think there is a structure (a place, a programme, screenings, audience composition, behaviour, and so on), there can be huge varieties within each model. One example is the sex cinema model. Going to a sex cinema triggers other kinds of cinema experiences than the mainstream theatrical model, one mostly characterised by transgression and an aura of forbiddenness (Biltereyst 2018). The sex cinema model is not a fixed entity and there are variations, but there is some common ground in terms of what was offered (daring films, genres, programming), in how they advertised, in the spatial strategies and arrangements in and around the venue (in red-light districts or not?), in the target group and audience composition (only men or not?), and so on.

Thinking in terms of cinematic models with a particular structure and variations opens opportunities for comparison, where, for instance, cinema experiences in Western Europe are compared with those in Latin America or the Arab world. The key issue here is that comparison is not only about adding information to the researcher's basket, but the point is to question some of the specific configurations in the cinematic experience, models and structures of feeling. An example is Mexico, where the model of open-air screenings for low-class audiences, known as 'terrazzas', is in many respects fundamentally different from what happens in Western Europe (Meers et al. 2018). Terrazas did not need to be located at a particular place, did not need bricks, were not often included in newspapers. This example is interesting because it questions some of the basic constituents of cinema like: what is a cinema in terms of place, space and a programme?

What about Sources and the Imaginative Dimension?

A final set of questions relates to the sources which are used in order to have relevant traces of the cinematic experience. One key question here is about whether, after all, we are using the right sources for understanding some of the key issues related to audience experiences. Thanks to digitisation processes, researchers now have easier access to historical data such as those in newspapers, magazines and trade papers, so that we are able to tell more complex stories about cinemagoers' experiences in the past. The variety of sources and traces of that past also includes audience-produced material like fan letters, film diaries, and other early forms of collecting and film-related DIY activities. We have industry-produced material like ledgers, and there is an urgency to use oral histories.

We need to remain critical and self-reflexive about those sources, though. One such issue is whether oral histories, which are often presented as deep interviews, are able to gain access to the more imaginative dimensions of cinema. Although oral histories offer us direct access to people's past cinema experiences, we have to admit that interviewees rarely talk about dimensions which are crucial in understanding cinema's imaginative power. Another issue is that some sources could be explored more creatively, like photos which are now often used as illustrations. But there is an overwhelming amount of pictures which contain rich data on how people behaved in a cinema, or how they were overwhelmed by what they saw on the screen. Think about Weegee's famous series of infrared photos made in the mid-1940s, when he ventured into the darkness of New York's movie theatres and turned a camera loaded with infrared film on the unsuspecting crowds (see Dundon 2017). Weegee captured shots of children, who are completely captivated by the film they are watching; there are images of sleeping adults, and of lusty lovers taking advantage of the darkness. These photos possibly are the only visible traces of the act of consuming pictures, and they mostly indicate that films were powerful, at least on some occasions for some people. The movies' imaginative power was so intense that people were intensively emotionally engaged with them; but on the other hand, films and the cinema were also places for doing other things. So, the photos graphically show us the range of audiences being active, passive and everything in-between – in sheer contrast to the idea of the homogeneous audience.

The same goes for the practices of cinemagoing like queuing, where photos can give us detailed and contextualised information on audience behaviour. Through the pictures we get visible evidence on audience composition where we often do not know from other sources who attended which cinema – with differences in terms of age, gender, class. The *Never Trust a Woman* newsreel is such a powerful illustration and a rich source for understanding how people in Amsterdam were dressed up for the occasion (the Tuschinski theatre was by far the most important and luxurious film palace in the city). It shows how they were disciplined, but also how they did not mind that there were guards or cinema stewards. It also shows how, for instance, people were offered a coffee or a tea, and when they were in the cinema, they received a programme with the lyrics of the songs. From shots taken at the back of the Tuschinski, we see how joyful people were when leaving the cinema. These tell us, again, something about the imaginative aspect of films, and of the intense pleasures involved in cinemagoing. It is strange to observe how film scholars often neglect such rich audiovisual material, and that it is not used enough as a primary source.

Mapping these types of rich audiovisual material is part of the work still to be done, not so much as illustrative material or ephemera, but just simply as primary sources. The same goes for postcards, cartoons, magazines, literature, and for other visual and artistic material like paintings, such as those by the Belgian surrealist René Magritte who once said that for him cinema was 'a trampoline for the imagination' (Fischer 2019). For Magritte – who made home movies, referred to films, stars and the cinematic in many of his paintings, and was an avid cinemagoer (Canonne 2020) – cinema was more than the place or the space, and he was deeply affected by cinema's imaginative world. It strongly influenced Magritte's worldview and structures of feeling, where cinema referred to childhood memories, innocence, and to a world that he opposed to bourgeois high culture.

Conclusion

This chapter has tried to raise questions about a broader research agenda on doing historical research on film audiences. One of its key ideas is that we need to take into account the multilayered character of audiences' cinema experiences, along with trying to find some structures in it, for instance by looking at varieties within cinematic models. Referring to Barbara Klinger's terminology in a groundbreaking article on film history and reception (Klinger 1997), this chapter is a call for self-reflexivity, as well as an attempt to underline the idea of an interminable history with multiple historicities. It is about Klinger's argument that we must try to understand the interaction between the semiotic and the social, or the relation between the imaginative and the social order of the total film experience.

Notes

1. This chapter is based on, and is a slightly revised version of, my keynote entitled 'Audience as Palimpsest. Mapping Historical Film Audience Research', given at Researching Past Cinema Audiences: Archives, Memories and Methods conference, Aberystwyth University, UK, 26–28 March 2018.
2. Following Richard Maltby (2007) and the New Cinema History perspective (Biltereyst et al. 2019: 2), I look at cinema as a multifaceted concept, referring not only to film, but also to the imaginative, sociocultural and economic realities within which films are produced, distributed, circulated, exhibited and received. The concept of cinema includes references to a place (the physical venue where movies are shown, and where other activities take place around film screenings), a space (people's experience of that place, or the imaginary and socially embedded version of the place), an industry (the production, distribution and exhibition of movies) and even a way of life (a particular way of talking, thinking, looking and perceiving the world).
3. See the wonderful book on the Payne Fund Studies, the parts on Cressey, and Cressey's manuscripts in *Children and the Movies* (Jowett et al. 1996).
4. See also Cressey's *The Taxi-Dance Hall*, published in 1932. This fine piece of sociological research on the 'recreational institution' of the taxi-dance hall was set up in 1925 because it was 'at the time a very new and questionable type of establishment' ([1932] 2008: xvii). In *The Taxi-Dance Hall*, Cressey combined an amazing amount of methodologies and approaches, which simply could be seen as a forerunner of his research agenda on cinema. Among the methods Cressey used, we can find geo-mapping techniques, participant observation, interviews and surveys, and other approaches.

5. This small case study on the historical reception of the German movie *Never Trust a Woman* was part of a wider New Cinema History project on the history of cinema cultures in the city of Ghent, Belgium ('Gent Kinemastad', 2009–12, funded by the Ghent University Research Council, BOF). The project used a triangulation of (1) an investigation of film exhibition venues, (2) a systematic analysis of film programming in sample years, and (3) oral histories with older cinemagoers. See Van de Vijver and Biltereyst (2010).
6. For an analysis of the movie's programming in the province of Oberschlesien, see Garncarz (2015: 226–9).
7. For information on the movie (*Ik Geloof niet meer in Vrouwen*) on the Cinema Context platform, see <http://www.cinemacontext.nl/> (last accessed 14 May 2021).
8. The film was put online by the Dutch Sound and Vision Institute and is available at <https://www.youtube.com/watch?v=se5YcGYwd6w> (last accessed 14 May 2021).

Bibliography

Altenloh, Emilie ([1914] 1977) *Zur Soziologie des Kino: Die Kino-unternehmung und die sozialen Schichten ihrer besucher*. Leipzig: Spamerschen Buchdruckerei.

Barefoot, Guy (2019) 'My Search for "Passion Pits with Pix": Cinema History and 1950s Drive-in Audiences', *Participations* 16(1), 824–43.

Biltereyst, Daniel (2018) 'Sex Cinemas, Limit Transgression and the Aura of "Forbiddenness": The Emergence of *Risqués* Cinemas and *Cinema Leopold* in Ghent, Belgium, 1945–1954', *Film Studies* 18(3), 14–33.

Biltereyst, Daniel, Richard Maltby and Philippe Meers (2019) *The Routledge Companion to New Cinema History*. London and New York: Routledge.

Biltereyst, Daniel and Philippe Meers (2011) 'The Political Economy of Audiences', in Janet Wasko, Graham Murdoch and Helena Sousa (eds), *The Handbook of Political Economy of Communications*. Malden, MA: Wiley-Blackwell, pp. 415–35.

Biltereyst, Daniel and Philippe Meers (2018) 'Film, Cinema and Reception Studies: Revisiting Research on Audience's Filmic and Cinematic Experiences', in Elena Di Giovanni and Yves Gambier (eds), *Reception Studies and Audiovisual Translation*. Amsterdam: John Benjamins, pp. 21–41.

Biltereyst, Daniel and Lies Van de Vijver (eds) (2020) *Mapping Movie Magazines: Digitization, Periodicals and Cinema History*. London: Palgrave Macmillan.

Blumer, Herbert (1933) *Movies and Conduct*. New York: Macmillan.

Bourdon, Jérôme (2015) 'Detextualizing: How to Write a History of Audiences', *European Journal of Communication* 30(1), 7–21.

Camus, Albert ([1942] 2013) *The Myth of Sisyphus*. London: Penguin Books. [First published as *Le Mythe de Sisyphe*. Paris: Gallimard.]

Canonne, Xavier (2020) *René Magritte: Les images révélées*. Ghent: Ludion.

Cressey, Paul G. (1938) 'The Motion Picture Experience as Modified by Social Background and Personality', *American Sociological Review* 3(4), 516–25.

Cressey, Paul G. ([1932] 2008) *The Taxi-Dance Hall: A Sociological Study in Commercialized Recreation and City Life*. Chicago: University of Chicago Press.

DeCordova, Richard ([1990] 2002) 'Ethnography and Exhibition: The Child Audience, the Hays Office, and Saturday Matinees', in Gregory Waller (ed.), *Moviegoing in America: A Sourcebook in the History of Film Exhibition*. Oxford: Blackwell, pp. 159–69.

Dibbets, Karel (2019) 'The Evergreens and Mayflies of Film History', in Daniel Biltereyst, Richard Maltby and Philippe Meers (eds), *The Routledge Companion to New Cinema History*. London and New York: Routledge, pp. 329–43.

Dundon, Rian (2017) 'Infrared Photos of 1940s Movie Audiences are a Candid Study of American Voyeurism: Imaging the Spectacle Like only Weegee Could', *Timeline*, 21 August. <https://timeline.com/weegee-photos-infrared-movie-ec9734a9d63e> (last accessed 14 May 2021).

Fischer, Lucy (2019) *Cinemagritte: René Magritte within the Frame of Film History, Theory, and Practice*. Detroit: Wayne State University Press.

Forest, Claude (ed.) (2017) 'Les salles de cinéma: histoire et géographie', *CINéMAS: Revue d'études cinématographiques/Journal of Film Studies* 27(2–3).

Garncarz, Joseph (2015) 'Frohe laune und ein hauch von tragik. Zur kulturspezifik regionaler filmpräferenzen in der preußischen provinz oberschlesien', in Brigitte Braun, Andrzej Dejbski and Andrzej Gwózdz (eds), *Unterwegs zum Nachbarn Deutsch-polnische Filmbegegnungen*. Trier: WVT, pp. 223–44.

Garncarz, Joseph (2021) *Begeisterte Zuschauer: Die Macht des Kinopublikums in der NS-Diktatur*. Cologne: Herbert von Halem.

Gelly, Christophe and David Roche (2012) *Approaches to Film and Reception Theories*. Clermont-Ferrand: Presses Universitaires Blaise Pascal.

Glen, Patrick (2019) 'Freak Scene: Cinema-Going Memories and the British Counterculture of the 1960s', *The Sixties* 12, 45–68.

Jernudd, Åsa (2013) 'Cinema Memory: National Identity as Expressed by Swedish Elders in an Oral History Project', *Northern Lights* 11, 109–22.

Jowett, Garth, Ian Jarvie and Kathryn Fuller (1996) *Children and the Movies*. New York: Cambridge University Press.

Juan, Myriam (2020) 'Looking at Movie Fans', in Daniel Biltereyst and Lies Van de Vijver (eds), *Mapping Movie Magazines: Digitization, Periodicals and Cinema History*. London: Palgrave Macmillan, pp. 201–20.

Klien-Thomas, Hanna (2019) 'Historical Disjunctures and Bollywood Audiences in Trinidad: Negotiations of Gender and Ethnic Relations in Cinema Going', *Participations* 16(2), 465–88.

Klinger, Barbara (1997) 'Film History Terminable and Interminable: Recovering the Past in Reception Studies', *Screen* 38(2), 107–28.

Kuhn, Annette (1999a) 'Memories of Cinemagoing in the 1930s', *Journal of Popular British Cinema* 2, 100–20.

Kuhn, Annette (1999b) 'Cinema-Going in Britain in the 1930s: Report of a Questionnaire Survey', *Historical Journal of Film, Radio and Television* 19(4), 531–43.

Kuhn, Annette (2002) *An Everyday Magic: Cinema and Cultural Memory*. London: I. B. Tauris.

Kuhn, Annette, Daniel Biltereyst and Philippe Meers (2017) 'Memories of Cinemagoing and Film Experience: An Introduction', *Memory Studies* 10(1), 3–16.

Lynd, Robert S. and Helen Merrell Lynd ([1929] 1956) *Middletown: A Study in Modern American Culture*. New York: Harcourt.

Maltby, Richard (2007) 'How Can Cinema History Matter More?', *Screening the Past* 22. <http://tlweb.latrobe.edu.au/humanities/screeningthepast/22/board-richard-maltby.html> (last accessed 14 May 2021).

Maltby, Richard, Daniel Biltereyst and Philippe Meers (eds) (2011) *Explorations in New Cinema History: Approaches and Case Studies*. Malden, MA: Wiley-Blackwell.

Mayer, Jacob-Peter (1946) *Sociology of Film: Studies and Documents*. London: Faber and Faber.

Meers, Philippe, Daniel Biltereyst and José-Carlos Lozano (2018) 'The Cultura de la Pantalla Network: Writing New Cinema Histories across Latin America and Europe', *Revista Internacional de Comunicación y Desarrollo (RICD)* 2(9), 153–7.

Morley, David (2009) 'For a Materialist, Non-media-centric Media Studies', *Television and New Media* 10(1), 114–16.

Münsterberg, Hugo ([1916] 2002) *The Photoplay: A Psychological Study*. New York: Routledge.

Peiss, Kathy (1986) *Cheap Amusements: Working Women and Leisure in Turn-of-the-Century New York*. Philadelphia: Temple University Press.

Richards, Helen (2003) 'Memory Reclamation of Cinema Going in Bridgend, South Wales, 1930–1960', *Historical Journal of Film, Radio and Television* 23(4), 341–55.

Rosenzweig, Roy (1983) *Eight Hours for What We Will: Workers & Leisure in an Industrial City, 1870–1920*. Cambridge: Cambridge University Press.

Sedgwick, John (2000) *Popular Filmgoing in 1930s Britain: A Choice of Pleasures*. Exeter: University of Exeter Press.

Stacey, Jackey (1994) *Star Gazing: Hollywood Cinema and Female Spectatorship*. Abingdon and New York: Routledge.

Thissen, Judith (2019) 'Faith, Fun and Fear in the Dutch Orthodox Protestant Milieu: Towards a Non-cinema Centred Approach to Cinema History', *Participations* 16(2), 436–64.

Thissen, Judith and Clemens Zimmerman (2016) *Cinema Beyond the City: Small-Town and Rural Film Culture in Europe*. London: BFI Publishing.

Treveri Gennari, Daniela and Silvia Dibeltulo (2017) '"It existed indeed . . . it was all over the papers": Memories of Film Censorship in 1950s Italy', *Participations* 14(1), 235–48.

Treveri Gennari, Daniela, Danielle Hipkins and Catherine O'Rawe (eds) (2018) *Rural Cinema Exhibition and Audiences in a Global Context*. Cham: Palgrave Macmillan.

Van de Vijver, Lies and Daniel Biltereyst (2010) 'Hollywood vs. Localiteit. Het ongelijke aanbod van Amerikaanse en Europese film in de jaren dertig in Gent', *Tijdschrift voor Mediageschiedenis* 13(2) (Spring), 60–79.

Wets, Paul (1920) *Une enquête sur les spectacles cinématographiques à Bruxelles*. Brussels: Office de la Protection de l'Enfance.

Williams, Raymond (1977) *Marxism and Literature*. Oxford: Oxford University Press.

2. FROM CINEMA CULTURE TO CINEMA MEMORY: A CONCEPTUAL AND METHODOLOGICAL TRAJECTORY

Annette Kuhn

The UK Economic and Social Research Council-funded project 'Cinema Culture in 1930s Britain' (CCINTB) was launched in the early 1990s with the objective of 'investigating the ways in which films and cinemagoing figured in the daily lives of people throughout the [British] nation in the 1930s, and situating cinemagoing and fan behaviour in this period within their broader social and cultural contexts'.[1] Alongside research in contemporary source materials relating to cinemagoing in the period, a key element of the project involved memory work with surviving 1930s cinemagoers. Over a period of twenty-five years and more, this memory work has generated, and continues to generate, fascinating and culturally significant insights concerning the nature of cinema memory as a distinctive subtype of cultural memory. This chapter traces a conceptual and methodological trajectory in this enduring project from a broadly cultural-historical approach towards a focus on cultural memory.

As the project's full title – 'Cinema Culture in 1930s Britain: Ethnohistory of a Popular Cultural Practice' – suggests, the originally intended substantive focus was cultural and historical. And indeed the inquiry, which started out with a focus essentially on a culturalist approach, was informed in part by Jackie Stacey's doctoral study of women's filmgoing in the 1950s, conducted at the Birmingham Centre for Contemporary Cultural Studies and published in 1994 as *Star Gazing*; as well as by Helen Taylor's work on *Gone With the Wind* – the novel and the film – and its female fans, which was published in 1989 (Stacey 1994; Taylor 1989). In a similar vein, in 1992 I had myself conducted a small-scale inquiry on cinema culture and femininity in the 1930s, based upon research in the many British film fan magazines of the period (Kuhn 1996). All three projects had in turn been inspired in varying degrees by 1980s debates within feminist film studies around female spectatorship in cinema, and on the ambition to focus on the female social audience as against film theory's implied 'spectator-in-the-text' (Stacey 1993).

Stacey and Taylor incorporated questionnaire surveys and other types of informant accounts into their inquiries. Stacey's work emerged from the ethnographic strand of the Birmingham Centre's output (such as Willis 2016), while Taylor's is rooted in the study of American literature and culture (for example Radway 1987). Both Stacey and Taylor were innovative in pursuing inquiries specifically into women as cultural consumers in tandem with a focus on popular culture, and in placing women's perspectives front and centre in terms of both substance and methodology. While neither work came out of a film studies context, the distinctive approach adopted in them undoubtedly influenced subsequent inquiries within film studies into screen audiences of the past.

'Cinema Culture in 1930s Britain' tried to do something new with this ethnographic approach to historical film reception; and besides including men as well as women it aimed to be more self-conscious (and, dare I say it, more rigorous) methodologically than this existing work. In this regard CCINTB's research design was guided by the methodological protocols of interpretive sociology, ethnography and oral history. As it turned out, in terms of methodology the project did not draw a great deal from either film studies or cultural studies. The research design, which is fully explained in *An Everyday Magic* (Kuhn 2002: 240–54; see also Kuhn 2020), was three-pronged, the main emphasis being on an ethnographic-style inquiry among surviving cinemagoers of the 1930s. Arguably one of the most distinctive features of 'Cinema Culture in 1930s Britain' is that it yielded data that is at once ethnographically 'thick' and relatively robust in terms of representativeness – data that has therefore been, and remains, qualitatively and interpretively rewarding.

A key – perhaps the main – element of the ethnographic inquiry took the form of depth interviews with eighty-six surviving 1930s cinemagoers living in four areas of the British mainland: two cities (Glasgow and Greater Manchester), one metropolitan suburb (Harrow in Greater London) and one rural region (East Anglia). The median birth year of interviewees was 1924. The bulk of the interviews were conducted during 1994 and 1995, and so most of the informants were in their seventies or older at the time. With one or two exceptions, all informants were interviewed at least twice. There were also two questionnaire surveys of self-selected informants, and many of those who took part in the project also donated essays, letters, diaries and other memorabilia.

Because transcription of interviews was ongoing throughout 1995 and 1996, it was possible to begin reviewing these materials from early on in the life of the project. In some respects, what interviewees recalled (and just as importantly what they did not recall) seemed surprising at first. Informants generally did not mention individual films very much, or indeed at all. What they did remember most vividly were the places where they went to the pictures in their childhood and adolescence and whom they went with. These things were typically recollected alongside other events in their young lives at the time – be it games of Cowboys and Indians played in the street, courtship rituals, or film star-inspired experiments with hairstyles and make-up. Interviewees would talk about stars of the period, usually with some prompting, but rarely had very much to say about particular films featuring their favourites. In other words, interviewees' accounts were focused on cinemagoing as opposed to filmgoing (Terrill 2021), on cinema culture as part of daily life. These testimonies focus on the social activity of going to the pictures, and cinemagoing is typically remembered as part of informants' everyday lives, routines, hobbies and relationships with family and friends. This Mancunian informant's memory is typical:

> [W]e'd only got the radio, not the television – every night on the radio there used to be a band from the London, one of the London hotels, so I used to do my home-, and I can remember this, it always used to be 10:30 at night till midnight, well I would do my homework. By then, I'd been to the pictures, played football and done my homework, 10:30 at night I'm doing my homework till probably one and two in the morning, listening to – well I can't be too sure about these – definitely Lew Stone and his band from the Monseigneur Restaurant on the Wednesday, definitely Roy Fox and his band from the Mayfair Hotel on another night.[2]

The raw substance of these recollections of a lived cinemagoing culture may be called *cinema memories*. Taken in aggregate, informants' cinema memories display a number of shared substantive and discursive attributes, and these are the soil in which the concept of *cinema memory* seeded itself early in the course of 'Cinema Culture in 1930s Britain'.

For example, the most striking, and perhaps the most intriguing, of these attributes is the centrality and the particular figuration of place and space in the cinema memories. During 1996, the first findings from 'Cinema Culture in 1930s Britain' were reported at a number of conferences at home and abroad. Among these was the Screen Studies Conference in Glasgow in the summer of that year. According to the abstract of a plenary lecture entitled 'Place, Space and Cinema Memory',

> Informants are keen to establish precisely where 'their' cinemas were situated, detailing local topographies which link locations of cinemas with other key places in their daily lives. Many recall in vivid detail the process of getting to the cinema and the people they went with . . . In

many of these accounts, narrators position themselves within their local topographies, moving freely in the telling from past to present and back again, as well as between remembered places: a sense emerges of narrators navigating mental maps, some of them extremely highly organised, of familiar remembered territory. (Conference Programme 1996)

Citing examples from CCINTB interviews, the lecture expanded on the instrumentality of place and space in cinema memory, and more broadly on the unique qualities of cinema memory as a subtype of cultural memory. This was one of the first public outings for this noteworthy finding. The workings of cinema memory have since been explored in greater depth in a number of conference presentations and publications (see, for example, Kuhn 1999, 2004, 2013).

In a characteristic example of the figuration of place in cinema memory, a seventy-nine-year-old interviewee who had lived in Bolton, Greater Manchester since the age of five offers a lengthy discursive 'walking tour' of the local cinemas that she remembers. In the course of the tour, she 'stops' to tell little stories about some of them:

> You get the main road, St Helen's Road. Eh there was the Rumworth, it was called. And then there was this eh Derby picture house which went to [became] the Tivoli. And that was all along that road. But going over to Deane Road, there was the Fern Cinema [probably referring to Plaza Cinema at the corner of Deane Road and Fern Street]. That's three isn't it, up to now? And then there was the Regent where we used to go. That's four. And then there was a big one. Eh . . . it turned into a skating rink after. And it began with R. It wasn't the Rialto and it wasn't the Regent. [pause 2 seconds] But it began with an R [probably referring to the Regal, aka the Astor aka the New Olympia, later the Navada skating rink] . . . And it was a big cinema that. And they used to say a lot of courting couples used to go there and sit on the back seat, you know. And that was to, I don't know. I never went in, so I don't know. Erm so that was like erm what, one, two, three, four, five. And then there was one on St George's Road called the Rialto. [pause 2 seconds] This was called the Imperial. That's six isn't it? There was the Queen's on Bradshawgate, that's seven. And then, there was one opened on Bradshawgate erm called the Lido. Now that's still going. I don't know if it's still called the Lido, but it's still going. And I can remember when it was being built. Now I was still at school when that was being built. They used to say, the workmen that were working on it said it would fall down within five years.[3]

From accounts like this there emerges a sense of navigation in embodied imagination of mental topographies of familiar, remembered territory. This 'topographical memory talk' evokes a set of spatial practices associated with very specific places, offering important clues as to some of the ways cinema memory works as a distinctive form of cultural memory. To summarise, in topographical memory talk: the starting place is home; the journey is on foot and is goal-directed; the journey is oft-repeated; it has a familiar, everyday quality; and the journey back home typically remains implicit.

These and other distinctive discursive features of 1930s cinemagoers' memories are reflected on in a chapter of *An Everyday Magic* which sets out the repeated themes in, and modes of narrating, recollections of cinemagoing (Kuhn 2002: 1–12). Some of these are discussed below. Meanwhile, it may be helpful to set out some reflections on how – or the methodology through which – the concept of cinema memory was arrived at. For it is, of course, a concept – an abstraction. But it is an abstraction grounded in empirical observation. It has not been conjured out of thin air, it is not an *a priori* notion. It is derived, through a process of induction, from the 'Cinema Culture in 1930s Britain' interviews and from other informant-generated memory materials assembled in the course of the project.

In other words, the concept of cinema memory presents itself in, and arises from, the project's empirical findings. It is not a prior assumption, nor is it a hypothesis. Before reviewing the corpus of informants' memory-stories, I had been unaware that there could be such a particular thing as cinema memory. To think about this in more concrete terms, you could say that cinema memory is like the essential oil derived from a plant. To start with you might have a sack of plant material – leaves, stems, flowers, seeds – from a rosemary bush, say. What you end up with is a tiny bottle of essential oil of rosemary. The two things, sack of plant materials and vial of essential oil, are clearly not identical. But they are different aspects or manifestations of the same basic stuff. Some kind of change or transformation has taken place: from the original plant materials oil has been conjured: extracted, reduced, distilled.

This is an analogy, not a scientific explanation; and an analogy that can be pursued for some distance. The original plant material may be likened to our 'raw' data – our cinemagoing memories, or cinema memories; and the essential oil to the reduction of these cinema memories to their fundamental features as cinema memory. What is important for present purposes is what has gone on in order to make the raw materials of cinema memories assume their essential form as *cinema memory*. If this begins to sound somewhat alchemical, it is worth remembering that underlying an apparently magical transformation there lies a scientific rationale – a method, in other words – to both the extraction of essential oils from plants and the inductive identification, from raw empirical data, of a cultural phenomenon, an abstraction, like cinema memory. What, then, are the fundamental features of cinema memory, as they emerge from the bundles of cinemagoing memories gathered in the course of 'Cinema Culture in 1930s Britain'?

Three *forms or modes* of cinema memory, in particular of early or childhood cinema memory, may be identified: firstly, remembered scenes or images from films; secondly, situated memories of films; and thirdly, memories of cinemagoing. The evidence suggests that these three forms of cinema memory are not separate or distinct from one another, but are more aptly regarded as occupying positions along a continuum. In particular instances, these may overlap, merge, or share characteristics. Also, since the project is still ongoing, this schema remains a work in progress. These categories may well therefore not exhaust our understanding of the nature and workings of cinema memory. There is always potential for further analysis.

Remembered Scenes or Images from Films

And it was a film, a silent film, about the sea. And these waves were uh making this ship roll, it was a sailing ship, and I was so frightened I got on the floor, and I was hiding my face in my mother's lap. I was scared stiff.[4]

Only a handful of memories of this kind emerged in 'Cinema Culture in 1930s Britain', but Victor Burgin recounts a striking one in his book *The Remembered Film*: 'A dark night, someone is walking down a narrow stream. I see only feet splashing through water, and broken reflections of light from somewhere ahead, where something mysterious and dreadful waits' (2004: 16). Burgin calls his own vivid and detailed earliest memory of a film a 'sequence-image', since he is recalling 'a sequence of such brevity that I might almost be describing a still image' (ibid.: 15). But in terms of content and feeling tone, both these examples have markedly distinctive qualities, and the fact that they are very early memories is important. In terms of the cultural significance of the finding, their intensity arguably more than compensates for their rarity.

Remembered scenes or images from films are distinctive in three respects, all of which are observable in these two examples. They are distinctive first of all in the vividness and the visual quality of the descriptions. These almost dreamlike memories are of individual, isolated shots, scenes and images from films whose titles are forgotten or unknown. And yet these images are obviously still resonant in informants' consciousness, in all their vividness, decades after the event. It seems clear that in the moment of telling *in the present* all the remembered feelings or sensations associated with these memories are in some sense being re-experienced.

A second marked feature of memories of this type is that the remembered scenes or images from films are characteristically very brief and are always recalled in isolation from the film's plot, which is not recounted and so is probably not remembered. Also, these memories are not as a rule accompanied by any details of the circumstances in which the film was seen: it is as if the remembered scene or image stands out in sharp relief against a background that is absent, or blurred and lacking in detail. Victor Burgin's remembered image is an extreme example of this. He notes that he can remember nothing more about the film than the scene or the image he describes: 'There is nothing before, nothing after' he says; 'no other sequence, no shot, no names of characters or actors, and no title' (ibid.: 16). As to the circumstances in which he saw the film, Burgin implies that he would have been in the cinema with his mother: 'my mother sought distraction at the cinema . . . I became her companion there' (ibid.: 16). But this is the adult Victor speaking, and there is no hint of his mother's presence within the telling of the memory itself. On the other hand, Tessa Amelan's remembered image, a frightening one, is associated with a memory of seeking comfort by burying her face in her mother's lap.

Miss Amelan's story calls attention to a third distinctive aspect of remembered scenes or images: their telling often re-evokes strong remembered emotions or bodily sensations on the narrator's part. Recollections of hiding or covering one's face, or of cowering under the seat, all point to an embodied, preverbal, response that has become tied in memory to the image or the scene itself. It is as if the remembered image or scene and the body of the person remembering it are fused together in the moment of recollection and in the feelings evoked by the memory.

In relation to all this, it is helpful to look at how the narrator constructs himself or herself in relation to these memories, as well as at the actual content of the memories and how they are narrated. For there is a sense in which the remembered scene or image *enfolds* the subject – who yet at the same time figures as an *observer* of the film scene and the scene of memory, in much the way Freud describes the subject of fantasy creating, and also placing himself within, a *mise en scène*; at once directing the fantasy scenario and helplessly caught up in it (Freud 1979).

All this lends support to Burgin's observation that the remembered film, as one instance of our everyday encounters with the environment of media, is analogous with such 'interior' processes as inner speech and involuntary association, and that it bears the hallmarks of the primary processes of the 'raw' dream, daydream or fantasy (2004: 14). This, along with the investment in the visual, and also the fragmentary and non-narrative quality observable in these memories, aligns them with the non-verbal or the preverbal, with the Preconscious or even the Unconscious.

Referring to his own remembered 'sequence-image', Burgin notes that this memory, which he associates with a 'particular affect' – a sense of apprehension – becomes somehow diminished when put into words, as if the process of articulation takes the *shine* off the unspoken, unarticulated, memory image. Elsewhere he mentions the 'brilliance' that surrounds this kind of memory; a word which captures the feeling of effulgence and vividness apparent also in (some of) the

1930s cinemagoers' remembered scenes. It is perhaps the bodily, primary process, preverbal, 'inner speech' quality that still attaches to these now verbalised memories that imbues them also with the directness and simplicity of the child's voice: a quality that is certainly apparent in 1930s cinemagoers' accounts of their remembered scenes or images.

To sum up, we may infer that the remembered film scenes or images described by Victor Burgin and by a few of the 'Cinema Culture in 1930s Britain' informants operate on the side of the inner world and the phenomenological. Burgin's rich and resonant descriptions of the experience of the remembered film (and of remembering films) make especially apparent the connection of these memories to psychical or mental processes, with their marks of interior speech, and of productions of the Preconscious or the Unconscious. Moreover, looked at discursively – in terms of their rhetoric or address – these memories display many of the formal qualities that distinguish a cultural genre or mode that I have elsewhere called the 'memory text' (Kuhn 2000). These include a non-continuous or non-sequential quality to the telling; a lack of specificity as to time; a fragmentary quality; and a sense of synchrony, as if remembered events are somehow pulled out of a linear time frame or refuse to be anchored in 'real' historical time. Memory texts, in short, share the generally imagistic quality of unconscious productions like dreams and fantasies. Significantly, Burgin notes that his own earliest memory of a film is sufficient ('sharply particular', 'brilliant', he says) within itself, and yet at the same time it is vague as to everything outside itself, unspecific as to 'who, where and what' (2004: 16).

The commonalities of observation and interpretation that emerge here indicate that if memories of this kind – remembered scenes or images from films – operate on the side of the phenomenological or the metapsychological and bear the marks of inner world processes, they are by no means to be dismissed as purely subjective, personal or idiosyncratic. There is clearly at some level something shared, even deeply cultural, about such 'inner-world' productions. However, the cultural is rather more obviously embedded in the second mode of cinema memory: situated memories of films.

Situated Memories of Films

In memories of this kind, films and scenes/images from films are remembered (or narratively situated) within a context of events in the informant's life:

> Oh, I remember the first film we went to see [Boris Karloff] in. Erm, at The Globe, in, where was it? Old Trafford, I think it was. And it was *The Mummy*. Well there were benches then, you know, not seats. I don't know whether I'd left school. Probably I'd left school. Anyway, I went to

see him. I was sat there, dead quiet. And when they opened the lid and it shows him like, you know, and he moves his hand. Well I let out one! I slid along the seat.[5]

[T]he first film I ever remember was going to a cinema in Maryhill Road called the Blythswood. And I had pleaded with my parents to let me go, and it must have been about nine and I was told I could go and it was *The Four Sons*. And we went, I went to the cinema on my own, and I was allowed to go to the first showing at 2 o'clock. And I went with a friend to the first showing and in these days you just sat right on. There was no change of, no going out. You just went any, in the middle, or any time you walked in, if you paid your fare. So at the end of that my friend said – 'I have to go, Helen.' And it just, as I say, went on again. I said 'I think I'll watch it again.' So I sat on and watched it again and I got out, got up to come out and was passing a friend with her parents and she said 'Aw, come on, sit beside me. Don't go out, Helen. Just sit with me.' [laughs] So I sat through it again! And at the end of it her parents were going and she said to her parents, 'Could I sit through this again?' and they said 'Well, if Helen'll stay.' [laughs] I sat through that film four times.[6]

In 'Cinema Culture in 1930s Britain', expressions of this type of cinema memory are rather more prominent than remembered scenes or images, though the detail and the nature of the remembered film and the associated life events, as well as the weight given to each and the relationship between the two, vary considerably across different instances.

The 'situated memories of films' quoted above are taken from CCINTB interviewees' accounts: Annie Wright's story about when she saw the 1932 version of *The Mummy* incorporates a vividly remembered image from the film – but this is set within a recollection of a cinema visit that also contains quite a lot of scene-setting detail (the name and location of the cinema, a description of its seating arrangements) as well as her own bodily response to the mummy's stirring into life. Helen Smeaton's recollection of seeing John Ford's 1928 family saga, *The Four Sons* (she tells this story in both her interviews), lacks the degree of detail about the cinema's facilities that marks Annie Wright's account, while emphasising the peer-group sociability of the occasion (being persuaded by her friend to stay longer) and conflating her discovery of the delights of continuous programming with her earliest remembered visit to a cinema. The story is also of a piece with this informant's concern, voiced throughout her interviews, to memorialise her mother, who is credited in this instance with indulgence of, rather than anger at, her daughter's late arrival home.

A further example of this mode of cinema memory – this one not from 'Cinema Culture in 1930s Britain'– is a recollection of a visit to the cinema in the 1950s, complete with scene-setting details. It hints at an explanation of the origin of an obsession with cinema that inspired the speaker's own artistic production in later life. The filmmaker Terence Davies remembers:

> When I was seven I was taken by my eldest sister to see *Singin' in the Rain*. Sitting in the dark brown, baroque interior of the Odeon, Liverpool watching Gene Kelly dance with an umbrella, I entered for the first time a world of magic: the cinema.[7]

In discursive terms, memories of this type are distinguished by what I term an 'anecdotal' rhetoric, a form of address that typically involves a story narrated in the first person singular about a one-off event or occasion, a story in which the informant constructs herself or himself as chief protagonist (Kuhn 2002: 10). The narrator, in other words, figures in the account both as the central character in the life events narrated and also as observer of what is on the cinema screen. While anecdotal address is relatively rare across the entire body of memories gathered for 'Cinema Culture in 1930s Britain' it is, unsurprisingly, a pervasive feature of situated memories of films.

In some narrations of these memories, informants deploy what may be called a 'weak' variant of the anecdotal to position themselves as central protagonists of life events or remembered film scenes/images that are in all likelihood (with apologies to *Blade Runner*) implants. Implanted memories might originate, for example – with or without acknowledgement on the informant's part – from family stories. For example, Glasgow interviewee Norman MacDonald retells a story that was told to him by his mother – about his unruly behaviour as an infant taken to a screening of the 1921 Chaplin film *The Kid*.[8]

While researching the reception of Disney's *Snow White*, released in Britain in 1938 (Kuhn 2010), I was contacted by Leonard Finegold, who grew up in Hackney, East London. In 1938, at the age of three, he was taken to see the film, and still retained a potent memory of 'the (green?) witch/stepmother/queen looking out of a frame. I ran out of the cinema. *My mother said* she didn't catch me for several hundred yards' (emphasis added).[9]

Sometimes, moreover, informants' 'memories' of seeing film scenes or images have clearly entered their stories after the event – as, for instance, where a particular image has acquired wide cultural currency in later years. For instance, a number of informants 'remember' iconic moments in the 1933 *King Kong* (Kuhn 2002: 77–8), above all the scene of the giant gorilla perched atop the Empire State Building.

Situated memories tend to lack the 'illumination' – the brilliance, the intensity – that marks the remembered scenes or images of the first variant of cinema memory. These anecdotal memories bear the traces of having been subjected to various forms of secondary revision, and they may well also have been embellished over the years through numerous retellings, and even by the retrospective addition of details. Unlike the intense, and apparently idiosyncratic, quality of remembered scenes or images, situated memories of films outwardly manifest an active, or at least a potential, social currency. They are stories which are – which have been – exchanged, negotiated, re-enlivened, and even embellished in retellings over the years.

As noted, in these memories the balance of emphasis in narration between memories of films on the one hand and memories of life events on the other may vary across different instances. Where the balance of emphasis rests predominantly on life events, this form of remembering begins to shade into the third type: memories of going to the cinema.

Memories of Cinemagoing

> The 'Ionic' was at the far end of the Golders Green and until modernised (sometime after the war, I think) was rather regarded as a flea pit ... Normally when I had a few coppers I would go with boys of my own age, occasionally with one of my brothers ... The 'Ionic' was the last cinema that I remember taking jam jars in lieu of entrance money ... Normally when we went to the Ionic, one of us would pay and then having been seated by the usherette would go to the toilet and open the emergency exit doors and let our friends in for free.[10]

> Used to be shelling the nuts on the floor, and then they'd take an orange, peel'd be on the floor. All these were going backwards and forwards. There was no peace. [And then there was them?] with clogs on. And erm, you sit next to some children you could smell camphorated oil. You know, they'd have their chests rubbed with camphorated oil. Or whatever stuff on there. You know, to keep it clean. And when I think back there was, there was no, no peace at all.[11]

Memories of this type do not involve 'remembered *films*' at all. They are actually memories of an activity: *going to the cinema*. Even when they are recollections of very early visits to 'the pictures', the name and the location of the picture house are often carefully noted, and there may be some detail also about the journey to it and of the routes taken. Informants also frequently recollect who their cinemagoing companions were, and sometimes also what it was like inside the cinema – the decor, the seating, the behaviour of staff and the audience, and even the smells.

In 'Cinema Culture in 1930s Britain', memories of this kind are the most prevalent by far; and they are normally recounted entirely separately from memories of actual films. In fact, as already noted, one of the key conclusions to emerge from the 'Cinema Culture in 1930s Britain' project is that, certainly in the memories of the vast majority of these cinemagoers of the 1930s generation, the essentially *social* act of 'going to the pictures' is of far greater consequence than the cultural activity of watching a film. For the project's informants, memories of cinemagoing are discursively marked by the deployment of a 'repetitive' type of narrative rhetoric. In 'repetitive memory discourse' – the stance, in fact, most commonly adopted by informants – the narrator does not implicate himself or herself in the events recollected, but (by contrast with the anecdotal) those events are represented as habitual rather than as singular or one-off. Often the narrator will adopt the first person plural ('we'), which brings with it a certain personal distance from the events being narrated, while at the same time imparting to the stories a strong sense of collective involvement. 'We used to' is the characteristic introductory turn of phrase here; and it is implicit in both of the stories quoted above. Although Mr Ryall sets the scene in a particular, named, picture house, his story is about what he and his friends habitually did in order to get into the cinema without paying. Mrs Casey's story about the behaviour of children at matinees suggests that she was part of the scene, as an observer of all the rowdiness; but in referring to her fellow picturegoers as 'they', she distances herself from it. Mr Ryall's setting the scene for his story by mentioning the name and the location of his picture house is an instance of another characteristic attribute of memories of cinemagoing: their investment in place. As already suggested, place repeatedly figures in informants' accounts as both a prompt and a *mise en scène* of memory.

The overwhelmingly repetitive and collective address of memories of cinemagoing is typically allied with a restricted set of repeated themes, contents and modes of expression. For example, variants of the 'jam jar' theme (memories of collecting drinks bottles or jam jars, returning them to retailers, and collecting the cash deposits to pay for entry to the cinema); references to rowdy children's matinees; and memories of getting random adults to help youngsters gain entry to 'A' films: all of these abound in informants' cinemagoing memories, which also deploy stereotypical turns of phrase and a circumscribed range of narrative tropes.

This highly consequential observation opens entry to a little-explored byway in the terrain of oral history studies. It has been observed that raw oral history interview material, especially from working-class or peasant informants, will often feature conventional forms of speech and modes of narration in a manner that melds the personal with the collective, or frames the personal within a collective experience. As the Italian historian Alessandro Portelli notes, the degree of 'presence of formalised materials', like 'proverbs, songs, formulaic language, stereotypes', can be a measure of the degree of presence of a 'collective viewpoint' (1981: 99).

The repeated themes and formulaic modes of telling that mark so many memories of cinemagoing, especially childhood memories, allied with the continuing and active currency of these much-told stories, seems to signal something significant about this form of cultural memory, and in all likelihood not only for a single generation in one country. The collective forms and currencies of memories of cinemagoing, along with their characteristically formulaic themes and contents, suggest a sliding together of the personal and the collective. It also aligns the memories on the side of the social (and the cultural), and of the social audience (as against the spectator as constructed in some branches of film theory), and locates them on the terrain of film and other popular media as they figure in everyday life. In her study of the cinemagoing habits of post-war immigrants from South Asia to Britain, the sociologist Nirmal Puwar (2007) has coined the evocative phrase 'social cinema scenes' to describe the sociality (and the place-related nature) of this noteworthy aspect of cultural memory, considering the role of social cinema scenes in forging a sense of collectivity and belonging.

Conclusion

Close examination of a corpus of *cinema memories* of members of a 'movie-made' generation, recorded some sixty years after the event, brings to the fore the distinctive features of *cinema memory*. In the process of distilling the raw data of cinema memories to the intensified essence of cinema memory, the focus of an inquiry into a past cinema audience shifts from cultural history to cultural memory. And attention to the most prevalent expression of cinema memory, remembered 'social cinema scenes', signals a return to a consideration of the cultural and the social. Cinema memories constitute the raw materials both for reconstructing a past cinema culture and for uncovering the fundamental features of cinema memory and its instrumentality as a component of cultural memory.

Notes

1. Part of the application to the ESRC can be found at <https://www.lancaster.ac.uk/fass/projects/cmda/wp-content/uploads/2020/01/OriginalProjectProposal.pdf> (last accessed 14 May 2021).
2. Houlston, Denis. Interview, Manchester, 26 April 1995. DH95-034-AT001, Cinema Memory Archive, Lancaster University Library Special Collections. For more from Mr Houlston's interviews, see Kuhn (1999).
3. McFarland, Freda. Interview, Bolton, 7 June 1995. FM-95-189AT001, Cinema Memory Archive, Lancaster University Library Special Collections.
4. Amelan, Tessa. Interview, Manchester, 29 May 1996. TA-95-183AT002, Cinema Memory Archive, Lancaster University Library Special Collections.

5. Wright, Annie. Interview, Manchester, 26 May 1995. AW-95-032AT002, Cinema Memory Archive, Lancaster University Library Special Collections.
6. Smeaton, Helen. Interview, Glasgow, 23 January 1995. HS-92-036AT001, Cinema Memory Archive, Lancaster University Library Special Collections.
7. From an exhibition panel accompanying Terence Davies retrospective at BFI Southbank, London, 2007.
8. MacDonald, Norman. Interview, Glasgow, 17 November 1994. NM-92-005AT001, Cinema Memory Archive, Lancaster University Library Special Collections. See Kuhn (2002: 39).
9. Finegold, Leonard. Snow White Questionnaire, May 2007, SW-07-008SQ001, Cinema Memory Archive, Lancaster University Library Special Collections.
10. Ryall, John. Participant letter addressed to Annette Kuhn and Valentina Bold, February 1995. JR-95048-DT-PL001, Cinema Memory Archive, Lancaster University Library Special Collections
11. Casey, Ellen. Interview, Manchester, 31 May 1995. EC-95-182AT001, Cinema Memory Archive, Lancaster University Library Special Collections.

Bibliography

Burgin, Victor (2004) *The Remembered Film*. London: Reaktion Books.
Conference Programme (1996) Screen Studies Conference, Strathclyde University, 28–30 June.
Freud, Sigmund (1979) 'A Child is Being Beaten (1919)', in *Pelican Freud Library, Vol. 10: On Psychopathology*. Harmondsworth: Penguin, pp. 159–93.
Kuhn, Annette (1996) 'Cinema Culture and Femininity in the 1930s', in Christine Gledhill and Gillian Swanson (eds), *Nationalising Femininity*. Manchester: Manchester University Press, pp. 177–92.
Kuhn, Annette (1999) 'Memories of Cinema-Going in the 1930s', *Journal of Popular British Cinema* 2, 100–20.
Kuhn, Annette (2000) 'A Journey through Memory', in Susannah Radstone (ed.), *Memory and Methodology*. Oxford: Berg, pp. 179–96.
Kuhn, Annette (2002) *An Everyday Magic: Cinema and Cultural Memory*. London: I. B. Tauris.
Kuhn, Annette (2004) 'Heterotopia, Heterochronia: Place and Time in Cinema Memory', *Screen* 45(2), 106–14.
Kuhn, Annette (2010) '*Snow White* in the 1930s', *Journal of British Cinema and Television* 7(2), 183–99.
Kuhn, Annette (2013) 'Home is Where We Start From', in *Little Madnesses: Winnicott, Transitional Phenomena and Cultural Experience*. London: I. B. Tauris, pp. 53–63.
Kuhn, Annette (2020) 'Annette Kuhn Talks about a Key Aspect of CCINTB's Research Design'. <https://www.lancaster.ac.uk/fass/projects/cmda/index.php/2020/10/23/ak-talks-about-a-key-aspect-of-ccintbs-research-design/> (last accessed 28 August 2020).
Portelli, Alessandro (1981) 'The Peculiarities of Oral History', *History Workshop* 12, 96–108.
Puwar, Nirmal (2007) 'Social Cinema Scenes', *Space and Culture* 10(2), 253–70.

Radway, Janice (1987) *Reading the Romance*. London: Verso.

Stacey, Jackie (1993) 'Textual Obsessions: Method, Memory and Researching Female Spectatorship', *Screen* 34(3), 260–74.

Stacey, Jackie (1994) *Star Gazing: Hollywood Cinema and Female Spectatorship*. Abingdon and New York: Routledge.

Taylor, Helen (1989) *Scarlett's Women: Gone With the Wind and Its Female Fans*. New Brunswick, NJ: Rutgers University Press.

Terrill, Jamie (2021) 'Filmgoing or Cinemagoing? The Role of the Film Text within Cinema Memory'. *Alphaville Journal of Film and Screen Media* no. 21. <https://doi.org/10.33178/alpha.21.11> (last accessed 28 August 2021).

Willis, Paul (2016) *Learning to Labour*. London: Routledge.

3. CONSTRUCTING CINEMA AUDIENCE HISTORIES: METHODOLOGICAL CHOICES AND CHALLENGES

Karina Aveyard

Researchers play an important role in defining and shaping the subjects they investigate – from identifying and defining objects of inquiry, to determining modes of investigation, and the selection of analytical and theoretical frameworks through which to make sense of different phenomena – meaning that reflection and self-awareness must always be part of good research practice. This chapter addresses the themes of this edited collection by engaging with the particular question of how, methodologically speaking, cinema audience histories are located, constructed and understood.

The reflections and analysis offered here are based on a case study of a research project completed in 2016 on the post-World War II histories of volunteer-led cinema ('Community Cinema') in the United Kingdom. In terms of 'locating and constructing' histories, this research asserted a new connection between the trajectories of formalised film societies and more recent, less structured models of community-run cinema. In doing so, it attempted to push existing accounts of the film society movement beyond consideration simply on its own terms (for example, MacDonald 2016, 2012, 2010; Sexton 2008). The research aimed to open a new frame of reference for understanding non-commercial cinemas and their audiences by highlighting patterns of continuity and interconnection, as well as those of rupture and differentiation between the past and present. This chapter discusses the rationale for this approach, the processes of analysis (including my ideological influences), and their impact on the conduct and outcomes of the research.

My project on 'Community Cinema' had two core areas of focus: first, to understand more about the circumstances in which volunteer-led cinemas have come into existence and what has sustained (and challenged) them; and second, to explore what kind of experience these cinemas provide to audiences and how and why people were (and continue to be) inspired to seek out this particular mode of public film consumption. There were a number of methodological challenges in this project, in particular how to integrate and balance historical and contemporary source material gathered via different mechanisms, the logistics of which are examined here. The reflective analysis in this chapter also looks at the ways ideological perspectives can guide and shape the objects and outcomes of critical research.

'FILM EDUCATION, TECHNOLOGY AND POPULAR CULTURE: COMMUNITY CINEMA IN RURAL AREAS OF THE UNITED KINGDOM SINCE THE 1950S'

Several years of research culminated in a book chapter with the above title, published in Judith Thissen and Clemens Zimmermann's edited collection *Cinema Beyond the City: Small-Town and Rural Film Culture in Europe* (2016). As outlined above, this project focused on the history of volunteer-led, non-commercial exhibition ('Community Cinema') in regional and rural areas of the UK since the end of World War II. One of the key outcomes of the research was to suggest that there had been two distinct phases of Community Cinema growth in the UK over the period in question, and that these had been shaped to a large extent by national and international level developments in film policy, advances in screening technology, and changing socio-political attitudes to education, cultural access and rural sustainability. Scholarship on small-scale cinemas (either community, rural or niche) has tended to emphasise the significance of local factors in determining the characteristics of such enterprises (for example, Bowles 2011, 2007; Caughie et al. 2018; Aveyard 2012a). However, in this case, particularly with regard to understanding the shifting rationale and modes of Community Cinemas over an extended historical period, the focus was broadened in order to offer a more comprehensive, meaningful account.

In the first phase of growth (or what I termed the 'first-wave'), volunteer cinemas flourished from the late 1940s to the late 1970s. Building on the work of 1920s and 1930s film culture pioneers (Donald et al. 1998; Sexton 2008), many non-commercial cinemas of this period were distinguished by their interest in film as an artistic and educational medium. These groups focused on screening art cinema, foreign language, and experimental and documentary films, *and* providing resources for fostering the appreciation of these films (for example, by distributing screening notes and hosting talks and lectures) (The Federation of Film Societies and the British Film Institute 1961). Typically, these kinds of cinemas were formally constituted as film societies and affiliated with the British Federation of Film Societies (BFFS), which had been established in 1937 just before the outbreak of war in Europe. The immediate post-war period saw BFFS memberships double from around 250 in the 1950s to reach 500 by the 1960s (BFFS 2014a).

While film societies grew over several decades, by the early 1980s the number of groups operating across the UK had declined significantly. This has been attributed, at least in part, to a decrease in the manufacture of 16mm prints and the greater availability of non-mainstream film following the arrival of home video and the launch of specialised movie channel Film4 (BFFS 2014a). However, the appearance of inexpensive and easy to use DVD (and later Blu-ray) exhibition technologies in the late 1990s helped turn this around and underpinned a sustained 'second-wave' resurgence in Community Cinema that has been particularly prominent in regional and rural areas.

In numerical terms, second-wave Community Cinemas have exceeded the zenith of the 1960s. The BFFS began tracking activity in this sector in the mid-2000s when it recorded 246 members and affiliates. By 2012/13 this had grown to 638 organisations (BFFS 2006, 2013). What is perhaps most notable about this second generation of Community Cinema is its departure from the ideals of high culture and aspirations of education and self-improvement that characterised the first wave. Instead these newer volunteer-led enterprises have embraced popular film and disarticulated film appreciation from their aims. Rather they have placed significant emphasis on film exhibition as a means of widening social participation, promoting inclusion, and improving the overall vitality and sustainability of small communities.

Overall, the two key periods of growth for Community Cinema can be understood at least in part as a creative repurposing of inexpensive, relatively user-friendly projection equipment (first 16mm and later DVD/Blu-ray). As Tom O'Regan observed in relation to VCR, DVD and the internet (although as a transitionary technology from 35mm, 16mm might be added to this as well), one of the features of these technologies has been the multiplicity of opportunities they have created for both large-scale corporate organisations as well as for small-scale, decentralised activity (2012: 385–6). However, it would be reductively deterministic to attribute the successes of volunteer-led cinema solely to advancements in technology. The organisation of regular film screenings is demanding work, requiring significant investments of time without the enticement of personal financial reward. The people who commit themselves to such enterprises create sites of consumption where commercial imperatives are set aside in favour of aspirations and ideals with more affective dimensions, such as self-improvement (through education and knowledge), cultural enrichment, social cohesion and community advancement. While these are often enacted, experienced and described at the level of the personal and the local, they are also unavoidably shaped by the language and priorities of the wider political, social and cultural environments in which they occur.

First-wave Community Cinemas in the UK were clearly connected with many of the ideals of a burgeoning national film culture movement and within the socially reformist political agenda of the early post-World War II period. The orientation of film societies towards education and appreciation had its origins in alternative film groups that had gained momentum over the first half of the twentieth century both in the UK and elsewhere (Donald et al. 1998; Sexton 2008). These movements defined themselves very much against the mainstream and tended to be highly dismissive of popular movies and what they perceived to be the undiscriminating masses that paid to view them.

In terms of national politics, a left-wing Labour government was elected in the UK in 1945 with a mandate for implementing significant social and economic change. The party pledged to foster greater social equality and was interested in increasing political awareness and participation (Child 2006: 10–27). As part of a general commitment to a 'raising up' of the working and poorer classes, education and access to knowledge and culture were seen as important means of self-improvement (MacDonald 2012: 87). Film offered an attractive conduit for engaging and teaching the perceived lower classes. Cinema was already a mass entertainment that attracted large audiences on a regular basis. However, the problem was that the movies to which they were attracted were deemed to be of little value by cultural elites. The goal then was to redirect this enthusiasm for cinemagoing towards more worthy films and in doing so raise the status of both the medium and its patrons (MacDonald 2012: 88).

Second-wave Community Cinemas, on the other hand, have tended to be driven by very different ideals. However, there is little evidence to suggest this has been in direct response to perceived problems of sustainability of the first wave. Traditional film societies, with goals of promoting appreciation of art and other specialised screen content, still operate in significant numbers, but this is no longer the dominant model for volunteer-led cinema. What has become more commonplace are groups that organise screening events in order to facilitate local social interaction and foster community cohesion by providing opportunities for people to get together in welcoming and informal public spaces. The volunteers who run these film groups and their supporters will often frame their activities as direct and positive responses to the everyday adversity of their local situation (Aveyard 2015a: 38–45, 114–18). In order to realise these goals, community groups typically aim for broad appeal in their film programming with an emphasis on mainstream movies that have already proved successful at commercial cinemas. Films with excessive sex or violence that might risk discouraging or offending local patrons are generally avoided. Activities centred explicitly on film education and appreciation are notably absent.

The sustained nature of this shift is underscored by the changing face of the BFFS, which renamed itself Cinema For All and widened the scope of its advocacy to the representation of volunteer cinemas in all forms, not just formally constituted film societies. Cinema For All articulates a much more open approach to Community Cinema with the emphasis on self-determination and local devolution as indicated in its mission statement:

> The British Federation of Film Societies (BFFS) is the national support and development organisation for the film society and community cinema movement.
> Established in its current form in 1946, *we enable communities across the country to develop the type of film screenings they want and can sustain*. (BFFS 2014b, italics mine)

This reorientation towards local devolution, and away from the strict designation of film as art, can be placed within wider political developments. Since the election of Conservative leader Margaret Thatcher (beginning in the late 1970s) the UK has shifted more towards the promotion of individual responsibility and a decreasing role for government. This tendency can be traced through successive Conservative governments as well as the era of 'New Labour' ushered in by Tony Blair in the late 1990s, but perhaps reaches its clearest distillation in David Cameron's idea of the 'Big Society' (Cameron 2010). In rural areas particularly, but also for other disadvantaged communities, these shifts have given rise to a transformation in the way socially and economically marginalised towns and villages are supported by the state. During the 1950s and 1960s, rural policy tended to be framed by a centralised bureaucracy. This was often problematic as policies were bestowed on communities rather than developed with them in response to their particular needs. In the decades that followed there was more interest in consultation and in partnerships with communities. However, this has, in turn, also placed greater emphasis on towns and villages doing things for themselves; successful community ventures are often celebrated within a rhetoric of empowerment and achievements of self-determination. In practice this approach has often also served as a pretext to reduce the provision of direct government support, financial and otherwise (UK Government 2014; Department of Agriculture and Rural Development 2014). This has created two significant issues. First, it has left many small communities reliant on volunteer labour that is neither properly acknowledged nor supported. Second, it has left community groups in situations where they are regularly having to raise funds for their social enterprises from *within* already disadvantaged populations.

Methodology

The foundations for this research on post-World War II Community Cinema came from a much larger project on contemporary screen exhibition in the UK and Australia. In particular, its antecedent can be found in the chapter on 'Grassroots Cinema' in *The Lure of the Big Screen* (Aveyard 2015a: 107–30). While the focus of that book was on present-day exhibition, it was in the process of researching historical contexts that I was alerted to the distinctive cycles of volunteer-led cinema in the UK, which I subsequently investigated further. Researching grassroots cinema in any form is always challenging, especially historically. These are the types of enterprises that can be hard to locate precisely because of their local focus. Their activities speak to and are promoted to a localised constituency and may not seek or require a presence beyond that. They rely on unpaid labour, which means they can be difficult to sustain over the long term, and groups can come and go leaving little trace they ever existed.

Researching the contemporary situation of Community Cinema was relatively straightforward and based primarily on field work: site visits, interviews and visual ethnography (see Aveyard 2012b for a detailed account of this). The historical component was more challenging, both from the perspective of gathering information and in combining different source materials for consistency in the analysis. Records of the BFFS are held in the UK National Archives in a special collection at the British Film Institute Library. However, the collection of available documents is relatively small and contains little information about the day-to-day activities of the BFFS during the 1950s to the 1970s. The records comprise primarily guides and other material published by the BFFS for film societies to assist them with the running of their events, and a collection of programmes for various film societies documenting the types of films that were chosen for screening. I also had access to Richard MacDonald's then unpublished PhD thesis (2010), which was immensely helpful in detailing the history of the BFFS as an organisation.

The issue of comparison was a significant one. While I had been able to visit, experience and talk to volunteer organisers and audiences of many of the contemporary cinemas upon which my research was based, I was not able to replicate this for the historical component. Participant observation was clearly not an option. It would have been possible to have found film society members and facilitators active in the post-World War II to 1970s period, but I did not have the resources to carry out this kind of work. The absence of experiential and direct observational perspectives for the first-wave period placed a distance between me and this part of the research subject. I was very aware of this inconsistency and reflected on it regularly in the process of analysis in an effort to ensure I was applying (as far as possible) similar tests of evidence and commensurate levels of criticality. I did interview a long-standing BFFS board member who had been involved in the organisation during the heyday of the 1960s. As Kuhn et al. (2017: 4–5) remind us, oral histories are continually constructed and reconfigured based at least partly on the experiences that follow them. In the case of my interviewee, it was apparent there remained a strong investment in the idea of film as art and the importance of audience education in learning to fully appreciate it. This limited the scope (in that interview) for comparative reflection between first- and second-wave community screen enterprises.

One area of the research that brought the issue of comparison into sharp focus was that of audience experiences. I had not actively set out to try to construct an account of film society audiences of the first wave. My interest was primarily in trying to understand the conditions that contributed to the rise and later fall of non-commercial cinema in this period. Film societies were undoubtedly popular, and their activities could be clearly located within broader political and cultural rhetorics of the period. However, it was intriguing to find substantial evidence that suggested audience enthusiasm for the educational zeal of film societies may have been more important at an intellectual level than at a practical one.

In the BFFS's *Forming and Running a Film Society* guides, societies were directed to provide written notes for every film screening they ran and arrange lectures and/or discussion groups. Provision of these resources is explicitly identified in the booklets as being crucial to realising the film society's educationally orientated goals. However, they also warn new community groups to expect only a small proportion of members to actually attend the supplementary educational events (1961: 16). Similar tensions between educational aspirations and attracting audiences are highlighted in an essay penned in 1950 by Gerald Cockshott, credited as founder of the Norwich and Sussex Film Societies, and included in the first edition of *Forming and Running a Film Society*. The essay includes some first-hand advice for new groups about getting started:

> It would be better not to suggest on your circular that you are founding an educational organisation: if you do, everyone will immediately think of the dullest documentary he has ever seen . . . If you say you intend to show good films, everyone will think he is going to see the sort of picture he already likes. He may be surprised by what you show him, but that does not mean he will be disappointed (Cockshott 1961: 19)

This and other comments in Cockshott's essay indicate a real resistance on the part of audiences to the aim of film societies to educate them, even among those who were sufficiently engaged to join a group and attend its screenings. This uneasy balance between education and entertainment was evidenced in other ways – for example, in a promotional film from the period (1956) made by the Ipswich Film Society, which mocks the lofty instructive aspirations of itself and other film societies. Collectively, these historical artefacts suggest that many members may have liked the *idea* of being educated more than the reality of it.

There was part of me that delighted in uncovering this evidence – a demonstration of active resistance to an elitist devaluation and disregard for popular culture and taste, and a small triumph against paternalism and centralisation. Yet at the same time, I recognise I was (and still am) invested in the idea of education as an important means of social and economic advancement for marginalised people and committed to the principle of equality of access. So, in that sense, it can be said that I was not completely opposed to the broad aims that film societies had and the outcomes they hoped to achieve. While not necessarily contradictory positions, these somewhat complicated sensibilities were important to recognise in the research process because of their potential bearing on selectivity and interpretation. Critical analysis must be always be evidence based – and thorough, thoughtful and rigorous in its scrutiny and consideration of source material. However, ontologies and epistemologies are unavoidably bound up with the personal. As Guba and Lincoln argue, these individual perspectives play a role in defining for the researcher 'what it is they are about and what falls within and outside the limits of legitimate research' (1994: 108). It shapes the kind of work a person will choose to do and the frameworks they adopt for analysis. With respect to my project, I recognise that it was precisely because of my political position that I was initially attracted to this evidence of resistance and non-compliance on the part of audiences, and at least partly attributable to why I subsequently prioritised this phenomenon and gave it sustained attention in the findings.

Similarly, in relation to second-wave Community Cinemas, the intersection of personal and critical philosophies has unquestionably shaped the way I have investigated and represented this contemporary phase of activity. However, for this part of the research what was perhaps most challenging was the absence, rather than presence, of resistance.

Community Cinemas rely on volunteers. They are defined by their cooperative management structures, dependence on an unpaid workforce, and their not-for-profit orientation. The energetic and inspirational people that lead Community Cinemas are very often vital to their success. These people typically invest huge amounts of time in these ventures and have an important role in encouraging other local residents to participate. Understanding what motivates people to devote their attention to the running of a Community Cinema is complex. My research suggests it is shaped in part by the characteristics and perceived needs of a particular locality, but it is also influenced by individualised factors such as personality, age and life experience. Among the many volunteers I have met and interviewed in nearly ten years of doing research on Community Cinema, there have been two reasons consistently advanced by volunteers in explaining their motivations. The first is to do something to address a local absence of access to public film exhibition – either to specialised content or to any screenings at all. The second, and often just as important, reason is to reduce the negative impacts of isolation and socio-economic disadvantage in their immediate area.

Operating under systems of cooperative work and management can be productive and rewarding. However, a workforce that is engaged on an informal and unpaid basis is also less stable, and the scope and boundaries of the work are not so well defined and regulated. Volunteers often work very hard, putting in long hours and making significant emotional investments in the groups they are part of. But they also get exhausted, burnt-out, they can get ill, or their financial position can change such that working voluntarily is no longer an option. There are also sometimes individual disagreements and rifts to deal with but without access to the kind of formal mechanisms for dispute resolution that one might find in a paid workplace. The lack of definition around volunteer work means the ways in which it is recognised and valued tend to be inconsistent and fragmented (National Council for Voluntary Organisations 2020) – unlike paid work that can arguably be more clearly understood through an exchange of labour for financial reward. Further, there is a gendered dimension to unpaid work, especially in relation to Community Cinema (for example, Aveyard 2015b), where women are consistently over-represented in committees and in the day-to-day work of screening groups.

Community self-direction and localised action can certainly contribute to a sense of enfranchisement for local residents. Taking positive and tangible steps towards alleviating a local problem can feel highly satisfying. This kind of activity might even be considered as a form of empowered creative functioning, what Michel de Certeau terms 'making do' (1984). He suggested 'making do' can be understood as more than the enforced or reluctant acceptance of circumstances that are inferior, inadequate, or unwelcome. While individuals are at times unavoidably restricted by the circumstances of their daily life, de Certeau contends they are not necessarily powerless. Even those in marginalised positions can, through subtle and sometimes unconscious resistance, construct positive affective spaces to operate within which do not necessarily challenge dominant social and economic structures.

While this may sound quite utopic, it would be short-sighted to be drawn into an uncritical celebration of Community Cinemas and in particular the volunteer labour that sustains them. While representing the importance of this work in research, it is necessary to also pay attention to the ways in which the successes underpinned by this labour are narrativised and appropriated by those beyond the local communities in which they originate, especially by governments and their agencies. Across my investigations into non-commercial cinema exhibition I have not encountered a single volunteer who has spoken about their work against these broader considerations. However, that does not mean that these are not legitimate questions to be asked in the context of doing critical research.

The endeavours of Community Cinemas and their volunteers are marked and applauded in various ways. Cinema For All promotes recognition through its annual Film Society of the Year competition culminating in a dinner and presentation evening (Cinema For All 2020). The Big Lottery scheme regularly posts information about the successful volunteer projects they fund, as do many local authorities and their funded organisations (for example, Creative Arts East n.d.; Flicks in the Sticks n.d.). The now defunct BFI Neighbourhood Cinema scheme had a section on its website whereby communities could join a listing of cinemas. This directory was eventually populated with several hundred venues – many of which the BFI could not lay claim to supporting but which nevertheless gave an impression of there being a vibrant non-commercial screening sector in the UK that the BFI was associated with.[1]

Public acknowledgements like this help to celebrate the contribution of volunteer cinema enterprises and give much deserved attention to the work of the people who make them possible. However, these processes also enable bureaucracies to attach themselves to stories of success in ways that may over-state their contributions, whether by perception or by direct claim. What also gets obscured in this kind of narrative is that those who are primarily doing the giving (in time and money) are often people who are already marginalised in some way. And this is perhaps one of the biggest flaws of individualised neoliberal concepts like the 'Big Society'. The devolved responsibility it advocates frequently asks more from those who are least able to give it, undermining claims that might be made regarding its potential to foster increased fairness and equality. Further, it contributes to rendering it acceptable for governments to do less in terms of social and cultural policy when there are many cases where they could and should do more. In highlighting the wonderful and selfless work of cinema volunteers it is also crucial to maintain criticality – without it academic scholarship risks becoming complicit in a system that is at once both enabling and exploitative. Research and its outcomes should be tempered accordingly and within a continued framework of questioning and reflection.

Conclusion

This relatively brief survey of the methodological and analytical approach to investigating Community Cinema has emphasised the importance of recognising and thinking critically about source materials *and* the role of ideology and personal perspectives in the research process. In practical terms this chapter describes one way in which the histories of film societies and other types of volunteer-led cinemas have been extended through comparative analysis and a combination of macro and micro perspectives deployed to form complementary rather than exclusionary means of doing research. This reflective analysis has also explored the tangible ways in which personal viewpoints are inevitably and unavoidably brought to bear in academic research. Rather than reading this as a problem of subjectivity and a weakness of rigour, I have suggested that the political is always present, in some way, in critically engaged endeavours. What is most significant perhaps is not that it is there, but that we, as researchers, can recognise and account for its influence in our work.

NOTE

1. The BFI Neighbourhood Cinema scheme ended in 2010. The website and its listings have been taken over by Cinema For All and moved to a new site at <https://mycommunitycinema.org.uk> (last accessed 17 May 2021).

BIBLIOGRAPHY

Aveyard, Karina (2012a) 'Cinema on the Edge: Improvised Film Exhibition and Digital Projection in Rural Australia', *Studies in Australasian Cinema* 6(2), 189–202.

Aveyard, Karina (2012b) 'Observation, Mediation and Intervention: An Account of Methodological Fusion in the Study of Rural Cinema Audiences in Australia', *Participations* 9(2), 648–63.

Aveyard, Karina (2015a) *The Lure of the Big Screen: Contemporary Cinema in Rural Australia and the UK*. Intellect: Bristol and Chicago.

Aveyard, Karina (2015b) '"Our Place": Women at the Cinema in Rural Australia', in Christine Gledhill and Julia Knight (eds), *Doing Women's Film History: Reframing Cinema's Past and Future*. Champaign: University of Illinois Press, pp. 232–43.

Aveyard, Karina (2016) 'Film Education, Technology and Popular Culture: Community Cinema in Rural Areas of the United Kingdom since the 1950s', in Judith Thissen and Clemens Zimmermann (eds), *Cinema Beyond the City: Small-Town and Rural Film Culture in Europe*. London: BFI Publishing, pp. 197–212.

Bowles, Kate (2007) '"All the Evidence is that Cobargo is Slipping": An Ecological Approach to Rural Cinema-Going', *Film Studies* 10, 87–96.

Bowles, Kate (2011) 'The Last Bemboka Picture Show: 16mm Cinema as Community Fundraiser in the 1950s', in Richard Maltby, Daniel Biltereyst and Philippe Meers (eds), *Explorations in New Cinema History: Approaches and Case Studies*. Malden, MA: Wiley-Blackwell, pp. 310–21.

British Federation of Film Societies (2006) *British Federation of Film Societies: 2005/06 Membership Survey*. <http://bffs.org.uk/export/sites/bffs_site/pdffolder/Survey_Report_2005-06.pdf> (last accessed 6 June 2014).

British Federation of Film Societies (2013) *British Federation of Film Societies: Community Exhibitor Survey 2012/13*. <http://bffs.org.uk/export/sites/bffs_site/pdffolder/BFFS_Community_Exhibitor_Survey_Report_2013.pdf> (last accessed 6 June 2014).

British Federation of Film Societies (2014a) 'History of the BFFS'. <http://www.bffs.org.uk/aboutus/aboutus/history.html> (last accessed 6 June 2014).

British Federation of Film Societies (2014b) 'About Us'. <http://www.bffs.org.uk/aboutus/> (last accessed 6 June 2014).

Cameron, David (2010) 'Big Society Speech', transcript, UK Government. <https://www.gov.uk/government/speeches/big-society-speech> (last accessed 17 May 2021).

Caughie, John, Trevor Griffiths and María A. Velez-Serna (eds) (2018) *Early Cinema in Scotland*. Edinburgh University Press: Edinburgh.

Child, David (2006) *Britain since 1945: A Political History*. Abingdon and New York: Routledge.

Cinema For All (2020) 'Film Society of the Year Awards'. <https://cinemaforall.org.uk/conference-and-awards/awards> (last accessed 17 May 2021).

Cockshott, Gerald (1961) 'An Informal Essay' (1950), in The Federation of Film Societies and the British Film Institute, *Forming and Running a Film Society*, 3rd edn. London: The Federation of Film Societies and the British Film Institute.

Creative Arts East (n.d.) 'Our Work'. <https://www.creativeartseast.co.uk/our-work> (last accessed 17 May 2021).

de Certeau, Michel (1984) *The Practice of Everyday Life*, S. Rendall (trans.). Berkeley: University of California Press.

Department of Agriculture and Rural Development (2014) 'Rural Development'. <http://www.dardni.gov.uk/index/rural-development.htm> (last accessed 16 May 2021).

Donald, James, Anne Friedberg and Laura Marcus (1998) *Close Up 1927–1933: Cinema and Modernism*. Princeton, NJ: Princeton University Press.

Flicks in the Sticks (n.d.) 'About Us', <https://www.artsalive.co.uk/About-Us.aspx> and 'Gallery', <https://www.artsalive.co.uk/Gallery.aspx> (last accessed 17 May 2021).

Guba, Egon G. and Yvonna S. Lincoln (1994) 'Competing Paradigms in Qualitative Research', in Norman K. Denzin and Yvonna S. Lincoln (eds), *Handbook of Qualitative Research*. Thousand Oaks, CA: SAGE, pp. 105–17.

Ipswich Film Society (1956) *Ipswich Film Society*, film, East Anglian Film Archive, catalogue no. 826. <http://www.eafa.org.uk/catalogue/826/> (last accessed 17 May 2021).

Kuhn, Annette, Daniel Biltereyst and Philippe Meers (2017) 'Memories of Cinemagoing and Film Experience: An Introduction', *Memory Studies* 10(1), 3–16.

MacDonald, Richard (2010) 'Film Appreciation and the Postwar Film Society Movement'. Unpublished PhD thesis, Goldsmiths, University of London, pp. 271–2.

MacDonald, Richard (2012) 'The Vanguard of Film Appreciation: The Film Society Movement and Film Culture, 1945–1965', in Geoffrey Nowell-Smith and Christopher Dupin (eds), *The British Film Institute, the Government and Film Culture, 1933–2000*. Manchester: Manchester University Press, pp. 87–101.

MacDonald, Richard (2016) *The Appreciation of Film: The Postwar Film Society Movement and Film Culture in Britain*. Exeter Studies in Film History. Exeter: University of Exeter Press.

National Council for Voluntary Organisations (2020) 'What the NCVO Does'. <https://www.ncvo.org.uk/centenary/> (last accessed 14 May 2021).

O'Regan, Tom (2012) 'Remembering Video: Reflections on the First Explosion of Informal Media Markets through the VCR', *Television and New Media* 13(5), 383–98.

Sexton, Jamie (2008) *Alternative Film Culture in Inter-war Britain*. Exeter: University of Exeter Press.

The Federation of Film Societies and the British Film Institute (1961) *Forming and Running a Film Society*, 3rd edn. London: The Federation of Film Societies and the British Film Institute.

UK Government (2014) *Rural Development Programme for England*. <https://www.gov.uk/rural-development-programme-for-england> (last accessed 16 May 2021).

PART II

RECONSIDERING NATIONAL AND TRANSNATIONAL CINEMAGOING HISTORIES

4. CINEMAS AND CINEMA AUDIENCES IN THE 'THIRD SPACE' IN WARSAW, 1908–1939

Karina Pryt

As the centre of the Polish film industry between 1908 and 1939, Warsaw also had a vivid cinema culture. As in many other urban regions around the world, cinema in Warsaw emerged as a commercial institution resulting from transnational transfers of technologies and films. Therefore, it was conditioned by spatial factors like geopolitical and geographical location, urban infrastructure, transportation networks and demographics. At the same time, it was shaped by ethnicity and sociocultural and sociolinguistic norms.

In this regard, the Polish capital presents a fascinating and challenging object of historical cinema and cinema audience study. Firstly, the geopolitical framework changed substantially, as cinema in Warsaw had emerged within the larger film market of the Russian empire. After 1918, it was embodied within the national film market of the newly independent Poland.

Secondly, in relation to size, Warsaw had been the third metropolis in the Russian empire and was continuously the largest Polish city, with a population that reached 797,093 by 1911 and 1,265,372 by 1938 (Wakar 1916: 10). Simultaneously, having the largest cinema numbers and seating capacities, Warsaw was the very centre of the cinema culture in the Polish territories.

Thirdly, like other Polish cities and towns prior to the hecatomb of World War II, Warsaw had a complex and differentiated population in terms of nationality, language and confessional community. So, approximately: the largest group consisted of the mainly Catholic Poles, who made up 55 per cent of the total population by 1911, rising to 68 per cent by 1938 (Wydział Statystyczny Zarządu

Miejskiego 1938: 11). Simultaneously, the smallest minorities, Russians, Germans, Ukrainians, Lithuanians and Tatars, taken together, declined from 7 per cent in the first decade of the twentieth century to 3 per cent (ibid.: 11). That left Jewish residents, belonging to Askenazim, as the second largest population group, one that constituted 38 per cent by 1914 and 29 per cent by 1938 of the total population measured by declaration of religion (ibid.: 11). Thereby, confessional community was the most reliable marker of distinction although only one element in the complex identity of the Polish Jews.

Hence, Warsaw was the largest Jewish city in Europe, and second only to New York on a global scale. In relation to the whole country, Jewish residents constituted less than 10 per cent of the total, and they were clustered primarily in large agglomerations in central and eastern parts of the Polish territories (Węgrzynek and Zalewska n.d.). On the whole, three quarters of the three million Polish Jews lived in cities and towns (ibid.). Unlike Jewish residents in Western Europe and the USA, only a small group of them were acculturated into the language and culture of the majority society. Called Poles of mosaic faith, they were distinct from the majority of co-believers who had begun to consider themselves as a separate nation since the end of the nineteenth century. Consequently, despite a trend towards Polonisation, the vast majority of Jews in Warsaw continued to speak Yiddish as their main language. Experiencing discrimination from the majority society, they showed a high level of self-organisation, keeping their own school system, hospitals, and cultural and social institutions. That turned Warsaw into the cultural capital of 'Yiddishland', the virtual area defined by the use of the vernacular language of the Ashkenazi Jews. Called *Warszawa* in Polish and *Varshe* in Yiddish, Warsaw was accordingly a divided city with Gentiles and Jews living largely side by side.

However, as a multilingual urban minority with experience in the transnational trade, Polish Jews contributed disproportionally to the general economic growth in Poland. Specifically, they were highly involved in the Warsaw-based film-production industry. Since its origin in 1908, Jewish entrepreneurs had constituted a majority of film producers, distributors and exhibitors (Gross 2002). Moreover, most Polish films, rooted in the culture and history of the Catholic Poles, were also made with largely Jewish production personnel (directors, screenwriters, musicians, scenographers) and occasionally with Jewish actors as well. In addition, since 1911, relying on the same infrastructure, the Polish film industry had also released Jewish films based on the culture and language of Ashkenazi Jews. Prior to World War I, Warsaw was even the leader of worldwide Jewish filmmaking, eventually falling slightly to second place in 1918 after New York (ibid.). Thus, both the strong Jewish involvement in the Polish film industry and the shared production basis of Polish films and Jewish films constituted intriguing social and cultural issues.

By shifting focus to cinemas and cinema audiences, this chapter touches on the history of people and places and the diverse relationships between them. Thereby, this investigation resembles the search for Atlantis, as Warsaw, which flanks both banks of the Vistula river, was severely damaged as a result of Nazi occupation during World War II. Beginning with the German air force attacks of 1939, the devastation continued after the Ghetto Uprising of 1943 and the Warsaw Uprising of 1944. While the right bank escaped destruction, the losses in urban architecture on the left bank at the end of the war were estimated at around 84 per cent in total and 95 per cent of theatres and cinemas (Łagodziński and Czerwińska-Jędrusiak 2012: 65). In addition, the Polish capital lost more than half of its citizens, including almost the entire Jewish population and the majority of the film producers, distributors and cinema owners (ibid.: 65). As a result, the site of the film industry had to be relocated to the more intact Łódź. After 1945, the Polish capital was rebuilt in accordance with the ideology imposed by the Soviet Union. Conceived as a model socialist city, Warsaw recovered from the cataclysm of World War II, but the continuity in terms of architecture and social and cultural life had been broken. Consequently, little in the present cityscape is reminiscent of its multicultural past.

Examining lost cinemas and cinema audiences in Warsaw therefore involves archaeological precision and critical academic self-reflection in order to uncover the object of research from the layers of destruction and forgetting. For this purpose, this chapter proposes an empirical bottom-up approach that is inspired by the interdisciplinary spatial turn and quantitative modes of analysis. Using mapping as a method and the free and open source geographic information system QGIS as a tool, the chapter discusses cinema topography and assesses the profile of cinemagoers in relation to class and confession. In order to grasp both geographical patterns in cinema landscape and their changes over time, this chapter uses three data sets: for 1911, 1922 and 1936. (The World War I period will be covered in a separate publication.) It starts respectively with the geopolitical framework, depicting the historical context and close detail of local cinema dispersion across the city. After showing cinema topography in relation to the urban infrastructure, these geographical patterns are linked with demographic information concerning the confessional composition of the local population. Finally, the contextualisation of geographical patterns enhances our understanding of cinemas as social spaces in this divided city.

Aligned with approaching history from below, this chapter questions the perspective of the classical film historiography, simultaneously benefiting from the New Cinema History and urban history. Essential input also comes from Jewish studies. Consequently, this investigation supports interdisciplinary and transnational broadening of research perspectives within the humanities.

State of Research and the Methodological Approach

Like other national film historiographies, the history of Polish film has been predominantly written as a history of domestic film production aiming to support a nation-state identity among their readers. Focused on film texts and aesthetic consideration, classical film historiography has paid little attention to the exhibition sector and audiences. In addition, it should be acknowledged that influential seminal works of Polish film history (Jewsiewicki 1951, 1966, 1967; Banaszkiewicz and Witczak 1966; Armatys and Stradomski 1988) were printed while Poland was ruled by a communist government post-1945. Like in other countries of the Soviet bloc, the ruling communist party in Poland referred officially to the idea of internationalism but leaned in praxis on nationalism in order to gain the missing social support among the Polish people. Following the example of the USSR, the Polish People's Republic replaced initial official support for the creation of Israel in 1948 with strong anti-Zionism. As a result, the educational and cultural policy dictated ignoring the impact of Jews, as well as the other minorities, on Polish history and culture (Zaremba 2001). Consequently, film historians had to overlook the contribution of Jews, and other minorities, to Polish film culture, whereas the domestic Yiddish-language production was described as a separate phenomenon linked exclusively to the anticipated insularity of Jewish social life and culture. It is only in the past three decades that the substantial Jewish impact on Polish film production has been underlined (Gross 2002; Mazur 2007; Silber 2008; Skaff 2008; Zajiček 2009a; Czajka 2013; Pryt 2013).

Correspondingly, older seminal works (and some newer publications) have described cinemagoers in general terms from the angle of the classical film history, usually overlooking the ethnic diversity of the audiences (Pacewicz 1989; Gębicka 1994) or dividing them along projected national boundaries. Thereby, Jewish cinemagoers were limited to being viewers of films with specifically Jewish plots (Stradomski 1988a). As a result, their contribution to the development of the Polish film industry was marginalised and underestimated in terms of demand (Stradomski 1988b; Zajiček 2009b, 2015).

Conversely, some newer works regarding local cinema cultures (Hendrykowska and Hendrykowski 1996; Biel 2002; Guzek 2004; Gierszewska 2006; Biskupski 2013) or cinemagoing (Sitkiewicz 2019) have stressed the confessional and linguistical diversity of cinema audiences. However, these analyses have drawn mainly on Polish newspapers or occasionally from Jewish newspapers printed in the Polish language, whereas exploiting written sources in Yiddish has remained within the domain of Jewish studies. Equipped with related linguistic skills, Martyna Steckiewicz (2013) has demonstrated through analysis of the local Yiddish paper *Lodzer Tageblatt* that Jewish residents were an integral part of Łódź's cinemagoers in the second decade of the twentieth century.

Evaluating several Yiddish newspapers from the 1920s, Ela Bauer has furthermore concluded that 'in some places, such as small towns on the periphery, Jews constituted the majority of movie viewers' (2017: 85). Without locating and concretising her reasoning geographically, she assumed later, 'In almost all cities and small towns movies were considered Jewish entertainment. Movie theatre owners and film producers relied on Jewish customers to fill the halls' (ibid.: 87).

Apparently, following different disciplinary traditions and relying on analyses of dissimilar written sources, film scholars and representatives of Jewish studies have come to opposing opinions regarding the ethnic composition of most cinemagoers in Poland. In order to prove both contradictory assumptions, empirical research shaped by spatial and statistical modes is needed in this field. To start with, this chapter adapts mapping in GIS with its potential to reveal information and detect connections hidden in texts. Uncovering spatial interrelations between the clustering of cinemas and settlement patterns of Jewish and non-Jewish residents in Warsaw, this suggested approach is also adjustable for further research on cinemagoing in multi-ethnic urban areas that characterised Poland and other Eastern European countries prior to the destruction caused during World War II. Thus, it adds also to the research on Jewish film audiences that has been conducted on interwar Britain (Toffell 2011, 2018) and on the USA (Hansen 1991; Singer 1995; Thissen 1999).

Thematically and methodologically, the chapter positions itself in relationship to New Cinema History (NCH). As a new subfield in film historiography, NCH has already yielded important works in the USA, Western Europe and Australia and is currently leveraging research in further parts of the world, as the growing numbers of the History of Moviegoing, Exhibition and Reception Network (HoMER) reveal.[1] Deliberately striking a contraposition to the classic film historiography, NCH meets my interest as a historian in the cinema as a commercial institution and in the sociocultural history of its audiences.

Thereby, this chapter follows Robert C. Allen, Jeffrey Klenotic and other representatives of the NCH who have pioneered research in using historical maps to retrace cinema locations and geographical patterns in moviegoing. In this regard, Klenotic's groundbreaking article on the usage of GIS in cinema historiographical research (2011) has introduced practical skills on how to integrate and visualise different types of information in order to create thematic maps. Generated using data from a wide assortment of historical sources, thematic maps thus offer the opportunity to visualise diverse connections and interrelations between the spread of cinemas and various factors like urban infrastructure, transportation systems, population density and more. Reflecting on the theoretical level, Klenotic has furthermore underlined that thematic maps must be taken as partial and limited representations of space as they convey a moment in the history of what the geographer Doreen Massey calls 'time-spaces' (Massey 2005: 177–95). Since then, mapping in GIS has enhanced a growing number of single and collaborative research projects (Hallam and Roberts 2014; Horak 2016; Porubčanská 2018; Klenotic 2019).

Inspired by these works, this investigation benefits furthermore from acknowledging the approaches of Jewish studies that have since the 1990s called for the writing of Jewish history to accord neither to the paradigm of a minority adapting to the non-Jewish majority society, nor to the pattern of a separate ethnic group to which the Gentile majority society was hostile. Dealing with the Polish Jews, Chone Shmeruk proposed the dynamic model of the trilingual polyculture that consisted of the Polish, Yiddish and Hebrew language subcultures. Some of them corresponded with political orientation, but none of them was independent of the other. Rather, they were all interactively connected (Shmeruk 1989). On this basis, further research has been conducted on the diverse processes of differentiation within the Polish Jews and their contradictory interactions with the non-Jewish environment.

Recently, scholars have adapted the concept of the 'third space' (Soja 1996) for conceptualising the social space in-between Jewish and Polish culture. Consequently, Silber (2008) has described Polish-Jewish film professionals as working in the 'third space', whereas Eugenia Prokop-Janiec (2013) and Alina Molisak (2016) have used that concept for Polish-Jewish literature. Building on these works, this chapter adopts the 'third space' as a public sphere where cultures met and mixed, breaking binary oppositions between them in contexts of asymmetrical relations of power (Bachmann-Medick 2010). This concept will be used for describing the public sphere of cinemas.

Sources and Methodological Problems

Many historians attempting to grasp past cinema cultures through spatial patterns begin by visiting the places in question. Looking at the current topography and at the buildings where cinema culture took material form can help to establish a basic orientation of the spatial dimensions. The 'strategy of digging into the past of the actual buildings', as Judith Thissen (2012: 298) has put it, is problematic in the case of the Polish capital due to the physical destruction of the city during World War II.

In addition, most primary sources, such as official documents of the municipal administration and of the film companies, private diaries and letters, which could have shed light on cinema culture and its participants, were damaged during the war. Furthermore, memoirs written by the few Holocaust and/or war survivors were subjected to the same communist censorship as every other published work. Not surprisingly, one can hardly find any mention of Jewish protagonists within the urban cinema culture in Poland in the relevant life stories, which were scripted by the decorator Józef Galewski (n.d.) and the travelling showman and founder of the first permanent cinema Antoni Krzemiński (1953). The same applies to the life story of Aleksander Hochman, a known distributor and exhibitor in pre-war Warsaw, which was published under the name Aleksander Jasielski (1958). It is telling that Hochman, who had escaped the Holocaust using the identity documents of Aleksander Jasielski, issued his memoirs under this name after the war in communist Poland.

Coping with layers of destruction and taboo, this chapter underlines the potential of QGIS and sources like maps and statistical data in the analyses of cinemas and cinema audiences in Warsaw. In addition, the chapter uses sources such as industry yearbooks, and film programmes that have been compiled from Polish newspapers (*Kurier Poranny, Kurier Warszawski*), the Polish-Jewish press (*Nowa Gazeta, Nasz Przegląd*) and the Yiddish press (*der moment, unzer ekspres haynt*). They are available online either on the Polish Federation of Digital Libraries (FBC) or on the Israeli site Historical Jewish Press.[2]

Cinema in the Third Metropolis of the Russian Empire, 1908–1914

Starting with the first shows in 1896 until the outbreak of World War I, cinema in the Polish lands unfolded within the economic and political parameters established by the partitioning of Poland in the late eighteenth century. Separated by borders and trade barriers from the Polish lands ruled by Prussia and Austria-Hungary, the cinema in Russian-controlled Warsaw benefited from free access to the large market of the multinational Russian empire. As the largest Polish city and an important railway and trade hub between East and West, Warsaw fast became a favourite stopover for showmen and housed its first permanent venue as early as 1903. However, the turbulent political situation linked to the 1905 revolution, also called the first Russian revolution, temporarily had an adverse impact on the further development of cinema. While urban areas in Western Europe and in the United States experienced a cinema boom between 1905 and 1907, strikes, demonstrations, martial law, and armed clashes between revolutionaries and the government forces dominated life in Warsaw and in other parts of the Russian empire. Only after the unrest had ceased did cinema fever spread in the capital of Congress Poland (as Polish lands under Russian rule were called) in the years 1907–8 and in smaller towns in the years 1910–11 (Hendrykowska 1993). Simultaneously, the first feature-length Polish-made film was produced in 1908, whilst cottage film production started on a regular basis by 1911.

This cinema boom coincided with general economic recovery and political liberalisation after the Tsar had conceded sharing his autocratic power with a newly established parliament. Simultaneously, restrictions on national minorities had been eased, bringing advantages for Polish and Jewish residents alike. The Russification policy was partially reduced, as a result of which Polish language returned to schools and administration, and an array of new Polish social and cultural associations was created. Similarly, Jewish self-organisation was prompted after the ban on the Yiddish language had been lifted. Thus, the Jewish theatre could openly perform in Yiddish, further theatres and cabaret were founded, and the Jewish press in Yiddish appeared in Warsaw. In sum, the cultural revival proceeded largely along languages and confessions, whereby the existing divisions between the Polish and Jewish residents of Warsaw deepened and solidified. The newly legalised public sphere was – as the historian Malte Rolf (2015) has convincingly described – deeply divided and full of conflicts.

Notwithstanding these political and social tensions, the public sphere in-between grew simultaneously. Prestigious music institutions, such as the Philharmonic and the Grand Theatre (Teatr Wielki), and further municipal theatres employed and relied on individuals from both confessional groups (Steinlauf 1987). An array of newly established private theatres and cabaret that performed in Polish and the emerging film production industry made the same contribution to the enlargement of the 'third space' in Warsaw.

Mapping cinemas onto the complex cultural landscape in the generally divided city appears as challenging as it is promising. Founded largely, though not exclusively, by Jewish entrepreneurs, film venues far surpassed in quantitative terms other forms of leisure, attracting thousands of viewers every evening. This huge demand was already reflected by the first local purpose-built venue, the Phenomenon, that was constructed by 1909 for 1,600 spectators. The Phenomenon opened by the end of April 1909 but was closed in January the following year as it had been rejected by the municipal authorities due to its wooden construction (Anon. 1910: 4). Nevertheless, no later than 1909 a non-permanent venue with 1,000 seats was installed in the hall of the Philharmonic.

Two years later, in 1911, according to the Russian film journal *Sine Fono*, there were already around thirty permanent cinemas operating for a population of 797,093. Unfortunately, data on seating capacities is missing, and *Sine Fono* provided only a two-stage categorisation without explaining whether this classification concerned the size or the standard of the venues. It can nevertheless be assumed that the division into first-class and second-class cinemas allows us to draw initial, cautious conclusions about the social hierarchy of cinemas. Accordingly, it can be assumed that the first-class cinemas were both larger and of a high standard; hence catered for upper-class and upper-middle-class audiences. Conversely, it cannot be assumed with the same probability that the second-class cinemas targeted lower classes of patrons only (Krzhizhanovsky 1911: 18). Matching this data on standard with information on location enabled me to generate a cinema topography using QGIS as a tool.

As Figure 4.1 visualises, cinemas in Warsaw in 1911 – like in other cities – were clustered in central areas near traffic hubs and in the main shopping streets. Most of the film venues were located on the left bank of the Vistula river, which was Warsaw's vital centre of economic and cultural life. In contrast, on the right

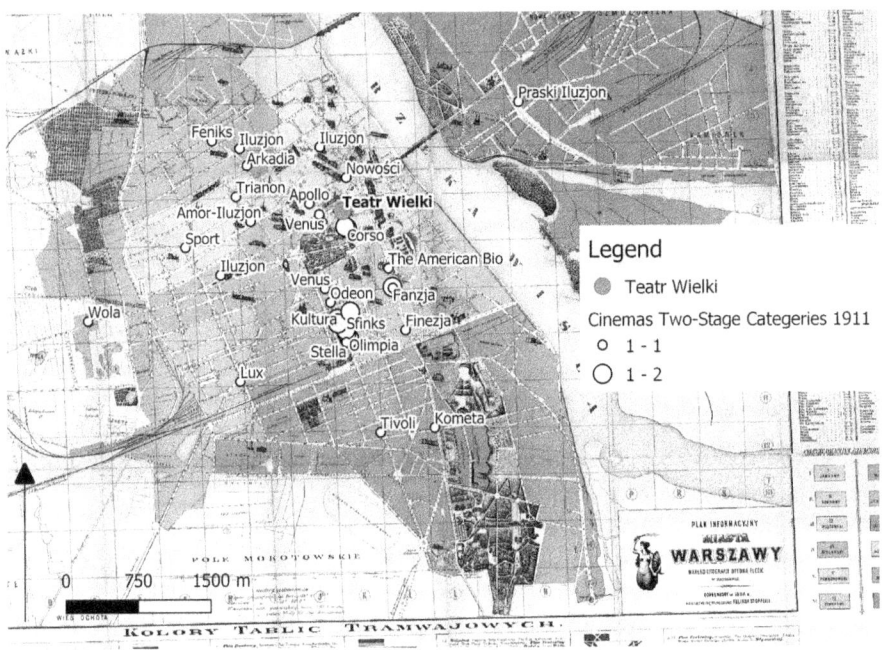

Figure 4.1 Layer of spatial information visualising location and categorisation of cinemas on a city plan of Warsaw for 1911. (Source: Author's own design.)

bank was only one permanent cinema. It was located near the station of the Saint Petersburg–Warsaw Railway line that provided imports of Russian film production, which had started by 1908. However, most films were imported from France, Denmark, Italy and Germany via Berlin. Not surprisingly, the preferable location was on the left bank as close as possible to the station of the Warsaw–Vienna Railway that connected Warsaw with the capital of the German empire over a further rail junction. Consequently, many of the nine first-class cinemas were clustered in the immediate vicinity of that central railway station on Marszałkowska. Further elegant cinemas were located both on this main artery leading from south to north and on the parallel artery constituted by the streets Nowy Świat and Krakowskie Przedmieście. To the north, two venues, Oaza and Corso, which were located on Wierzbowa Street just opposite the Grand Theatre, they were roughly on the northern border of the area of high-standard cinema. Located in these central areas with their pronounced middle- and upper-class character, the elegant venues addressed consumers of highbrow culture, who were usually seen in theatres, at the opera or in the Philharmonic (Anon. 1914).

Conversely, the second-class venues (or the lower-quality venues) that relied generally on lower-middle- and working-class patrons, were more dispersed across the city. Most of them were spread further to the north and to the west of the Grand Theatre. A few smaller cinemas were in the city centre, whereas there were only two venues further to the south of the Warsaw–Vienna Railway station.

Whilst information on cinema standards provides quite a clear distinction in relation to class, the estimation of audiences with respect to confession appears more complicated. In general, press articles did not usually give information on that issue. A rare hint to the confessional background of cinemagoers could be found in only one article in another Russian film journal, *Kine Zhurnal*, which described the cinema topography in Warsaw (Samter 1910). In doing so, the Russian journal argued that almost all cinemas outside the city centre were located in Jewish districts.

To prove this, it must be clarified what should be understood as Jewish districts in the case of Warsaw. Whereas *Kine Zhurnal* used the plural form, Polish sources usually mentioned only one Jewish district. Located to the north, this neighbourhood was usually referred to as the Northern District (*Dzielnica Północna*). Formally, however, a Jewish district never existed in Warsaw (it was only introduced in 1940 and destroyed in 1943 by the German occupiers). Until 1862, formal restrictions described only areas where Jews were not allowed to live, and not where they should live. After their abolition, Jewish residents could legally settle throughout the city; however, they clustered in certain areas for economic, sociocultural and religious reasons (Zalewska 1996; Bergman 2009). Therefore, I refer here to areas with predominantly Jewish populations and identify them using statistical data giving the average spread of Jewish inhabitants across administrative districts in 1913 (Wakar 1919: 9).

As Figure 4.2 shows, districts on the left bank to the east of the city centre, with a lower percentage of Jewish residents, had indeed the lowest cinema density. Conversely, there were more cinemas clustered to the north of the city centre, where Jews comprised at least 25 per cent of the total population. Moreover, the so-called Northern District, where approximately two-thirds of all Jewish inhabitants in Warsaw lived (Zalewska 1996: 278), had seven cinemas. Three of them – Feniks, Iluzjon and Arkadia – were located in both districts, where Jews comprised 70 per cent and 90 per cent of the total population, whereas a further four – Trianon, Apollo, Nowości and Iluzjon – were situated at the culturally estimated borders of the Northern District. Surprisingly, the main artery of this area, Nalewki street, did not have any venues.

Regarding first-category venues in the city centre, only venues on Nowy Świat and Krakowskie Przedmieście streets were located within a primarily Christian neighbourhood. Conversely, cinemas on Marszałkowska touched the areas with a population that was composed in equal numbers of Jews and non-Jews. Similarly, the two first-category cinemas in the northern city centre, Corso and Oaza at Wierzbowa street, were situated within a mixed population of which Jews constituted more than 35 per cent. Relying also on

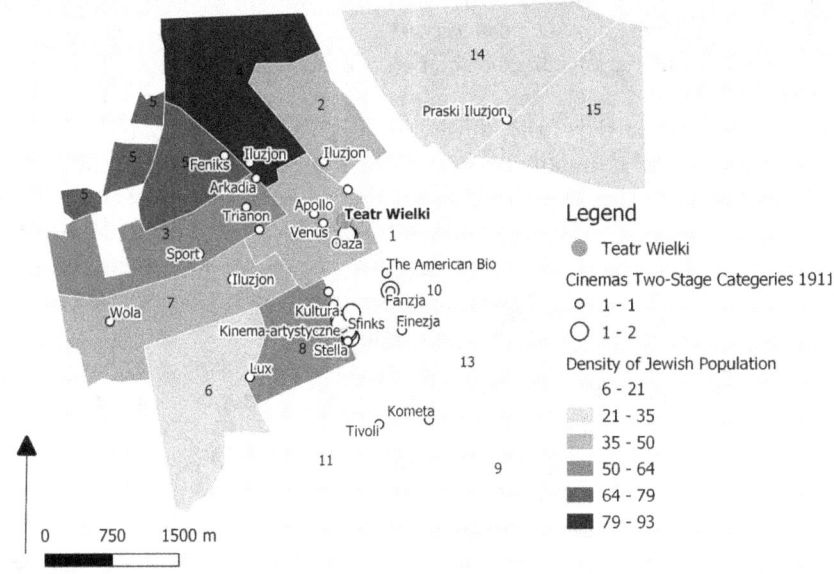

Figure 4.2 Thematic map using census data to visualise the ethnic context of cinema dispersion created for 1911. (Source: Author's own design.)

visitors coming from further districts, all first-category venues were likely to host patrons from both groups, as sighting of advertisements in the Polish press and Jewish press proved.

Whereas *Kine Zhurnal* suggested a strong correlation between venue clustering and the density of Jewish residents in areas outside the city centre, the thematic map presents a more ambiguous picture. Nonetheless, geographical patterns show quite clearly that Jewish viewers were significant not only in the rise of cinema outside the city centre, but also in the case of cinemas in the city centre. In addition, only a few second-category venues were likely to have patrons belonging to one confessional group, whereas most venues were more like to address mixed audiences. As such, they functioned in the 'third space' in this divided city.

Cinema in the Capital of the Polish Republic, 1918–1939

World War I, and the proclamation of an independent Polish state in late 1918, fundamentally altered the position of Warsaw within the transnational film trade. Having lost access to the huge Russian market, the Polish film industry had to adapt to the circumstances created during the war and then to the consolidation of the three film markets of the former partitioning powers after

1918. Unlike in the USA and Western Europe, the exhibition sector developed slowly and at a very low level in regard to seating capacities, reflecting both the predominantly agrarian character and economic problems of the newly independent Poland. Most permanent venues were situated in cities and towns where only one-quarter of the Polish citizens lived, whereas only some agrarian regions were occasionally frequented by travelling cinemas (Zajiček 2015: 174). Remaining a largely urban phenomenon, watching films was for the overwhelming majority still not an available luxury. To give an example, by 1936, the proportion of people who never visited a cinema was estimated as being as high as 85 per cent, which was almost three times higher than the ratio of non-cinemagoers in neighbouring Germany (Anon. 1936b).

The share of cinemagoers in Warsaw, which had been enlarged in 1916, was obviously much larger, reflected in annual attendance rates that varied between 7.3 to 12.7 ticket sales per capita (Zajiček 2015: 99). However, after the peak had been reached in 1929, Warsaw lost its leading position in terms of attendance rates in favour of other cities as soon as 1930. Notwithstanding this alteration, cinemagoing remained by far the most preferred form of entertainment in the Polish capital, surpassing, for example, theatre-going ticket sales by no less than a factor of ten sales (Anon. 1938: 109). Acknowledging this popularity, the municipal administration, the army, the Catholic Church and various Polish social institutions established their own exhibition places that accounted for about one-third of all venues in Warsaw. Unlike the Catholic organisation, the rabbinical authorities remained sceptical towards moving pictures (Gross 1990: 23). But several Jewish associations used to rent cinemas for special screenings or non-film related purposes.

Analysing private venues that accounted for the remaining two-thirds of the city's cinemas, this chapter uses maps created from two samples. Figure 4.3 captures the situation in 1922, with thirty-four cinemas and 15,260 seats operated for a population of approximately 937,000. Conversely, Figure 4.4 shows the situation in 1936 when fifty-five venues with 29,794 seats served a population of approximately 1,200,000 people (Anon. 1922, 1936a). Accordingly, in the time that the population rose by a third, seating capacities almost doubled.

As both maps show, the remarkable growth of cinema applied to both the enlargement of seating capacities and the extension of cinema's geographical spread. Starting with first-class cinemas, Warsaw had only four cinemas with seating capacities over 1,000 in 1922. The number increased threefold as twelve venues of this category operated in 1936. The largest cinema, the Colosseum, which had already been established by the end of the war, hosted more than 2,200 visitors. As in 1911, most of these venues were in elegant central areas along Marszałkowska and Nowy Świat street, whereas two venues, Adria and Splendid/Sfinks near the Grand Theatre, marked roughly the north end of the high-standard cinema area.

THE 'THIRD SPACE' IN WARSAW, 1908–1939

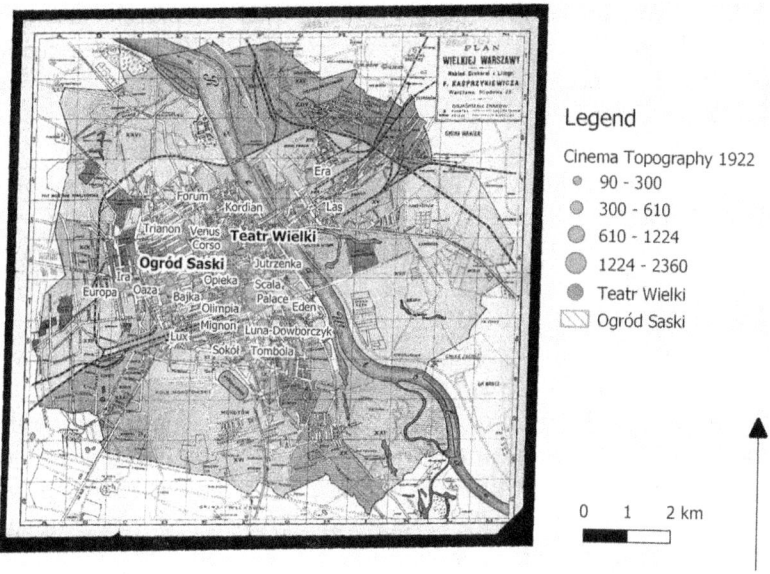

Figure 4.3 Layer of spatial information visualising location and categorisation of cinemas according to their size created on a plan of Warsaw for 1922. (Source: Author's own design.)

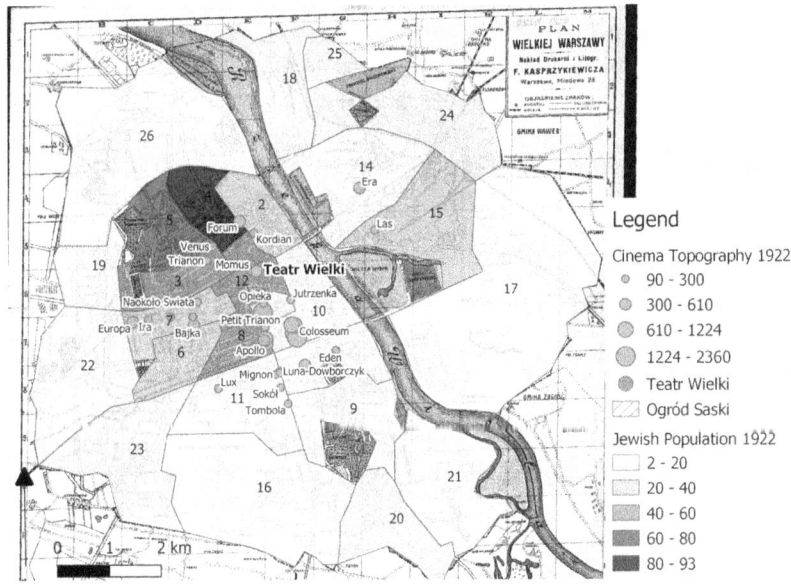

Figure 4.4 Layer of spatial information visualising location and categorisation of cinemas according to their size created on a plan of Warsaw for 1936. (Source: Author's own design.)

Middle-sized and small cinemas, which relied on patrons from lower-middle- and working-class neighbourhoods, likewise experienced significant growth. In this respect, both maps show further geographical dispersion in areas to the north and south of the city centre and on the right bank of the Vistula. Moreover, both maps visualise the appearance and then the stabilisation of a third cinema line with Italia, Helios, Kometa, Czary and Amor along the horizontal artery comprised by the streets Chłodna and Wolska.

Coming to the analysis of cinema dispersion in relation to the confessional composition of the potential audiences, it should be noted that Warsaw remained, during the 1920s and 1930s, a generally divided city, with Polish Jews and Polish Gentiles living largely side by side. Simultaneously, being exposed to the Polish language and culture, more Jews were entering the mainstream of Polish civil society. Not only did a growing number of Jewish children and youths attend Polish state schools, but also an increasing number of Polish Jews listened to the state radio broadcasting, visited Polish theatre, and read Polish literature and press. Consequently, linguistic acculturation progressed fast, and most Polish Jews felt that it was appropriate to use that language in public. Although in the 1931 census, 88.9 per cent of Jewish residents in Warsaw stated Yiddish as their main language, most of them even felt embarrassed to use their vernacular language outside their neighbourhoods. Deemed by advocates of the Yiddish language as a sin of 'shmendrikism', this sociolinguistic phenomenon was quite common among young upwardly mobile parts of Jewish society (Weiser 2015). As had been passed down in Jewish literature, the residents of the Northern District in Warsaw used to change their vernacular language to Polish while going southwards before entering the area of the Saxon Garden (Molisak 2016: 238). Linking this information with cinema topography, it becomes clear that this informal sociolinguistic line was slightly below the northern border of the high-standard cinemas' area that was marked by the elegant venues Adria and Splendid/Sfinks.

This unwritten sociolinguistic border was situated in an area where Jewish residents consisted of more than 40 per cent of the total local population, as can be seen in Figure 4.5, which portrays the density of Jewish residents for the year 1922 (Rocznik Statystyczny Warszawy, 1924: 20). As the proportion varied only slightly, the same statistical data has been taken for creating the thematic maps displaying cinema topography for 1922 and for 1936. Both thematic maps demonstrate clearly that most venues were still located in mixed areas. From these maps, we can conclude that only areas in the south, where the proportion of Jewish residents was only between 2 and 20 per cent, were likely to have predominantly Catholic patrons. Conversely, all other private venues were likely to accommodate Jewish cinemagoers too.

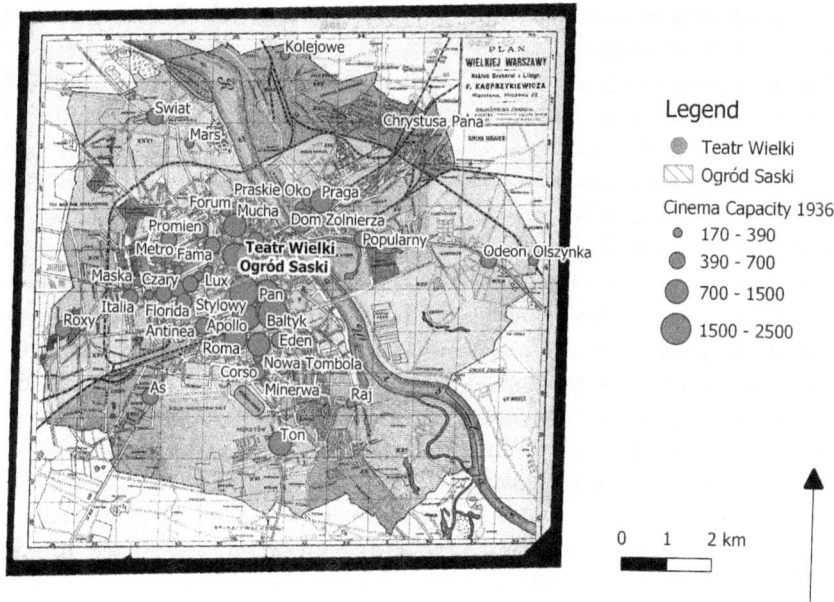

Figure 4.5 Thematic map using census data to visualise the ethnic contexts of the cinema dispersion created for 1922. (Source: Author's own design.)

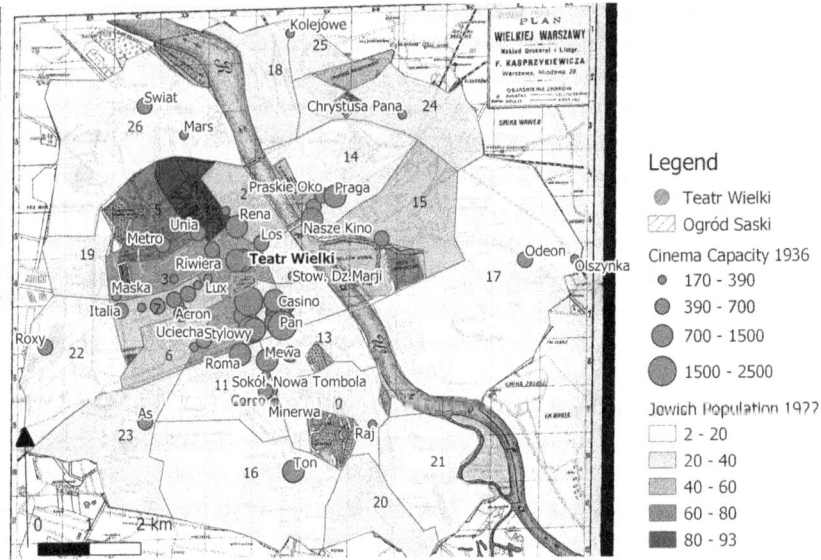

Figure 4.6 Thematic map using census data to visualise the ethnic contexts of the cinema dispersion created for 1936. (Source: Author's own design.)

Residents of the so-called Northern District admittedly lost three cinemas that had been in the fourth and fifth districts in 1911, very likely as a result of the general impoverishment of the Jewish residents during World War I. In this respect, the situation did not change until the end of the research period in the fourth district, whereas the fifth district received its own middle-sized cinema with 650 seats by 1928 that functioned as Broadway, later Europa and finally as Metro (Magistrat m.st. Warszawy 1930). Located in the border areas of the so-called Northern District, small and middle-sized venues such as Unia, Promień (Venus, Skala), Forum, Fama and Riwiera likewise relied chiefly on Jewish cinemagoers, as analysis of cinema programmes in Jewish dailies (*Nasz Przegląd*, *unzer expres* and *der moment*) indicates. The same applied to venues situated in the districts where Jews made up 38 per cent of the total population like Mucha, Rena, Miejskie, Adria and Splendid/Sfinks. As a result, it is notable that the public sphere of cinemas in the Northern District was shaped by both languages, Yiddish and Polish. Both languages were on film posters, whereas films were screened only with Polish subtitles despite the demands of Jewish cinemagoers in the 1920s (Bauer 2017). Offering an extra translation into Yiddish in silent and in sound film was very likely not worth it for economic reasons.

Other private second- or third-run venues spread across the city likewise addressed Jewish audiences, as occasional advertisements in Jewish dailies confirm. Similarly, the first-run cinemas in the city centre on Marszałkowska and Nowy Świat street advertised regularly in both Polish and Polish-Jewish dailies and occasionally in Yiddish-language newspapers. Thus, they functioned within the growing 'third space', simultaneously contributing to its enlargement. Although shaped primarily by the Polish language, these cinemas in the 'third space' occasionally hosted screenings of Jewish films or provided space for non-film-related events for Jewish societies.

In the 1920s, even some of these centrally located first-run venues organised premieres of Jewish films. For example, owners Szymon Lejman and Maurycy Lilienfeld showed the feature film *Pojlisze welder/In the Polish Woods* (1928) simultaneously in their venues Światowid and Wodewill on 18 January 1929. By giving space to Yiddish on the screens and billboards on Marszałkowska and Nowy Świat street, both entrepreneurs challenged the common sociolinguistic and cultural norm.

The rising anti-Semitism of the 1930s, however, increased pressure on the Yiddish language and culture, displacing screenings of Jewish films out of the centre to the north of the city. Located at the unwritten cultural and sociolinguistic border, Sfinks therefore served as the first-run cinema for the popular musical film *Yidl Mitn Fidl/Yiddl With His Fiddle* (1936) or the masterpiece of Yiddish film *Dybuk/The Dybbuk* (1937). Situated further to the north, the middle-sized Fama venue functioned as the further first-run cinema for Jewish films until the end of the period under investigation here.

CONCLUSION

Researching cinema and cinema audiences in Warsaw, this chapter coped with the paucity of sources caused by World War II, and with the heritage of communist censorship within the Polish film historiography. QGIS proved to be a very efficient tool in uncovering the object of research from the layers of destruction and taboo. In all samples (1911, 1922 and 1936), information on size and standard of cinemas was quite a distinct indicator for the social background of audiences, whereas the estimation of the confessional compositions of cinema audiences appeared more ambiguous. However, thematic maps displaying cinema topography in relation to confessional composition of the local population showed quite clearly that only middle-sized and small cinemas in the southern areas of the city were likely to have predominantly Catholic patrons. Conversely, all private venues in the city centre and in the northern area were likely also to have Jewish cinemagoers, as entries in Polish, Polish-Jewish and Yiddish-language newspapers confirmed. Cinemas that were situated in the so-called Northern District relied mainly but not exclusively on Jewish visitors, as they could also have been frequented by Catholic residents from the neighbourhood.

Simultaneously, it has been proved that Jewish cinemagoers cannot be thematically limited to viewers of films with specifically Jewish plots, nor can they be geographically reduced to patrons of venues in the Northern Districts. They were, on the contrary, an integral part of the local spectatorship, and contributed substantially to the rise of cinema in Warsaw. Thus, the contribution of Jewish residents to the Polish film industry should be acknowledged not only at the site of production, but also at the site of exhibition and reception. However, since the percentage share cannot be estimated exactly, it is difficult to assess whether Jews constituted the majority of all cinemagoers. Moreover, it could not be confirmed that the social praxis of cinemagoing was considered exclusively a Jewish entertainment. On the contrary, addressing viewers from both confessional groups, most venues functioned in the 'third space' of this generally divided city, contributing simultaneously to its enlargement.

This finding has implications beyond the local cinema culture in Warsaw for both film studies and Jewish studies. Mapping in QGIS offers the chance for further investigations to reveal the correlation between cinema dispersion and settlement patterns of Jews and other national minorities such as Germans or Ukrainians. Furthermore, a closer cooperation between these two disciplines through the evaluation of sources in Polish, Yiddish and other languages of national minorities is needed to overcome the national paradigm and to offer cross-perspectives resulting in the creation of new ways of observing. This suggested approach has the potential for cinema historiographical inquiries that would mirror the complex multinational population that was characteristic of Poland, as it was for other East European countries, prior to the hecatomb of World War II.

Notes

1. See <http://homernetwork.org/about/> (last accessed 17 May 2021).
2. See <https://fbc.pionier.net.pl/?lang=en> and <https://web.nli.org.il/sites/JPress/English/Pages/default.aspx> (both last accessed 17 May 2021).

Bibliography

Anon. (1910) 'Zamknięcie Kinematografu', *Kurier Warszawski*, 17 January, p. 4.
Anon. (1914) 'Taśma i publiczność', *Kino-Teatr i Sport* 1, 2.
Anon. (1922) 'W świecie ekranu: Kina warszawskie', *Przegląd Teatralny i Kinematograficzny* 4(47–8), 17.
Anon. (1924) 'Procentowe rozmieszczenie ludności, gęstość zaludnienia i procent żydów według Komisariatów w latach 1921–1922', in *Rocznik Statystyczny Warszawy 1921 i 1922*. Warszawa: Magistrat m. st. Warszawy, p. 20.
Anon. (1936a) 'Spis kinoteatrów w Polsce: Warszawa', *Kalendarz Wiadomości Filmowych* 11, 171–7.
Anon. (1936b) 'Sytuacja kinematografii w Polsce', *Wiadomości Filmowe* 3(28), 1 February, 2.
Anon. (1938) 'Frekwencja w teatrach, kinach, na koncertach, widowiskach sportowych i w Miejskim Ogrodzie Zoologicznym', in *Rocznik Statystyczny Warszawy 1936 i 1937*. Warszawa: Magistrat m. st. Warszawy, p. 109.
Armatys, Leszek and Wiesław Stradomski (1988) *Od niewolnicy zmysłów do czarnych diamentów: Szkice o polskich filmach z lat 1914–1939*. Warszawa: Centralny Ośrodek Metodyki Upowszechniania Kultury.
Bachmann-Medick, Doris (2010) *Cultural Turns: Neuorientierungen in den Kulturwissenschaften*. Reinbek bei Hamburg: Rowohlt-Taschenbuch-Verlag.
Banaszkiewicz, Władysław and Witold Witczak (eds) (1966) *Historia filmu polskiego*. Warszawa: Wydawnictwo Artystyczne i Filmowe.
Bauer, Ela (2017) 'The Jews and the Silver Screen: Poland at the End of the 1920s', *Journal of Modern Jewish Studies* 16(1), 80–99.
Bergman, Eleonora (2009) 'The "Northern District" in Warsaw: A City within a City?', in *Reclaiming Memory: Urban Regeneration in the Historic Jewish Quarters of Central European Cities*. Materials from the international conference held on 25–26 June 2007, Kraków. Kraków: International Cultural Centre, pp. 287–99.
Biel, Urszula (2002) *Śląskie kina między wojnami, czyli, przyjemność upolityczniona*. Katowice: Wydawnictwo Śląsk.
Biskupski, Łukasz (2013) *Miasto atrakcji: Narodziny kultury masowej na przełomie XIX i XX wieku: kino w systemie rozrywkowym Łodzi*. Warszawa: Narodowe Centrum Kultury and Szkoła Wyższa Psychologii Społecznej.
Corrsin, Stephen D. (1990) 'Language Use in Cultural and Political Change in pre-1914 Warsaw: Poles, Jews, and Russification', *The Slavonic and East European Review* 68(1), 69–90.
Czajka, Katarzyna (2013) 'Kina żydowskie w Warszawie w dwudziestoleciu międzywojennym', *Kwartalnik Historii Żydów* 3(247), 561–70.

Galewski, Józef (n.d.) 'Wspomnienia filmowe'. Unpublished memoirs. Zespół Dokumentacji Teatralnej IS PAN Archiwum Warszawa.
Gawryszewski, Andrzej (2009) *Ludność Warszawy w XX wieku*, vol. 10. Warszawa: PAN IG i PZ.
Gębicka, Ewa (1994) 'Sieć kin i rozpowszechnianie filmów', in Edward Zajiček (ed.), *Film, kinematografia: Encyklopedia kultury polskiej XX wieku*. Warszawa: Instytut Kultury, Komitet Kinematografii, pp. 415–51.
Gierszewska, Barbara (2006) *Kino i film we Lwowie do 1939 roku*. Kielce: Wydawnictwo Akademii Świętokrzyskiej.
Gross, Natan (1990) *Tôledôt haq-qôlnôa' ha-yehûdî be-Pôlîn, 1910–1950*. Jerusalem: Magnes Press, The Hebrew University.
Gross, Natan (2002) *Film żydowski w Polsce*. Kraków: Rabid.
Guzek, Mariusz (2004) *Filmowa Bydgoszcz, 1896–1939*. Toruń: Dom Wydawniczy 'Duet'.
Hallam, Julia and Les Roberts (eds) (2014) *Locating the Moving Image: New Approaches to Film and Place*. Bloomington: Indiana University Press.
Hansen, Miriam (1991) *Babel and Babylon: Spectatorship in American Silent Film*. Cambridge, MA: Harvard University Press.
Hendrykowska, Małgorzata (1993) *Śladami tamtych cieni: Film w kulturze polskiej przełomu stuleci 1895–1914*. Poznań: Oficyna Wydawnicza Book Service.
Hendrykowska, Małgorzata and Marek Hendrykowski (1996) *Film w Poznaniu i Wielkopolsce: 1896–1996*. Poznań: Ars Nova.
Horak, Laura (2016) 'Using Digital Maps to Investigate Cinema History', in Charles R. Acland and Eric Hoyt (eds), *The Arclight Guidebook to Media History and the Digital Humanities*. Brighton: Reframe Books in association with Project Arclight, pp. 65–102.
Jasielski, Aleksander (1958) *Wyprawa po celulidowe runo*. Warszawa: Filmowa Agencja Wydawnicza.
Jewsiewicki, Władysław (1951) *Przemysł filmowy w Polsce w okresie międzywojennym (1919–1939)*, no. 3. Łódź: UŁ.
Jewsiewicki, Władysław (1966) *Polska kinematografia w okresie filmu niemego*. Łódź: Zakład Narodowy im. Ossolińskich.
Jewsiewicki, Władysław (1967) *Polska kinematografia w okresie filmu dźwiękowego*. Łódź: Zakład Narodowy im. Ossolińskich.
Klenotic, Jeffrey (2011) 'Putting Cinema History on the Map: Using GIS to Explore the Spatiality of Cinema', in Richard Maltby, Daniel Biltereyst and Philippe Meers (eds), *Explorations in New Cinema History: Approaches and Case Studies*. Malden, MA: Wiley-Blackwell, pp. 58–84.
Klenotic, Jeffrey (2019) 'Roll the Credits: Gender, Geography and the People's History of Cinema', in Daniel Biltereyst, Richard Maltby and Philippe Meers (eds), *The Routledge Companion to New Cinema History*. London and New York: Routledge, pp. 202–16.
Krzemiński, Antoni (1953) *Jak powstało pierwsze kino w Polsce: Ze swoich wspomnień spisał Antoni Krzemiński*. Unpublished memoirs in Zespół Dokumentacji Teatralnej IS PAN Archiwum Warszawa.

Krzhizhanovsky, G. A. (1911) 'O gorodah: Varshava', *Sine-fono: zhurnal, posviāshchennyĭ sinematografam, govoriāshchim mashinam i fotografīi* 1(2), 18.
Łagodziński, Władysław W. and Barbara Czerwińska-Jędrusiak (2012) 'Warszawa Fenkisem XX wieku. Statystyka Warszawy w 1945r.'. <http://www.warszawa-stolica.pl/inne/feniks.pdf> (last accessed 17 May 2021).
Magistrat m.st. Warszawy (1930) *Rocznik Statystyczny Warszawy 1928*. Warszawa: Magistrat m. st. Warszawy.
Massey, Doreen B. (2005) *For Space*. London: SAGE.
Mazur, Daria (2007) *Dybuk*. Poznań: Wydawnictwo Naukowe UAM.
Molisak, Alina (2016) *Żydowska Warszawa, Żydowski Berlin: Literacki portret miasta w pierwszej połowie XX wieku*. Warszawa Instytut Badań Literackich PAN – Wydawnictwo.
Pacewicz Tadeusz (1989) 'Zeroekrany przedwojennej Warszawy', *Iluzjon. Kwartalnik Filmowy* 1(33), 41–6.
Porubčanská, Terézia (2018) 'Approaches to Spatial Analysis in a Local Cinema History Research', *Journal for Media History | Tijdschrift voor Mediageschiedenis* 21(1), 54–75.
Prokop-Janiec, Eugenia (2013) *Pogranicze polsko-żydowskie: Topografie i teksty*. Kraków: Wydawnictwo Uniwersytetu Jagiellońskiego.
Pryt, Karina (2013) 'Nationale Mythen: Heimatvorstellungen der multikulturellen Warschauer Filmbranche', in Konrad Klejsa, Schamma Schahadat and Margarete Wach (eds), *Der polnische Film: Von seinen Anfängen bis zur Gegenwart*. Marburg: Schüren, pp. 52–67.
Rolf, Malte (2015) *Imperiale Herrschaft im Weichselland: Das Königreich Polen im Russischen Imperium (1864–1915)*, vol. 43. Berlin: De Gruyter Oldenbourg.
Samter, S. (1910) 'Kronika Varshava', *Kine-zhurnal: zhivaiā fotografīiā* 1(24), 14–15.
Shmeruk, Chone (1989) 'Hebrew-Yiddish-Polish: A Trilingual Jewish Culture', in Israel Gutman (ed.), *The Jews of Poland between Two World Wars: International Conference: Papers*. Hanover, NH: Published for Brandeis University Press by University Press of New England, pp. 285–311.
Silber, Marcos (2008) 'Narrowing the Borderland's "Third Space": Yiddish Cinema in Poland in the Late 1930s', *Simon Dubnow Institute Yearbook* 7, 229–51.
Singer, Ben (1995) 'Manhattan Nickelodeons: New Data on Audiences and Exhibitors', *Cinema Journal* 34(3), 5–35.
Sitkiewicz, Pawel (2019) *Gorączka filmowa. Kinomania w międzywojennej Polsce*. Gdańsk: Słowo Obraz Terytoria.
Skaff, Sheila (2008) *The Law of the Looking Glass: Cinema in Poland, 1896–1939*. Athens, OH: Ohio University Press.
Soja, Edward W. (1996) *Thirdspace: Journeys to Los Angeles and other Real-and-Imagined Places*. Cambridge, MA: Blackwell.
Steckiewicz, Martyna (2013) 'Lodż hot gehuljet. Łódź hulała: Obraz kina i kultury atrakcji w żydowskiej gazecie codziennej "Lodzer Tageblt" w latach 1908–1914', *Kultura Popularna* 3(37), 62–77.
Steinlauf, Michael C. (1987) 'Jews and Polish Theater in Nineteenth Century Warsaw', *The Polish Review* 32(4), 439–58.

Stradomski, Wiesław (1988a) 'Film żydowski', in Barbara Armatys, Leszek Armatys and Wiesław Stradomski (eds), *Historia filmu polskiego*, 6 vols, Volume II: 1930–1939. Warszawa: Wydawnictwa Artystyczne i Filmowe, pp. 305–16.

Stradomski, Wiesław (1988b) 'Kino a społeczeństwo: Publiczność kinowa. Młodzi i kino. Kościół i film', in Barbara Armatys, Leszek Armatys and Wiesław Stradomski (eds), *Historia filmu polskiego*, 6 vols, Volume II: 1930–1939. Warszawa: Wydawnictwo Artystyczne i Filmowe, pp. 51–9.

Thissen, Judith (1999) 'Jewish Immigrant Audiences in New York City (1905–1914)', in Melvyn Stokes and Richard Maltby (eds), *American Movie Audiences from the Turn of the Century to the Early Sound Era*. London: British Film Institute, pp. 15–28.

Thissen, Judith (2012) 'Early Cinema and the Public Sphere of the Neighborhood Meeting Hall: The Longue Durée of Working-Class Sociability', in Marta Braun, Charlie Keil, Rob King, Paul Moore and Louis Pelletier (eds), *Beyond the Screen: Institutions, Networks, and Publics of Early Cinema*. Bloomington: Indiana University Press, pp. 297–306.

Toffell, Gil (2011) 'Cinema-Going from Below: The Jewish Film Audience in Interwar Britain', *Participations* 8(2), 522–38.

Toffell, Gil (2018) *Jews, Cinema and Public Life in Interwar Britain*. London: Palgrave Macmillan.

Wakar, Włodzimierz (1916) *Ludność Warszawy wobec wyborów do Rady Miejskiej. Szkic statystyczny*, Warszawa: Drukarnia Noskowskiego.

Węgrzynek, Hanna and Gabriela Zalewska (n.d.) 'Demografia', <https://sztetl.org.pl/pl/slownik/demografia> (last accessed 18 June 2021).

Weiser, Kalman (2015) 'The Capital of "Yiddishland"?', in François Guesnet, Glenn Dynner and Antony Polonsky (eds), *Warsaw. The Jewish Metropolis: Essays in Honor of the 75th Birthday of Professor Antony Polonsky*. Boston: Brill, pp. 298–322.

Wydział Statystyczny Zarządu Miejskiego (ed.) (1938) 'Ludność według okręgów', in *Warszawa wczoraj, dziś, jutro: przewodnik i plan wystawy: Warszawa w liczbach: październik-grudzień*. Warszawa: Wydawnictwo Wydziału Statystycznego Zarządu Miejskiego w m. st. Warszawie.

Zajiček, Edward (2009a) 'Film żydowski w Polsce', in Grażyna M. Grabowska (ed.), *Sto lat polskiego filmu: Kino okresu wielkiego niemowy*. Warszawa: Filmoteka Narodowa, pp. 52–63.

Zajiček, Edward (2009b) *Poza ekranem: Kinematografia polska, 1918–1991*. Warszawa: Filmoteka Narodowa.

Zajiček, Edward (2015) *Zarys historii gospodarczej kinematografii polskiej*. Łódź: Państwowa Wyższa Szkoła Filmowa, Telewizyjna i Teatralna im. L. Schillera.

Zalewska, Gabriela (1996) *Ludność żydowska w Warszawie w okresie międzywojennym*. Warszawa: PWN.

Zaremba, Marcin (2001) *Komunizm, legitymizacja, nacjonalizm: Nacjonalistyczna legitymizacja władzy komunistycznej w Polsce*. Warszawa: Wydawnictwo Trio and Instytut Studiów Politycznych Polskiej Akademii Nauk.

5. GERMAN FILMS IN BRAZIL: IMMIGRATION, ASSOCIATIONS AND NATIONAL FILM CULTURE

Wolfgang Fuhrmann

In the context of the substantial immigration within South America, Brazil has been one of the most important destinations of German immigrants since the eighteenth century. It has been estimated that in the 1930s the number of immigrants of German origin in Brazil was around a million (Nazario 2007: 85) but the role of immigrants, immigrant associations and their contribution to national cultures in the country and on the continent has hardly been reflected in national film historiographies.

This chapter focuses on how German educational associations in Brazil informed Brazilian cinema culture in many regions of the country during the 1930s (Fuhrmann 2016, 2015).[1] It questions the common assumption in Brazilian film historiography that German films that were shown by associations were just aimed at a German immigrant public, to establish a bond between Germany and the immigrants' territories, and that they are examples of Nazi propaganda in the country (de Moraes von Simson 2005; Blank 2008). In contrast, it will be argued that the reception of German films in Brazil should be understood also in the context of a dynamic national Brazilian film culture. Applying a transnational perspective to the history of German films in Brazil, the chapter shows how records of immigrant associations provide important sources for an understanding of a national film culture and its audience.

The chapter is based on research of records such as annual reports and correspondence of the Association of German Teachers in São Paulo (Deutscher Lehrerverein São Paulo), the Film Service of the National Association of German-Brazilian Teachers (Filmdienst des Landesverbandes Deutsch-Brasilianischer Lehrer, L.D.L.), the German-Brazilian Cultural Film Service (Deutsch-Brasilianischer Kulturfilmdienst, D.K.D.) and German journals in Brazil, roughly between 1930 and 1938. The records and journals are archived at the Martius-Staden Institute in São Paulo, which is the biggest archive on German immigration in Brazil.

Rural regions have been less well covered in traditional Brazilian film history, which usually focuses on urban film cultures in Rio de Janeiro and São Paulo and the investigation of genres and movements like the *Chanchada* musical comedies in the 1940s and 1950s, the Cinema Novo in the 1960s and early 1970s or the rise of the New Brazilian Cinema in the 1990s (Ramos 1985; Stam and Johnson 1995; Shaw and Dennison 2007).[2] The following investigation throws light on a less known aspect in film history. It provides important information on the distribution of German films and their reception in Brazil in an extra-theatrical context for German and Brazilian film historiography.

Voluntary Associations

Voluntary associations played an important role in the distribution of German films between 1931 and 1938, especially in the southern states of Brazil. Together with public cinemas, associations form part of the public sphere. In response to Jürgen Habermas's revisionist approach to the concept of the public sphere as a domain of social life in which access is guaranteed to all citizens, scholars such as Nancy Fraser and Geoff Eley have argued that, despite all the rhetoric of openness and accessibility upon which the official public sphere rests, in fact it is constituted by a significant number of exclusions (Fraser 1992: 113). The revisionists' approach recognises the existence of competing public spheres in each phase of history and stresses the heterogeneity of these spheres as an arena of continuous conflict. Therefore, according to Geoff Eley, it makes more sense to understand the public sphere 'as the structured setting where cultural and ideological contest and negotiation among a variety of publics takes place . . .' (1992: 306).

In the context of this research, a more nuanced understanding of the exclusionary character, as well as the diversity, of the public sphere can be provided through the study of the network of voluntary associations and associative life. According to Eley:

> The public sphere [. . .] was linked to the growth of urban culture – metropolitan and provincial – as the novel arena of a locally organized public life (meetinghouses, concert halls, theaters, opera houses, lecture halls, museums), to a new infrastructure of social communication (the press, publishing companies and other literary media; the rise of a reading public

via reading and language societies; subscription publishing and lending libraries; improved transportation; and adapted centers of sociability like coffee houses, taverns, and clubs), and to a new universe of voluntary associations. (Eley 1992: 291)

The importance of associations in German history has been emphasised by Roger Chickering, who saw the proliferation of voluntary associations as 'one of the most remarkable cultural phenomena of the Wilhelmine era' (1984: 183). Most of the associations were driven by non-political objectives, such as entertainment, self-training and articulation of a common welfare policy.

Membership of an association has had a great significance in German daily life, which extends to the countries of German immigration. German immigrants took their language, customs and traditions to their new homeland and set up an infrastructure to practise and preserve culture in sports clubs, orphanages, charities, schools, chambers of commerce or religious associations (Müller 1997: 150). Showing and watching films was a way of maintaining and caring for traditions and culture, connecting the new homeland with the country of origin. The important aspect of associations that they adapted themselves to the dynamics of modern social processes (Nipperdey 1976: 182) is particularly significant for the German-Brazilian context since associations played an important role in the modernisation of Brazilian rural regions. Film screenings of associations very often were the very first film experience for small-town citizens and villagers, as reported by Karl Otto Müller, the head of the Cultural Film Service, in 1934 (1934: 76).

The Transnational

In order to analyse the reception of German films in Brazil, however, a transnational perspective is necessary, which considers the associations' particular situation in the context of Brazilian national cinema. Archival records of the teacher organisations show that the audience of German films was more heterogeneous. German schools were not attended just by German children or children of German origin. Film screenings in villages and districts addressed the broad public, and Brazilians attended the screenings as well and sometimes even made up the majority of the film audience.[3]

Film has always been and continues to be an international means of communication, which, especially in the context of distribution and reception, is always transnational. In his article 'The Limiting Imagination of National Cinema' (2000), Andrew Higson submits his canonical text 'The Concept of National Cinema' (1989) to a new critical reflection. Starting from Benedict Anderson's (1991) concept of an imagined community, Higson asks about the usefulness of the concept of a national cinema that is a helpful taxonomic labelling device but also 'to some degree tautologous and fetishizing the national' (2000: 64). The analysis of national cinema can lead to a limitation on films that show the nation as a demarcated geopolitical space with a homogeneous community, closed off to other identities.

What national cinema is not able to show is the cultural diversity and the exchange that characterise the cinematographic activities in a country. Borders are not only a means of state demarcation, but also passages that enable migration and exchange (ibid.: 67). The transnational seems to be much more adequate to describe social, cultural and economic formations that do not stop at national borders. Transnational phenomena can be studied in all areas of film: the coproductions or the effect of migrating filmmakers on the production side; censorship, dubbing, subtitling and marketing issues in the sphere of distribution; and the ways audiences receive films in their specific cultural context. In addition to the reception of films in a new cultural context, one must add the specific exhibition context for foreign films, an aspect that is not mentioned by Higson but is particularly important for the analysis of German films in Brazil (Fuhrmann 2015: 181).

Screening German Cultural Films in Brazil

The aim of film screenings of the Association of German Teachers in São Paulo, the D.K.D. and the L.D.L. was to screen mainly non-fiction films, so-called Cultural Films (*Kulturfilme*) from Germany to German immigrants. Cultural Films were a didactic documentary film form characteristic of German cinema since the beginning of the 1920s until the end of World War II. They were an early form of audiovisual infotainment and covered all kinds of cultural topics or aspects of natural sciences (Kreimeier et al. 2005).

A special promotion of the Cultural Film seemed to take place in the rural German-speaking areas at the end of the 1920s, initiated by the visit of Edgar Beyfuß to Brazil in August 1925. Beyfuß was the head of the UFA's Cultural Division (Kulturfilmabteilung), and ran the Organisation for Film Education (Filmunterrichts-Organisation). One of the stops on his tour was the German School, also known as Olinda School,[4] in São Paulo, where he gave a lecture about the Cultural Film and showed a short film about their production. In the following years, the German schools in Brazil – headed by the Olinda School – reinforced their film-programming activities, which were decisively influenced by political changes in Germany and by a private film network in Brazil.

In 1931, two years before Hitler took power, the Association of German Teachers in São Paulo purchased a Zeiss-Ikon film projector to increase the number of film screenings in and around the city.[5] The purchase of the projector was necessary after the association received two donation films from the German Association for Image Use (Deutsche Bildspielbund), a central organisation in Germany, which was dedicated to the coordination of visual education in German schools and educational institutions.[6] Three other films, *Oh, du mein Vaterland/Oh, My Dear Fatherland*, *Frohe Menschen/Happy People* and a film about a sporting event in Cologne in 1928 were donated to the L.D.L. The fact that this association was dependent on donations rather than acquiring films on a regular basis by itself indicates that it did not follow specific selection criteria. The uncertainty in the supply of new films was a continuous problem for the associations.[7]

In May 1931, the association released the first information about an upcoming film tour. It started in Presidente Venceslau during the Easter festivities (5–8 April), in Campinas (25 April), in the city of São Paulo at the Olinda- and Vila Marianna School (2 May),[8] in the German Sports Club of 1890 (Deutsche Turnerschaft von 1890) in São Paulo (7 May), in Monte Mor (9 May), in Cosmópolis (4 June) and in São Caetano (12 June). All shows were successful, very well attended, and ticket sales were an important source for improving the financial situation, as for example in Presidente Venceslau or São Caetano. Because of the lack of electricity, film screenings in rural regions generally required great skill from the organisers. In Presidente Venceslau the association had to use a power plant from a nearby carpenter's shop that was installed on a truck;[9] other exhibitions were transferred to public cinemas due to the lack of electricity; and a show in the Friedburg Colony, now Fribourg, a district of the city of Campinas, had to be cancelled for lack of electricity, a problem that the city managed to resolve only in 1935.[10]

In the following years the São Paulo association continued its very successful screenings with films supplied by the Deutsche Bildspielbund: *Ein Besuch bei Hindenburg/A Visit at Hindenburg*, *Das arbeitende Hamburg/Working Hamburg*, *Das schöne Hamburg/Beautiful Hamburg*, *Die Lüneburger Heide/The Luneburg Heath* and *Ein Turnfilm/A Physical Education Film*. The news of the work and the success of the association caught the attention of other states. In June 1932, the *Lehrerzeitung: Vereinsblatt des Katholischen Lehrervereins in Rio Grande do Sul* (Teachers' Journal: Publication of the Catholic Teachers Association of Rio Grande do Sul) published an article on the annual assembly of the São Paulo association, which included the screening of films in the state of São Paulo.[11] With reference to the journal's article, Walther Kosche from the Pre-Theological Institute in São Leopoldo, Rio Grande do Sul, contacted his colleagues in São Paulo and offered a collaboration between his film service and the São Paulo film service.[12] Kosche already had experience with film screenings and the management of a film service. Being interested in cinematography, he had operated the D.K.D. since April 1932. The organisation of the D.K.D. was different from that of the São Paulo film service. From the central office in São Leopoldo, Kosche established a network of film agencies that was open to everyone who wanted to become a partner. To join the network, new members paid a fee that was used to finance the purchase of new films and projectors and to cover administration costs. The concept of the D.K.D.'s film service was based on the constant circulation and exchange of films among the agencies.

The expansion of the D.K.D. in 1933 was the result of Kosche's great personal commitment. The amount of correspondence indicates that he must have travelled extensively throughout the state, contacting colleagues, clubs and other associations in order to provide a quality film programme to its members. In his correspondence with the São Paulo association, Kosche requested information on films such as Arnold Fanck's generic mountain film *Der Berg des Schicksals/ Mountain of Destiny* (1923/4), *Tertianerstreiche/Secondary School Pranks* or 'any other film'.[13] Kosche's exchange of correspondence also made it possible for his associations to exchange films with other film enthusiasts. A contact from Bom Jesus in Rio Grande de Sul offered Kosche several films, among them the film he was looking for, Fanck's *Der Berg des Schicksals/Mountain of Destiny*, as well as *Kakteen- und Orchideenblüten/Cacti- and Orchid Blossom, São Lourenço und Umgebung/Saint Lawrence and Surrounding* (120m), *Rosario-Prozession und Navegantesfest/Rosario Procession and Navegantes Celebration* (850m), *Spiessbraten/Spit Roast* (40m) and four 30m films with Charlie Chaplin and Jackie Coogan.[14]

The D.K.D. exclusively worked with reduced-format films (16mm) that made organisation faster and more economical. In cases where the D.K.D. had the chance to show standard-format films that were offered to the service, it organised screenings in local public cinemas. The collaboration between the D.K.D. and São Paulo did not take place until 27 March 1934, after an agreement that had been reached at an assembly held during the celebrations of the national Schoolday in Blumenau at the end of September 1933. With this collaboration, from 1934 onwards, the service was administered by the L.D.L. In 1935, the service was restructured and renamed L.D.L.-Film Service of the National Association of German-Brazilian Teachers.

The administration of the service changed from São Leopoldo to São Paulo, under the direction of one of the Olinda schoolteachers, Dr Karl Otto Müller. In order to facilitate the administration of the São Paulo office, the Film Service set up a provincial sub-office in Porto Alegre that managed the southern states of Brazil.[15] Later, the new service branched out throughout the country with district and regional offices, reaching Bahia, in the Brazilian north-east. In Rio Grande de Sul, offices were located in the cities of São Leopoldo, Santa Cruz, Cachoeira, Santa Maria, Santo Ângelo, Belo Centro, Burica, Ijuhy, Neu Württemberg, Carasinho, Boa Vista de Erechim, Erechim, Marcelino Ramos, Porto Novo, Porto Felix, São Lourenço, Pelotas and Bagé; in Santa Catarina: Blumenau, Joinville, Porto União and Florianópolis; in the state of Paraná: Curytiba, Ponta Grossa and Rio Negro-Mafra; in Minas

Figure 5.1 Exhibition of the L.D.L.-Film Service at the annual school festivity of the Olinda School in 1936. (Source: Arquivo do Instituto Martius-Staden, São Paulo, Brazil.)

Gerais: Burnier and in Rio de Janeiro. Two mobile agencies operated by the associations of Evangelical and Catholic teachers supported the network in Rio Grande do Sul. An agency in Espírito Santo was formed in 1936.[16]

Films from the L.D.L.-Film Service could be rented for free or just with a cover fee to pay the exhibition costs. Screenings of standard-format films (35mm) were made by the Foreign Organization of the Nazi Party (N.S.D.A.P.) and the official representation of the German Reich Railroad (Deutsche Reichsbahn) in Rio de Janeiro. Screenings of the Teachers Association in São Paulo, and of the D.K.D. and the L.D.L.-Film Service were all very popular. For the period between 1931 and 1938 it is possible to evidence numerous requests from associations and clubs that were planning exhibitions and suggested new acquisitions of film. According to the Olinda School Report, in the first year the D.K.D. organised ninety-nine nights of film presentations, thirty-one of them in the state of São Paulo (Müller 1934). By the following March, the total number of screenings had grown to 121. The films were supposed to 'help maintain nationality as a living link with the homeland' and strengthen German public education in Brazil (Müller 1936: 88). On the other hand, the films produced by the D.K.D. were to inform in the homeland (*Heimat*) about the 'German nationality in Brazil' (Müller 1934: 75).

In her investigation of historical photographs, Olga Rodrigues de Moraes von Simson points out that the aim of these film services was to provide national socialist ideology to the German immigrants:

> The aim of the work of distributing educational films was, according to the expansion programme of the national socialist ideology for the German colonies that were spread over the five continents, to maintain the Teuton tradition among the settlers that were spread all over the continents, to report about the political, social and educational achievements obtained by Nazism in the motherland [. . .]. (de Moraes von Simson 2005: 27)

From 1933 on, the L.D.L.-Film Service could not avoid the influence of the N.S.D.A.P., and local Nazi groups tried to influence the German-Brazilian associations in the following years. However, limiting film screenings to Nazi ideology and propaganda means to exclude the films' historical audience, which positions the films in a rather ambivalent reception context.

It is important to look at the relationship between Germans who were living in Brazil and joined the Nazi Party and German-Brazilians who opposed the Nazi hegemony in the country. Most German-Brazilians cared about their language, art and tradition, but showed little interest in Nazi ideology, as Luiz Nazario writes in his survey article about Nazi film politics in Brazil (2007: 86). There were voices in Brazil that criticised the party's actions for being insensitive and running the risk of threatening the reputation of German-Brazilians as 'good Brazilian citizens' (Müller 1997: 296). The number of N.S.D.A.P. members outside Germany was never significant. Only 5 per cent of Germans living outside Germany joined the Nazi party (ibid.: 47). Of the 90,000 Germans who were living in Brazil as Germans with German citizenship (*Reichsdeutsch*), members of the Nazi Party in Brazil numbered only about 3.2 per cent (Dietrich 2007: 159). Brazilian historian René Gertz recalls that 'among those who joined the party was probably a significant number who were in direct economic dependence on German companies (from Germany) operating in Brazil, for whom joining the party was almost an obligation' (Gertz 1996: 89). The great majority of Germans in Brazil were ethnic German (*Volksdeutsch*) of German origin with a Brazilian citizenship, a group that considered themselves as German-Brazilians (Dietrich 2007: 157). German historian Jürgen Müller has argued that although many German-Brazilians considered the Versailles Treaty as a national humiliation and believed in a new and strong German nation after the end of World War I, correspondence and newspaper reports indicate that the nationalism of this group did not necessarily mean being a national socialist, nor being subordinate to the aims of the National Socialist Party (Müller 1997: 203–5).

Considering this background of the ambivalent political orientation of Germans and German-Brazilians, film programmes should be understood at best as being in an ambivalent position between propaganda, visual information from Germany and entertainment. An example can be analysed with the L.D.L.'s most popular film of 1934, *Der Tag von Potsdam/The Potsdam Day*. The film shows the festivities of the meeting between Adolf Hitler and German President Paul von Hindenburg, two weeks after the election of Hitler as the new Chancellor of Germany in 1933. No source exists to tell us how the audience responded to the film at the time, but different readings of the film are possible. Being of an important historical event in German politics, the film could be understood as what it was: a topic of particular interest for people of German origin. It is also possible that the audience understood the film as a glorification of Adolf Hitler. However, we could also understand it as an encounter between the old and the new Germany. German immigration to Brazil peaked after World War I so that to many German-Brazilians Hindenburg was much more a biographical reference than Hitler. In addition, every city film offers sites that can be of general interest to an audience that is not familiar with the history of the city (see Jung 2002). To argue for a more nuanced understanding of the films and their ambivalent interpretation, the films that were shown by the associations between 1931 and 1935/6, however, have to be placed in an additional broader cultural propaganda context.

Cultural Propaganda

The screening of films in Brazil resulted from an effort by the Association of Teachers Abroad (Verein Deutscher Lehrer im Ausland, V.D.A.) in Germany in 1930. In January, the newspaper *Die Deutsche Schule im Auslande* (The German School Abroad), the official organ of the V.D.A., published its first article on cultural propaganda in schools abroad (Schmidt 1930). In the article the author remarks that, though the war is over, a new struggle has started. Besides the economic competition over resources and new markets in the world, there exists a cultural struggle between nations, which deserves the same attention. In addition to Asia, Europe and the East, South America is the fourth 'battlefield' for cultural propaganda – a German cultural policy without threatening indigenous culture. The author emphasises that knowledge of German culture is not intended to alienate non-German students from their own culture, but to use German education as a 'reinforcement' between cultures (ibid.: 9).

Another article reports on the exhibition of Cultural Films as part of this cultural propaganda. The German Reich Railway provided the V.D.A. with a film of 1,500m about Germany, to be shown in all schools and associations in South and Central America (Prinzhorn 1930). Including explanatory texts in Spanish and Portuguese, the film was intended not only for immigrants of

German origin, but also for students and relatives who were not German and who could see the film during a social event. The aim of the film, that 'really is a propaganda film' (ibid.), was not simply to depict Germany, but to establish the country as a competitor to France, which attracted the majority of tourists from South America. The first premiere of the cultural propaganda film was planned to take place in Brazil. It is quite possible that the propaganda film was *Oh, My Dear Fatherland*, which was donated to the L.D.L., and the association's tour in May 1931 the film's premiere.

Addressing the Local Public

Films that were shown by the D.K.D. and the L.D.L.-Film Service in areas of German immigration and in German schools during the 1930s were not exclusively filmed in Germany. Films such as the aforementioned *Saint Lawrence and Surrounding*, *Rosario Procession and Navegantes Celebration* or *Spit Roast* were clearly addressing a national, local public. A film such as *O Brasil Grandioso/Grand Brazil*, screened in September 1931 at the Olinda School, did not address an exclusively German audience. Germans made up the smallest part of the Olinda School students, which was mostly attended by German-Brazilians, and a quarter of the audience was composed of Brazilian and other nationalities.[17] Following the reports and correspondence about cinematic events in the cities and in the rural regions, the target public was also not exclusively German or of German origin. In rural regions, it was practically impossible to organise film screenings without the Brazilian-Portuguese-speaking population. As the cultural propaganda was directed at the public in Brazil, as recommended in 1930, a photograph of a board at the entrance of the Cine Casari in Presidente Venceslau reads: 'Today Great Success. UFA presents two interesting films of great culture. Part 1: Sport in General in two fine parts; Part 2, *Minha Patria/My Fatherland*, in eight parts, demonstrating the most beautiful landscapes of Germany' (Soares 2009: 90).

The combination of a sports film and the title *My Fatherland* suggests that the photo was probably taken during the tour of the São Paulo Association on 8 April 1931. Bruno Pinto Soares points out the contradiction of the text on the sign:

> *My Fatherland* intends to show the most beautiful landscapes of Germany, and the name itself invites to imagine that it is a production with a nationalist tenor. The interesting thing in this matter is the intention to show the film in the urban area of the city, after all the overwhelming majority of the German community lived in the rural area. It can be noted that the film was not addressed to the Germanic public of the city, because if it was, it would be shown in the colony itself. The intention of programming a film, which has the purpose of showing the 'most beautiful landscapes of

Germany', had a greater purpose for the city than just to learn about the fatherland of many Venceslau inhabitants. In this case, it could work two goals: to nourish the far from their fatherland Germans with the national-socialist ideology and to make it sympathetic to the inhabitants in places that give shelter. (Soares 2009: 90)

Soares concludes that 'the sign itself, in Portuguese and not in German or bilingual, demonstrates that the target audience for reproduction would be the non-Germanic community of the city' (ibid.). Soares describes how the film screening with all its ideological purpose also functioned as kind of a neighbourhood link between the two communities, Brazilian and German-Brazilian, in a small town like Presidente Venceslau. Other sources support Soares's observation. In June 1931, due to the lack of electricity, it was necessary to relocate a film projection in Cosmópolis, in the interior of São Paulo, to the local cinema. Only thanks to the presence of the Brazilian population was it possible to avoid a financial loss. A report remarks:

Though the stories of the films were easy to comprehend, it is interesting that especially the Brazilians lamented that the texts were just edited in German and not in Portuguese. Without any doubt we could be even more successful, if we considered this request in future.[18]

An exhibition on 25 June 1934 in Araçatuba, in the interior of São Paulo, was almost exclusively attended by Brazilians. Of 500 spectators, only 100 were of German origin. The exhibitions in Congonhas do Campo and Casa de Pedra in Minas Gerais, in 1938, were also almost a Brazilian event: of 200 spectators only ten to fifteen were of German origin.[19] A unique connection between German and Brazilian films in a screening in March 1935, in São Caetano, Minas Gerais, shows that the Brazilian public was taken into consideration at least in the planning of the screenings. Next to films like *Von Ammergau zum Staffelsee/From Ammergau to Lake Staffel*, *Die Ostsee, 5. und 6. Teil / The Baltic Sea, Part 5 and 6* and *Sport im Schnee/Snow Sports* were shown the films *Os 3 Cavalheiros/The Three Gentlemen* and *Koko e o Cacique/Koko and the Chief*. It is not only remarkable that the programme included German and Brazilian titles, but also that the German titles referred to the Cultural Film genre, while the other two titles were animation films. The evening programme can be seen as an alternative to the dilemma in Cosmópolis. Although it is not known in what language the event was presented or introduced, or whether intertitles of the first three German films were translated into Portuguese, the animation films did not require any explanatory text or introduction. They had the goal of being amusing, entertaining films for a broad audience, regardless of the audience's origin, German or Brazilian.

Another example combines an ambivalent reception on the German spectators' side with a mixed audience. In May 1934, at the Olinda School, the screening began with the animation film *Wupp lernt das Gruseln/Wupp Learns to be Scared* (Hermann Diehl, 1932), followed by *Mit dem Condorflugzeug von Natal bis Santos/With the Condor Aeroplane from Natal to Santos* and *Der schöne Rhein. II. Teil/The Beautiful Rhine, Part II*. The animation film was hardly suitable to strengthen Germanhood in Brazil, but its function was first of all to start an entertaining film evening. The subtitle 'From Koblenz to Rotterdam' in *The Beautiful Rhine* was able to demonstrate that German landscapes reached beyond national borders to the Netherlands. In the same way, the German public could interpret the flight in a Condor aeroplane along the Brazilian coast as a masterpiece of German technology that measured aeronautically the new *Heimat*. The view of a Condor plane flying over Brazilian territory, travelling 3,000km along the Brazilian coast, from the north-east (Natal) to São Paulo (Santos), in contrast to 400km from Koblenz to Rotterdam in *The Beautiful Rhine*, certainly corroborates the Nazi ideology of people without space (*Volk ohne Raum*). However, considering the critical position of many German-Brazilians in relation to Nazi ideology, it was thus possible to reach the conclusion that Brazil and Germany represented different periods in the life of the German-Brazilians: the great Brazil as the aspiration for a new and better life and the small Germany for the outdated memory. However, for the Brazilian public, the programming of the film could have had a different effect: they could have appreciated the film for its demonstration of Brazil's enormous size in comparison with the small European country. Moreover, the film contrasted modernity and technology, the Condor plane over Brazil, with a traditional and old transport system, a boat on the river Rhine in Germany. Film shows of the associations could be an experience of taking part in progress and modern life. Due to the lack of electricity, it took four years before the people in Friedberg could watch films from the L.D.L.-Film Service. The first projection in 1935 suggests that the film show was not only the first contact for German immigrants and Brazilians with the medium of film but also a celebration of modern life that had finally reached the small town.[20]

In her investigation of *Wochenschau*, the German newsreels about Brazil that were shown in Germany, Thais Blank argues that newsreels helped to consolidate the bond of a Nazi 'imagined community'. German viewers in Germany would see how the world was marked by Germanic traits even if this world was thousands of kilometres away (Blank 2008: 11). In analogy to Blank's argument, it can be argued that German Cultural Films that were shown in Brazil had a similar function: the films were supposed to produce a feeling of belonging, being German and being part of the Nazi community. The examples, however, show that the exhibitions of the São Paulo association, the D.K.D. or the L.D.L. should not be seen exclusively as an extraterritorial extension of German or national-socialist cinematographic propaganda, but also as part of the Brazilian cultural offering. An interpretation of the film screenings that focuses exclusively on Nazi propaganda, which undoubtedly reached German immigrants in Brazil, underestimates the exhibition context and the dynamics of the film programmes that addressed the broad public, including Brazilians. The work of associations and services in the Brazilian regions shows that the associations' exhibitions could strengthen the bond of an imagined community. However, it was not necessarily the bond only of an imagined German community but also that of a Brazilian one.

The cinematographic activities of the Association of German Teachers in São Paulo, of the D.K.D. or of the L.D.L. were not the only ones in Brazil or in South America. The Association of German Teachers in Rio de Janeiro, for example, organised a show at the Cine Alhambra, in Rio de Janeiro, where 700 children watched films such as *Besuch bei Hindenburg/Visit to Hindenburg*, *Kinderland-Sonnenland/Children's Land – Sunland* (in two parts) and *Ceylon* (a Cultural Film from UFA). The Faulhaber Foundation (Faulhaber Stiftung) in Neu-Württemberg, now Panambi, regularly organised screenings of standard-format films and operated a travelling cinema, *Wanderkino*. In 1930, the Association of German Teachers in Chile reported on their efforts to acquire Cultural Films for free.[21] In 1934, The Humboldt German school in Buenos Aires organised sound film screenings.[22]

Conclusion

Without challenging the propagandistic efforts of Nazi Germany abroad, this case study shows that German Cultural Films were not just shown in public cinemas abroad but were an important source for the work of German educational associations. German Cultural Films might have followed an ideological aim, to bring Nazi propaganda to German immigrants, but the programming and the composition of the audience indicate that the films are better understood as part of a dynamic Brazilian film culture. Associations were present in regions where cinema culture was less developed or even absent. The film screenings were attended by Germans and by Brazilians. Further research in local archives in towns or municipalities with populations of German origin could give additional information and data to the records at the Martius-Staden Institute. Together they could produce an even more detailed picture of the audience composition and the reception of German films in Brazil.

This case study also illustrates the need for more comparative analysis. German immigration to Brazil was not insignificant in numbers but was outmatched by Portuguese, Italian and Spanish immigration. Further research could show if the different immigration groups, or any other nation that was active in Brazil, joined the struggle for cultural propaganda and made similar efforts in the regions that were dominated by the respective immigrants. One major counterargument in the discourse of national cinema is the danger of cultural imperialism through foreign films and culture (Jarvie 2000). Research results would not play down the significance of national genres and movements in Brazilian film history but present Brazilian film history as an example of a dynamic, multi-ethnic cinema culture. To reach a more detailed understanding of national and transnational cinematographic relations in film history, associations and their activities could therefore play a key role.

NOTES

1. This chapter is based on an earlier version of the article 'Cinema nacional, para quem? Associações, recepção e Transnacionalismo', *História: Debates e Tendências* 16(2), July/December 2016, 328–43.
2. Already in its fifth year, the Pre-SOCINE workshop of the annual conference of the Brazilian Society of Film and Audiovisual Studies, Sociedade Brasileira de Estudos de Cinema e Audiovisual (SOCINE), which precedes the conference in October each year, illustrates the growing interest and change in Brazilian film and cinema historiography. Presentations that are given at this workshop often cover rural regions, for example the Sertão in the north-east of Brazil.
3. 'Bericht des Deutschen Lehrervereins-São Paulo über die Filmvorführungen vom 22.5.1931'. GIVf, 25/Schubert-Chor, Arquivo do Instituto Martius-Staden, São Paulo [henceforth AIMST].
4. Today known as Colégio Visconde de Porto Seguro.
5. Correspondence, 'Deutscher Lehrerverein São Paulo, 4 Aug. 1931'. Akten des Landesverbandes deutsch-brasilianischer Lehrer, Mappe 5, AIMST.
6. Ibid.
7. 'Kulturfilmdienst' (May 1936). Correspondência Deutscher Lehrerverein São Paulo, 1936, AIMST.
8. Today known as Colégio Benjamin Constant.
9. Correspondence, 'Bericht des Deutschen Lehrervereins – São Paulo über die Filmvorführungen, 22 Mai 1931'. Deutscher Lehrerverein São Paulo und Ruhegehaltskasse Bezirk São Paulo. Protokolle vom 29.08.1925 bis 25.10.1931 (samt Anlage), AIMST.
10. Correspondence, Richard Gübels(?), 8 December 1935. Correspondência Deutscher Lehrerverein São Paulo, 1935/II, AMIST.
11. 'Jahreshauptversammlung des Deutschen Lehrervereins S. Paulo', *Lehrerzeitung: Vereinsblatt des Katholischen Lehrervereins in Rio Grande do Sul*, Porto Alegre, 31(6), June 1932, 6–7.
12. Correspondence, Dr. Kosche, São Leopoldo, 2 July 1932. Correspondência Deutscher Lehrerverein São Paulo, 1932, AIMST.
13. Ibid.
14. Correspondence, Gustav Holl, Bom Jesus, 14 June 1933. Akten des Landesverbandes Deutsch-Brasilianischer Lehrer, 1933, AIMST.
15. 'Landesverband Deutsch-Brasilianischer Lehrer, 46. Rundbrief'. Akten des Landesverbandes Deutsch-Brasilianischer Lehrer, 1935, AIMST.

16. 'Bericht über die Lehrertagung in St. Maria (Espírito Santo), am 8. und 9. September 1936'. Akten des Landesverbandes Deutsch-Brasilianischer Lehrer, 1936, AIMST.
17. In 1923 the school had 426 students: 259 Brazilian of German origin, 79 German, 88 Brazilians and other nationalities. In 1938 the school was attended by 947 students: 520 Brazilian of German origin, 126 German, 249 Brazilians and 52 of other nationalities.
18. 'Bericht des Deutschen Lehrervereins-São Paulo über die Filmvorführungen am 22 May 1931'. GIVf, 25/Schubert-Chor, AIMST.
19. 'Deutschbrasilianischer Kulturfilmdiens (DKD)'. GIVf, 31/12, AIMST.
20. Correspondence, Richard Gübels(?), 8 December 1935. Correspondência Deutscher Lehrerverein São Paulo, 1935/II, AIMST.
21. 'Verein Deutscher Lehre in Chile. 1. Rundschreiben'. End of March 1930. Correspondência Deutscher Lehrerverein São Paulo, 1930, AIMST.
22. 'Deutschbrasilianischer Kulturfilmdienst. São Paulo'. Letter from 5 September 1934. GIVf, 31/12, Allgemeiner Schriftwechsel 1934–1936, II, AIMST.

Bibliography

Anderson, Benedict (1991) *Imagined Communities: Reflections on the Origin and Spread of Nationalism*. London: Verso.

Blank, Thais (2008) 'O papel dos cinejornais alemães sobre o Brasil na "Comunidade Imaginada" Nazista'. Paper presented at the XXXI Congresso Brasileiro de Ciências da Comunicação, Natal, RN, Brazil, 2–6 September, pp. 1–13. <http://www.intercom.org.br/papers/nacionais/2008/resumos/R3-1708-1.pdf> (last accessed 17 May 2021).

Chickering, Roger (1984) *We Men Who Feel Most German: A Cultural Study of the Pan German League, 1886–1914*. Boston: George Allen & Unwin.

de Moraes von Simson, Olga Rodrigues (2005) 'Imagem e memória', in Etienne Samain (ed.), *O fotográfico*, 2nd edn. São Paulo: Hucitec, pp. 19–32.

Dietrich, Ana Maria (2007) 'Nazismo tropical? O partido nazista no Brasil'. PhD thesis, Universidade de São Paulo. <http://www.teses.usp.br/teses/disponiveis/8/8138/tde-10072007-113709/> (last accessed 17 May 2021).

Eley, Geoff (1992) 'Nations, Publics and Political Cultures: Placing Habermas in the Nineteenth Century', in Craig Calhoun (ed.), *Habermas and the Public Sphere*. Cambridge, MA: MIT Press, pp. 289–339.

Fraser, Nancy (1992) 'Rethinking the Public Sphere: A Contribution to the Critique of Actually Existing Democracy', in Craig Calhoun (ed.), *Habermas and the Public Sphere*. Cambridge, MA: MIT Press, pp. 109–42.

Fuhrmann, Wolfgang (2015) 'The Ufa Universe: German Cinema in Brazil', in Anke Finger, Gabi Kathöfer and Christopher Larkosh (eds), *KulturConfusão: On German–Brazilian Interculturalities*. New York and Berlin: de Gruyter, pp. 179–97.

Fuhrmann, Wolfgang (2016) 'Cinema nacional, para quem? Associações, recepção e Transnacionalismo', *História: Debates e Tendências* 16(2), 328–43.

Gertz, René E. (1996) 'Influência política alemã no Brasil na década de 1930', *Estudios Interdisciplinarios de América Latina y el Caribe* 7(1), 85–105.

Higson, Andrew (1989) 'The Concept of National Cinema', *Screen* 30(4), 36–46.

Higson, Andrew (2000) 'The Limiting Imagination of National Cinema', in Mette Hjort and Scott Mackenzie (eds), *Cinema and Nation*. London and New York: Routledge, pp. 63–74.

Jarvie, Ian (2000) 'National Cinema: A Theoretical Assessment', in Mette Hjort and Scott Mackenzie (eds), *Cinema and Nation*. London and New York: Routledge, pp. 75–87.

Jung, Uli (2002) 'Local Views: A Blind Spot in the Historiography of Early German Cinema', *Historical Journal of Film, Radio and Television* 22(3), 253–73.

Kreimeier, Klaus, Antje Ehmann and Jeanpaul Goergen (2005) *Geschichte des dokumentarischen Films in Deutschland 1895–1945. Band 2: Weimarer Republik (1918–1933)*. Stuttgart: P. Reclam Jun.

Müller, Jürgen (1997) *Nationalsozialismus in Lateinamerika: Die Auslandsorganisation der NSDAP in Argentinien, Brasilien, Chile und Mexiko, 1931–1945*. Stuttgart: Hans-Dieter Heinz.

Müller, Karl Otto (1934) 'Kulturfilmdienst in São Paulo', in *Deutsche Schule São Paulo: Bericht über das Schuljahr 1933 und 1934*. São Paulo: Deutsche Schule, pp. 74–7.

Müller, Karl Otto (1936) 'Der Kulturfilmdienst', in *Deutsche Schule São Paulo: Bericht über das 59. Schuljahr*. São Paulo: Deutsche Schule, pp. 87–91.

Nazario, Luiz (2007) 'Nazi Film Politics in Brazil, 1933–1942', in Roel Van de Winkel and David Welch (eds), *Cinema and the Swastika: The International Expansion of the Third Reich*. New York: Palgrave Macmillan, pp. 85–98.

Nipperdey, Thomas (1976) 'Verein als soziale Struktur in Deutschland im späten 18. und frühen 19. Jahrhundert. Eine Fallstudie zur Modernisierung', in Thomas Nipperdey (ed.), *Gesellschaft, Kultur, Theorie: Gesammelte Aufsätze zur neueren Geschichte*. Göttingen: Vandenhoeck and Ruprecht, pp. 175–205.

Prinzhorn, [?] (1930) 'Kulturfilmpropaganda', *Deutsche Schule im Ausland*, 22(12), 405.

Ramos, Fernão (ed.) (1985) *História do Cinema Brasileiro*. São Paulo: Art Editora.

Schmidt, Franz (1930) 'Kulturpropaganda und deutsche Auslandschulen', *Die Deutsche Schule im Auslande* 21(1), 1–10.

Shaw, Deborah and Stephanie Dennison (2007) *Brazilian National Cinema*. London and New York: Routledge.

Soares, Bruno Pinto (2009) 'Germanismo e nazismo na colônia alemã de Presidente Venceslau' (1923–45). Master's thesis, Universidade Estadual Paulista, São Paulo. <https://repositorio.unesp.br/handle/11449/93344> (last accessed 17 May 2021).

Stam, Robert and Randal Johnson (eds) (1995) *Brazilian Cinema*, expanded edn. New York: Columbia University Press.

6. EMOTIONAL COMMUNITIES IN THE CINEMA: TRACING EMOTION IN MASS OBSERVATION CINEMA RECORDS, 1937–1950

James Jones

In 1937, a commercial clerk replied to a Day Survey issued by the social research organisation Mass Observation (MO), detailing a recent trip to a Birmingham cinema to see Alfred Hitchcock's *Sabotage* (1936). 'We would have preferred to be going to the Royalty, a modern cinema, only a stone's throw away', explained the respondent, 'but we had come over to see *Sabotage*. I had not been in Harborne Picture House since the "penny crush" days of my childhood, but the same raddled and wrinkled blonde who pulled a lever to release our metal checks in the old days was in the pay box.'[1] Aside from nostalgic reflections on his cinemagoing past, the Observer noted the 'strong expressions of emotion throughout the audience' which consisted of 'Ahs! Ohs [sic] and a general breathiness'.[2] This record illustrates how, in his eyes, the intersection between emotion, modernity and space could define the cinema in the twentieth century. Recent scholarship on the history of emotions offers illuminating approaches to MO material such as this, and work on emotional communities is particularly useful in exploring the emotional returns of cinemagoing.

This chapter examines a range of Mass Observation documentation in order to explore how the cinema was used as a site for emotional experience, the tensions between group and individual feelings, and the ways in which emotional communities (defined as a group of people who adhere to the same norms of emotional expression and who value or devalue a set of emotions within a specific context) were formed (Rosenwein 2007: 2). This chapter also illustrates how methodological approaches from the history of emotions can help to enhance an understanding of past cinema audiences and their cinemagoing motivations. More broadly, it contributes to wider discussions in movements such as New Cinema History which advocate a multifaceted, multidiscipline approach, concerned 'with the cinema as a commercial institution and with the socio-cultural history of its audiences' (Maltby et al. 2011: 9).

Mass Observation, Cinema and the History of Emotions

Mass Observation was established in 1937 by Tom Harrisson and Charles Madge with an aim to record the everyday lives of 'ordinary' Britons and to bridge the 'undoubted gap of knowledge and understanding between the small group of people who direct our civic and national life . . . and the vast majority of ordinary folk'.[3] One could argue that, for MO, the 'ordinary' Briton was quite a broad term: in many cases, it was engendered by the volunteer correspondents who put themselves forward to contribute to the project. Those volunteers were often relatively well educated and, especially in the case of MO diarists, drawn from the middle classes. Some scholars, such as James Hinton, have argued that Tom Harrisson was acutely aware of his own privileged background and never positioned himself outside the social elite, believing instead that his education and class gave him a responsibility to provide the working class with a voice (Hinton 2013: 12). MO constructed itself as the 'other' and its volunteer Observers (even those who identified themselves as working class) self-consciously set themselves apart from those under study. Although a noble aspiration, MO's ambition to become a mouthpiece for the working man was arguably weakened in its projection of middle-class values on the working class: in some cases, by the judgements it cast on those under observation.[4] More widely, MO came under criticism at the time, and in the years after, for its rather disordered qualitative approach, perceived invasions of privacy, erratic research methods, and openly acknowledged political motivations. The data gathered was often incomplete, unrepresentative, collected in a non-systematic manner, and was far from objective. That the project was not without flaws or critics does not detract from its value as a unique historical social record, and the unwieldy nature of the archive acts as an enticing challenge for the social historian.

Mass Observation's varied research methods included questionnaires, personal diaries, monthly investigations on specific topics, and the collection of ephemera. The reports collected by MO are frequently framed by a subjective and intensely personal tone which may be absent in other sources. Naturally, this presents difficulties for the historian trying to navigate documents which contain subjective descriptions of other people's emotions and then attempting to extrapolate this into a meaningful assessment of historical feeling. Moreover, the accounts given, although often very personal, were written by people who knew that their writings were going to be read by an outside organisation, and this may have had an influence on what they chose to reveal or suppress about their cinema trips. Unsystematic data collection frequently led to missing information about the respondents, and for every detailed diary or directive reply, there is another which sketches out only the barest of information: often frustrating for the historian. Nevertheless, the eclectic cache of MO material gives texture and depth to historical embodied and lived emotional practices. The loyalty given to the organisation by many of its correspondents often provides raw and explicit accounts of emotion, and the introspection induced by contributing to such a project draws out more nuanced and considered reflections than might be found elsewhere in the historical record. As with any historical source, the challenges are not insurmountable, and MO material is extremely valuable in assessing emotional experiences of past cinemagoing.

Similarly, the burgeoning field of emotions' history is certainly a useful way to uncover – and re-evaluate – the past. Key in this field are the works of William Reddy, Peter Stearns and Barbara Rosenwein, and each has brought their own methodological and conceptual tools to the sub-discipline. Reddy explored the role of emotions in political life, aiming to unpick the 'sticky relationship between language, culture, and the feelings . . . asking whether emotions exist apart from culture and the words used to describe them' (Matt 2011: 119). Reddy proposed the term 'emotives' as a way to describe the act of expressing emotion through speech, as well as establishing the notion of 'emotional regimes' which are a 'complex of practices that establish a set of emotional norms and that sanction those who break them' (2001: 323). Stearns, on the other hand, championed the 'emotionology' of a culture which gave shape to, and controlled the expression of, emotion.[5] Rosenwein's research into emotion in the Middle Ages suggests that it has always been subject to control through emotional communities and that different emotions 'come to the fore at various times' in history (2014: 78). One method by which Rosenwein identifies these shifting patterns of specific emotions is by analysing the frequency of certain 'emotion words' in medieval documents, demonstrating how such words appear in greater concentration at different moments in time. Such a methodology creates something of a 'map' which tracks how emotional responses and their expression modulated to a great extent, dependent on the place and context in which they occurred.

Rosenwein, Reddy and Stearns are united in the belief that 'culture gives some shape to emotional life and that consequently, feelings vary across time' (Matt 2011: 117). Other scholars such as Peter Burke suggest that historians have to decide

> whether they believe in the essential historicity or non-historicity of emotions. Either it is the case that specific emotions, or the whole package

of emotions in a given culture . . . are subject to fundamental changes over time; or that they remain essentially the same in different periods. (Burke 2004: 109)

Whilst such a proposition may at first appear to be the only choice for the historian of emotion, it is rather reductionist and threatens to eradicate the nuances of studying past feeling. It is more fitting to argue that scholars can adopt both strategies: whilst emotions have a biological basis (and are, therefore, essentially the same throughout time), these physiological reactions are expressed (or repressed) according to the context and time in which they are felt. For instance, the feeling of intense sadness at the death of a loved one in Ancient Greece would have, fundamentally, been the same as that experienced by a mother losing a child in Victorian England. The expression of this grief, however, would have been inflected by the different beliefs prevalent at the time, and would have altered how it was viewed by both the person experiencing the emotional act and by those witnessing it.

The Cinema Auditorium as an Emotional Space

The cinema auditorium in the mid-twentieth century was, as now, simultaneously a private and a public space, charged with emotion both on and off the screen. In her ethnographic study of cinemagoing memories, Annette Kuhn argues that the 'pleasure of looking at the cinema screen is but a small part of an all-encompassing somatic, sensuous and affective involvement in the cinema experience' (Kuhn 2002: 147). For many, this cinema experience was emotionally subtle, guided by the film being screened and shaped by the context of the cinema auditorium.

Before examining the experience of individual emotion and how it fits with the development of a cinemagoing emotional community (either physically located within an auditorium or, in a more general sense, constructed as a film fan culture emerged), it would be useful to consider the value of MO material in analysing the historical emotional landscape. One of the main strengths of the methods employed by MO is the way in which it questioned its respondents. The numerous directives issued by the organisation often contained questions which sought to uncover not only the public's opinions on topics but, significantly, how they felt about such issues. For example, respondents were asked how they felt about the monarchy, drinking beer, swearing and, in a 1950 survey, if they cried in the cinema and, if so, 'how far, if at all do you feel ashamed on such occasions?'[6] The foregrounding of emotion in the questions may have aided in teasing out the feelings of respondents in their writing, feelings which may have otherwise remained hidden. The material is also valuable in tracing how respondents contextualised and theorised understandings of emotional selfhood, and how they negotiated the rapidly changing social boundaries between public and private spheres, as upheavals such as World War II effected significant social and cultural change (Langhamer 2016).

The cinema was viewed by some as a unique route into the psyche of the everyday man or woman. In a report on film research, one Mass Observer wrote that if 'fundamental attitudes' about life were to be understood, investigations must 'penetrate below the superficial words' of interviews.[7] The Observer argued that study of 'the film, in its environment of the cinema, is practically the ideal medium for the study of private opinion'.[8] Such a record is an apposite example of one of the frustrations of using MO: the Observer in this case is simply identified as 'TM' and it is not possible to tell whether they had any special interest or knowledge in the area. As a general statement, however, it shows how the cinema auditorium could be considered a somewhat anonymous space in which individual emotion could be freely expressed, and it became a prime example of the new meanings of space which had emerged during the first half of the twentieth century. Existing between the private and the open, the inside and the outside, and the domestic and the public, cinema auditoria were fluid spaces which helped to erode the divisions between public and private spaces and experiences of leisure. The cinema was self-evidently a public space: it was located outside the domestic home; it was a recreation experienced in the company of strangers; films entered the public discourse; and, as buildings, cinemas occupied a prominent position in the urban landscape. Simultaneously, however, a visit to the cinema offered the chance for private emotionality in a space allied with a safety found in the darkness of the auditorium. Through habitual attendance, this assumed a reassuring familiarity and a quasi-domestic dimension which extended domestic spheres for the working class. Notions of 'comfort' and 'safety' were ascribed to the cinema by MO participants, feelings most frequently associated with the home; and such readings support the argument that the cinema became an extension of the domestic which lay 'beyond the worlds of home and neighbourhood while still remaining part of a real and accessible world' (Kuhn 2002: 141). Importantly for MO, the cinema auditorium also muted some of the social constraints on the display of feeling which existed in mid-twentieth-century public life (typified, as shall later be explored, by the 'stiff-upper-lip' mentality).

The analysis of MO cinema material elicits comparisons with work on memory and ethnography. The area of memory reclamation has been gaining popularity within film studies in recent years, and was initially championed by scholars such as Annette Kuhn and Helen Richards as a way to understand people's experiences and relationships with the mid-century cinema (Allison et al. 2013: 181). As Carrie Hamilton has suggested, oral history 'would seem to have a privileged relationship to the history of emotions', built upon not only the physical relationship between interviewer and interviewee but also the 'wider range of emotional evidence' offered by interviewees (their changes of pace, tone, facial expressions, silences and gestures: obviously absent in documentary evidence) (2010: 86). The methodology of oral history certainly allows an immediate access to emotion – which often dominates recollections of past events – but, unlike MO, some clarity can be lost for the simple reason that participants were recounting events which took place many decades before. Accounts of cinemagoing in MO, on the other hand, were much closer to the event in temporal terms and, whilst not academic, they offer a useful record of leisure practices and contemporaneous emotion as they occurred, rather than being affected by the passing of time. This is not to reduce the importance of using memory studies in conjunction with documentary evidence to reconstruct historical cinemagoing, but, rather, to substantiate the notion that memory is a 'text to be deciphered, not a lost reality to be discovered' (Richards 2003: 341).

Beyond those emotions normally associated with cinemagoing (such as amusement, fear, sadness or excitement), MO panellists frequently defined the cinema as a force capable of changing their mood for the better. As a leisure activity, cinemagoing became, for some, an opportunity for emotional reinvigoration: 'I felt very morbid and almost at the end of the proverbial tether', wrote one woman to *Picturegoer* magazine, but after visiting a cinema, she left 'refreshed, feeling I could carry on once more'.[9] This restorative quality was attributed to the cinema time and again in MO. Another keen cinemagoer even suggested that the pictures were a miraculous tonic for her health: 'if I had a headache or felt sick, I went to a cinema and forgot all about it and I found that cinema going was much cheaper than doctor's bills'.[10] Such an endorsement of cinemas (as public spaces capable of enhancing the very well-being of patrons) is advanced by Jeffrey Richards, who argues that picture houses in the interwar period became the focus for individual emotional expression, allowing people to be 'taken out of themselves and their lives' (2010: 1).

Emotives in the Cinema

In more general terms, many Observers recorded the overall 'mood' of cinema audiences, couching their interpretations in terms of the vocal reactions (or lack thereof) of an audience. The noting of oral responses was perhaps the only way of uncovering emotional reactions to films through pure observation. The vocalisation of emotion (through laughs, comments directed at the actors, and hisses, for example) was the main way in which internal feelings were brought into the public arena, and became a means by which Observers could access the emotional economy of an audience. Reddy's work on 'emotives' can become a useful tool in assessing this opportunity for MO to examine audience emotion. Asserting that emotives are the ways in which emotions are linguistically expressed, Reddy's framework places great importance on the dynamic relationship between emotives and emotion. Importantly, emotives have the ability to shape, repress or intensify feelings and, as a result, the vocal expressions of emotion from individual cinemagoers may have, in particular circumstances, perpetuated and strengthened feelings of enjoyment for the audience as a whole (Reddy 1999: 270).

The reliance of emotives on language does slightly weaken their application to the MO material as specific words uttered by audience members were not frequently recorded by Observers. Nevertheless, the proposition can be advanced that emotives, as a theory, can be taken further than linguistics. The non-vocal manifestations of emotion can also be emotives which translate inner feelings into observable displays of emotions, influenced as they are by context and social expectation. For example, one Observer, Leonard England, used laughter as a route to evaluate the emotive experience of both a man seated near him and of the wider audience. England observed the Ministry of Information film *Miss Grant Goes to the Door* (1940) on six occasions for MO in different London cinemas, noting that in one screening

> a man thought the whole film was a great joke and laughed loudly throughout. At first he had the audience with him and there was a great deal of laughter . . . but the rest of the film gripped, and the man laughed alone.[11]

The man's laughter acted as an emotive because it outwardly signified, if not enjoyment, his obvious amusement. The reduction in audience laughter was interpreted by England as a sign that the audience's emotions had changed from amusement to excitement. Naturally, using this methodology presents some problems, not least because it may not be able to capture the meanings of any audience reactions between noise and silence, as it relies on the subjective process of an individual impressing their own emotional interpretations onto others. It serves as an illustration, however, of how the emotion of an audience may be indicated not through the existence of an emotive, but by the distinct absence of one.

The Emotional Threshold and Group Emotionality

Mass Observation correspondents clearly marked out the auditorium in direct contrast to other public spaces and, in general terms, the cinema acted as a unique space: simultaneously both private and public. One MO panellist suggested that most people 'under cover of a dark theatre . . . can indulge in a little sentimentality in a similar way as we react to great sorrow – in the quietness of one's own room'.[12] Ostensibly a public leisure venue, the cinema became a locus of private emotion for many people and an extension of the privacy and emotional exclusion which was found in domestic settings. Any autonomous emotional reaction in the cinema was, of course, positioned within – and influenced by – the responses of other people. Evidence in MO relating to the cinema continually contrasts individual emotion with the emotion of the cinema audience as a whole, creating a dynamic relationship between the two. Moreover, MO correspondents record how their emotionality was influenced by those with whom they went to the cinema. Whilst some felt that the strength of their emotions was enhanced by their friends displaying similar affective responses, others considered attendance with a friend to be inhibitive: 'I am usually ashamed', wrote one MO respondent, 'if I am with somebody [and cry at a film] . . . I cry as much as I like if I go to the pictures by myself.'[13] Another female respondent viewed a trip to the cinema with a friend as having a positive effect on her feelings: 'it makes a great difference to my physical reactions whom I see a film *with* – seeing one with a sensitive and affinitive type of friend the emotion I feel is immensely enhanced and vice versa'.[14]

Interestingly, another respondent suggested that it was not her own emotional response of which she was embarrassed, but that of her husband who accompanied her to the cinema: 'although my husband does not weep he has on innumerable occasions squeezed my hand so tightly in emotional scenes that he has nearly broken my fingers. Of course I feel ashamed at such crackpot behaviour!'[15] In this case, an emotional response was stimulated by the emotionality of those with whom one went to the cinema, rather than by the film itself. Again, this suggests the multiplicity of emotional experience which was to be found in mid-century cinemas, as well as the range of reactions to that very emotional expression. Not every MO respondent, for example, viewed emotion as a negative result of a cinema visit. One panellist declared that he was not ashamed of his emotional reactions and that 'on the contrary I feel rather disappointed if the film leaves me cold'.[16] Emotional stimulation was marked out as a central goal of cinemagoing, and many judged the success of a film on its ability to excite emotion.

Cinematic Emotional Communities

Any group emotions which were elicited during a film screening helped to contribute to an emotional community in the cinema: a community defined by its broad emotions which guided and modulated the feelings of individuals within the audience. Such a thesis runs counter to Ute Frevert's argument that, because emotional responses are essentially personal, 'a group, a community or an institution . . . cannot by nature have emotions' (2011: 213). Rosenwein conversely suggests that, whilst group emotions do exist, they are not defined by one or two feelings, but are composed of 'constellations' of emotions to which individuals contribute their own affective experiences (2007: 26). Using this framework to explore the mid-century cinema audience, it becomes clear that emotionality was determined by, and reinforced with, experiences of individual and collective feeling. The sociability of a cinema visit was an important facet of people's cinemagoing motivations. '"The more we are together, the happier we shall be" is a phrase justified by experience in the cinema', wrote a Londoner to *Picturegoer* in 1940, suggestive of the manner in which people found pleasure and reassurance in participating in shared emotional experiences.[17]

The reassuring nature of being part of a group became a stark reality during the Blitz. Many MO volunteers wrote how bombing raids during a screening would do little, if anything, to disrupt proceedings. At first, it may seem rather strange that people frequently preferred to remain in the cinema during an air raid rather than leave for an official shelter. MO respondent 'GW' reported a conversation between his sister and another woman which exemplifies many wartime cinema experiences:

> Sister: The other night when we were in the cinema, the sirens went and the manager said his little piece and I don't think one person left.
> Woman: I'm not surprised . . . I've noticed hardly anyone leaves, after all one is as safe in a cinema as out in the streets.[18]

Confidence in the protection offered by cinemas was, inevitably, shown to be misplaced. In July 1943, a German bomber released eight bombs over the Sussex town of East Grinstead, hitting the Whitehall Cinema during a matinée screening, resulting in the deaths of 108 people. Although perceptions that a cinema auditorium was effective shelter against an air raid were somewhat naïve, they indicate how cinemas were again viewed as comforting and domestic spaces in which people found safety in a group. Indeed, an air raid warning notice was displayed to the East Grinstead audience, but few chose to heed it. Curiously, the passivity of a cinema audience during an air raid became a point of nationalistic pride for one MO respondent who recalled how

> a bomb fell somewhere near and the building rocked. No one moved, there was scarcely even a murmur. When we came out Jules said, 'I am not given to singing the praises of the British nation but when I see the way we can behave when something like that happens I begin to think we are not such a bad race after all'. Abroad there would have been pandemonium.[19]

Another correspondent for MO recorded an air raid notice screened in a London cinema which read: 'Don't panic. Remember you are British.'[20] Just as the English were perversely proud of their emotional reticence, this much-debated stiff-upper-lip mentality evidently extended itself to leisure practices.[21]

Again, people's emotional reactions were moderated by their fellow audience members and MO respondents remained alert as to how they were viewed by others. One woman recounted how she 'was nearly convulsed with laughter and I felt that people nearby were laughing at me and the noise I was making, rather than at the news reel', highlighting how deviating from the emotional norms of one's fellow cinemagoers could produce a feeling of embarrassment.[22] Another respondent used the cinematic emotional community to simultaneously validate emotion and hide any embarrassment: 'almost everyone in the cinema was crying . . . so nobody took much notice of anybody else'.[23] Whilst some were reluctant to publicly display their feelings when watching a film – 'I never like betraying emotion in a crowd' – the emotional responses of others were expedited and enhanced by being part of an audience and by the cinema building itself.[24] Cinemagoing additionally brought, as Robert James suggests, 'a sense of camaraderie and belonging that may have otherwise been denied' to many people; the social aspect was equally as important as the entertainment (2010: 17).

The temptation to treat the cinema audience as a homogeneous group, all conforming to the same emotional style and response to a film, should, however, be avoided. There were always a few in an audience for whom the emotional experiences of those around them were antithetical to their own: and this minority was largely disregarded by MO in its reports. This group often defined its emotionality in direct contrast to the dominant emotions of the wider audience: 'I am more embarrassed at my hardheartedness [sic] among weepers. It makes me feel arrogant and conspicuous.'[25] Such observations again bring the tension between individual feeling and group emotion into focus. In 1937, the coronation of George VI was screened in cinemas across the country, and one MO Day Survey panellist highlighted how, by watching the film with others, he was 'surprised how much I responded to the atmosphere of the crowd', explaining that his fellow audience members encouraged positive feelings towards the King and Empire which were quite opposite to his usual opinions.[26] Interestingly, he suggested that the cinema visit allowed him to experience unfamiliar 'emotion and be in and of a crowd', explaining that 'one becomes very weary of always being in the minority . . . one is fighting against the herd instinct all the time'.[27] An experience such as this indicates how the mood of a cinema audience had the potential to affect individual emotion, and how people were very much aware of this influence.

A Gendered Emotional Space?

Much of the free and open emotionality displayed in the cinema can be attributed to its physical environment. Many MO volunteers identified the darkness of the auditorium as a key – and unique – feature of a cinema visit: a specific characteristic which afforded patrons a degree of privacy in their emotional and physiological responses even when in the company of others. A report on the influence of film remarked that 'the whole set-up of the cinema, the darkness, the reasonably comfortable seats are all conducive to a mild sort of hypnotism'.[28] This link between darkness, emotional concealment and the distancing of fellow audience members is most evident in the August 1950 directive which asked if people cried in the cinema. Many respondents said they only felt embarrassed by their weeping in the cinema when the house-lights were turned on, suggesting that the darkness during the film offered protection against openly losing their emotional reserve in public. Whilst a forty-year-old housewife wrote that she 'always felt thoroughly and absolutely ashamed when the lights went up', a female civil servant of a similar age recorded how she did not often cry in films, but if she did, she 'shouldn't mind . . . as it's so comfortably dark!'[29] Another hinted at the emotionally permissive atmosphere constructed in the cinema, one which was destroyed the moment the lights were illuminated: 'I don't feel ashamed but I would rather the lights should not go up while the tears are rolling.'[30] For many, the darkness allowed explicit emotionality, as long as any tears were dry by the time the film finished. As previously noted, others extended this relaxed, personal emotional economy further, choosing to remain in their seats once the lights had been turned back on until they had composed themselves, to avoid venturing out 'into the light with red-rimmed eyes'.[31]

The expectations of society – particularly for women in respect of their appearance, and for men in conforming to ideas of rational masculine behaviour – determined to a great extent attitudes to the dark film-watching environment. Weeping in the cinema, even under the cover of darkness, remained for some an unacceptable action. Replies from men to the August 1950 directive 'admitted' to crying (emotional display was, evidently, something to which men guiltily confessed), with one man writing that 'tears come readily in moving scenes. I also feel it (perhaps wrongly) to be a sign of weakness.'[32] The tension between public emotional expression and public restraint was significantly inflected by dominant codes of masculine emotional culture, and was certainly not limited to the cinema auditorium, as Martin Francis highlights in his exploration of emotion in post-war British political life (2002: 355). It is interesting to note that there appears to be little correlation between the age of respondents and their opinions on public emotion. Older generations, perhaps surprisingly, appeared less hostile to the idea of men crying in response to films.

A seventy-four-year-old clergyman, for example, differentiated the social expectations of male emotion from those of the wider cinema audience, exclaiming 'being a man, I don't cry. But being a human being, I find tears come behind the eyes sometimes.'[33] One thirty-year-old customs officer was less charitable: 'of course I felt ashamed afterwards; what man wouldn't', whilst a twenty-two-year-old bank clerk dubiously claimed, 'I never cry at the pictures – it's only the Welsh that do that – and a lot of silly women . . . if I did cry I should be ashamed and anyway a gentleman always keeps his emotions to himself.'³⁴ Assertions about women and the population of Wales aside, such a reply indicates the extent to which particular social codes of male behaviour were dominant in the post-war era, engendered by the stiff-upper-lip mentality. Even in the context of the cinema, many MO respondents believed that a man should still maintain strict control over his feelings, underscored by the 'traditional British training' in emotional restraint which one schoolmaster said kept him from 'giving way' in the cinema.³⁵ Cultural reinforcement of this reserve extended across society in different ways including, as Hera Cook has highlighted, class experiences of emotional discipline. Arguing that 'men of the upper classes combined "stoicism" with positions of authority . . . [whilst] for those lower down in the hierarchy, emotional control was part of accepting the control of them by others', Cook advances the case that emotional restraint was a gendered practice (2014: 635). Sadness (let alone weeping) was certainly not an emotion to which the mid-century man, whether middle or working class, had easy access in the public arena.

Women, on the other hand, were much more uninhibited in, and revealing of, their emotional practices in the cinema. The majority of female MO respondents were forthcoming in their cinemagoing autobiographies: one teacher recalled 'tears popping out of my eyes and cascading down to my lap', as opposed to many male responses which noted a mere 'moistening of the eye', lest they be accused of uncontrolled emotion.³⁶ This was not universal, however, and some women expressed their 'annoyance' at their public 'weakness and sentimentality' in the cinema.³⁷ Another female MO diarist took exception to *Sentimental Journey* (1946) – in which a husband wrestles with the death of his wife – and criticised the producers' 'nerve and the licence to make and distribute such harrowing, nauseating films for the sole entertainment of silly women who "like a good cry" in the shilling seats', subscribing to the notion that *any* emotional display in public was frivolous, regardless of gender.³⁸ This response also highlights how class (as well as gender) was a key factor in the emotional experiences of cinemagoing.

Stereotypically, women were viewed as more emotionally volatile, and in contrast to men's recollections, female responses abhorred the physical results of weeping, rather than the semiotic, social concerns about public crying. Whilst feelings of shame or embarrassment at one's emotional reactions were ascribed to cinemagoing by female MO correspondents, the physicality of emotion, and how it was viewed by others, was equally prominent in their responses. The recollections of a middle-aged housewife are typical in this respect: she wrote that emotional displays in the cinema made her feel 'uncomfortable – not because of the emotion I feel, but because I look a sight crying'.³⁹ Other women echoed this aspect, explaining that any shame was a result of their looking 'so ghastly afterwards', rather than being embarrassed by emotional arousal itself.⁴⁰ Again, individual emotion in the cinema was moderated, suppressed and developed by the emotional community of the cinema audience. The August 1950 directive is revealing of the tensions between male and female modes of emotional expression in English society, which again reinforce Rosenwein's notion of 'constellations' of emotions (male and female) operating within a single emotional community (2007: 26).

Cinemas as Emotionally Permissive Environments

The mid-century cinema was exceptional in its atmospheric construction of intimate private spaces in public places: few other mass-leisure venues offered such a malleable emotional environment. For some, the cinema acted as a vent for private emotions (such as sadness or anger) which they were reluctant to express elsewhere, and one Observer praised the cathartic nature of cinemagoing: 'I am rather relieved and pleased that I have been able to rid myself of the emotions.'[41] It would be valuable to briefly consider how this idea fits in with different models of emotion. The belief conveyed by this MO respondent (that emotions could be 'jettisoned') runs counter to theories from psychologists such as William James who, at the start of the century, claimed that emotions were fundamentally linked with rational thought and action. One could not experience fear, so their thinking went, without an external threat; consequently, emotions were necessarily *about* something rather than being abstract physiological phenomena (Deigh 2001: 1253). In this model, emotion in the cinema was inextricably linked to the affective events in a film, rather than existing as an underlying psychological state which could be eliminated from people's everyday lives.

More widely, those hostile to the social value of the cinema argued that it served little emotional purpose: 'why pay money to weep when you can do it free?' asked one MO contributor, whilst another argued there was little wisdom 'in paying to sit in the dark to watch other people's ideas of sordidness ... [when] there are enough tears in daily life'.[42] Emotional experiences were also tied to the perceived worthiness of films, and many cinemagoers only felt comfortable with expressing emotion if a picture was deemed to be of an appropriate quality. Indeed, the apparent quality of a film acted as a determinant of people's attitudes towards their own emotionality: one could feel unashamed about emotional expression if a film was sufficiently commendable and worthy of an emotional response. A useful example of this can be found in an MO reply from 1950 in which a male student recalled

> crying quite a bit in one film ... I didn't feel embarrassed because the film seemed worth it, but I did feel I was a bit silly when I nearly did the same recently over *Silent Dust* which was less worthy of any great emotion.[43]

In the same directive, another panellist wrote: 'I don't hate myself for crying in say *Brief Encounter* but I do bitterly for succumbing to some of the emotional clichés in 2nd rate films.'[44] Such resentment about being emotionally 'manipulated' was fairly common in MO material.

It would now be useful to return to William Reddy's work on emotional regimes and refuges. If wide-reaching emotional regimes emerge at different times in history, each with its own set of normative emotions and specific emotives, then set within these overarching structures are emotional refuges. Reddy suggests that these refuges offer a space in which emotional 'norms are relaxed or even reversed [and where] mental control efforts may be temporarily set aside' in a context conducive to the development of affective connections with others (2001: 128). The cinema certainly operated as an emotional refuge, set within the restrictive and stifled emotional regime which arguably dominated much of the twentieth century. Thomas Dixon has argued in his study on weeping in Britain that this extreme of emotional restraint – which has become something of a stereotype – was, in fact, 'an aberration in our national history': it was quite removed from the more permissive and open emotional regimes which came before and after (2015: 5).

Nevertheless, social expectations of individual emotional restraint assured the cinema a discrete place in the lives of many in the twentieth century; it became both a physical and imagined emotional refuge where one could freely express feelings which were often incompatible with the main emotional regime. When a secretary was asked by MO if she cried in the cinema, her response centred on this opportunity for emotional sanctuary:

> one just did not cry for personal sorrow in front of the servants or young children, or at public school (in which latter place one had to lock oneself in the lav. for the luxury of a good cry) . . . but in films, what matter![45]

For this woman, crying was clearly an indulgence, and cinemas thus became emotional refuges which, Reddy concludes, 'helped to make the current order more liveable for some people, some of the time' (2001: 128).

A Public Space Defined by Emotion

The general picture which emerges from the Mass Observation material on emotional experiences in the cinema is a subtle and complex one. The application of methodologies from the history of emotions, however, permits a better understanding of the cinema's place in the affective landscape of England. This chapter often refers to 'English', rather than 'British', cinemas and society. This is largely a result of MO's focus on England, where its investigative heart lay and, therefore, from where most of the records originate. In some cases, the two terms could be used interchangeably, as debates about leisure affected the whole of the British Isles, and emotional reactions found in English cinemas could quite naturally have also occurred in other parts of the United Kingdom. The framework of the history of emotions, however, could be used in future work about cinemas in these other geographical areas.[46]

Historical cinemagoing practices reflect the ways in which public emotion was enhanced in the twentieth century, as tensions between individual feeling and group emotion manifested themselves in cinema auditoria around the country. Emotional communities (centred on the film) were formed as patrons crossed the emotional threshold of the box office; these communities were also developed by the physical environment of the cinema. The darkness, the exoticism and, conversely, the familiarity of cinemas marked them out as emotionally hospitable spaces in cities and towns, where feeling was still subject to the accepted norms of English culture; crucially, such feeling was allowed to develop in a more permissive and anonymous space. Many MO cinemagoers viewed their emotional experiences in the cinema as rather atypical in their lives, and their affective responses to the films (and to their own emotionality) were influenced by a range of factors including class, gender and the collective nature of the cinema audience. Although the cinema, as a public arena of emotion, elicits comparisons with other mass entertainments, it was clearly viewed by many people as a distinctive form of leisure which underscored their private – and public – emotional practices. Indeed, to quote one MO diarist, many were 'surprised at the vigour' of the emotions they felt in the cinema, just as another diarist mused that it was 'strange how feelings get the better of you. I surprised myself by almost jumping to my feet and cheering.'[47] It seems that surprises were not only to be found in film narratives on the big screen, but also in the personal emotional narratives of millions of cinemagoers.

Notes

1. Mass Observation Day Survey Respondent 409, 1937. SxMOA1/3.
2. Ibid.
3. 'Mass-Observation in Bolton: A Social Experiment', draft articles. SxMOA1/5/1/1/C/2.
4. Peter Gurney has explored this notion in his work on the construction of working-class women's sexuality. He suggests that MO's research methods were debilitated by an explicit agenda brought to investigations which, in turn, produced results more representative of middle-class attitudes towards sexuality, rather than of those being observed. See Gurney (2013).
5. For an insightful overview of the different methods employed by these academics, see Plamper (2010).
6. August 1950 Directive, Question 4. SxMOA1/3/128.
7. Report on 'Social Research and the Film' by TM, 08/10/1940. SxMOA1/2/17/2/H.

8. Ibid.
9. Letter to *Picturegoer* from Olga Townend, Halifax, Yorkshire, 06/10/1940. Recorded in SxMOA1/2/17/5/3.
10. 'Personal note on film going' by Joyce Ausden, Watford. SxMOA1/2/17/1/B.
11. 'Memo on *Miss Grant Goes to the Door*' by Leonard England, 13/08/1940. SxMOA1/2/17/8/A/6.
12. Directive Respondent 4582, August 1950. SxMOA1/3/128.
13. Ibid. Respondent 4750.
14. Ibid. Respondent 3474.
15. Ibid. Respondent 4305.
16. Ibid. Respondent 4483.
17. Letter to *Picturegoer* from a Mr Reynolds, Westminster, 1940. Recorded in SxMOA1/2/17/5/3.
18. Conversation Report by GW, 25/09/40. SxMOA1/2/17/2/H.
19. Mass Observation Diarist 5401, 12/01/41.
20. Mass Observation Respondent. SxMOA1/2/17/4/1/4.
21. Typical of such debates are Capstick and Clegg (2013); Heathorn (2004).
22. 'Report on cinema in wartime' by Joyce Ausden. SxMOA1/2/17/1/B.
23. Directive Respondent 2316, August 1950. SxMOA1/3/128.
24. Ibid. Respondent 4304.
25. Directive Respondent 4568, August 1950. SxMOA1/3/128.
26. Mass Observation Day Survey Respondent Unidentified, May 1937. SxMOA1/3/6.
27. Ibid.
28. 'Film and family life' Report by Leonard England. SxMOA1/2/17/3/I.
29. Directive Respondents 1016 and 1066, August 1950. SxMOA1/3/128.
30. Ibid. Respondent 3426.
31. Ibid. Respondent 1981.
32. Ibid. Respondent 3634. For an in-depth study of the August 1950 Directive on cinema crying, see also Harper and Porter (1996).
33. Directive Respondent 3204, August 1950. SxMOA1/3/128.
34. Ibid. Respondents 4114 and 4475.
35. Ibid. Respondent 2795.
36. Mass Observation Diarist 5412, 26/02/1943.
37. Directive Respondent 4361, August 1950. SxMOA1/3/128.
38. Mass Observation Diarist 5270, 12/10/1946.
39. Directive Respondent 1362, August 1950. SxMOA1/3/128.
40. Ibid. Respondent 4299.
41. Ibid. Respondent 2975.
42. Ibid. Respondents 3034 and 2994.
43. Ibid. Respondent 3860.
44. Ibid. Respondent 4223.
45. Ibid. Respondent 3474.
46. There are excellent works which focus on Scottish, Welsh and Northern Irish cinemas, such as Richards (2003); Griffiths (2012); Manning (2016).
47. Mass Observation Diarist 5212, November 1940 and Diarist 5236, February 1942.

Bibliography

Allison, Deborah, Hiu M. Chan and Daniela Treveri Gennari (2013) *The Phoenix Picturehouse: 100 Years of Oxford Cinema Memories*. London: Picturehouse Publications.

Burke, Peter (2004) *What is Cultural History?* Cambridge: Polity Press.

Capstick, Andrea and David Clegg (2013) 'Behind the Stiff Upper Lip: War Narratives of Older Men with Dementia', *Journal of War and Cultural Studies* 6(3), 239–54.

Cook, Hera (2014) 'From Controlling Emotion to Expressing Feelings in Mid-Twentieth-Century England', *Journal of Social History* 47(3), 627–46.

Deigh, John (2001) 'Emotions: The Legacy of James and Freud', *International Journal of Psychoanalysis* 82(6), 1247–56.

Dixon, Thomas (2015) *Weeping Britannia: Portrait of a Nation in Tears*. Oxford: Oxford University Press.

Francis, Martin (2002) 'Tears, Tantrums, and Bared Teeth: The Emotional Economy of Three Conservative Prime Ministers, 1951–1963', *Journal of British Studies* 41(3), 354–87.

Frevert, Ute (2011) *Emotions in History: Lost and Found*. Budapest: Central European University Press.

Griffiths, Trevor (2012) *The Cinema and Cinema-Going in Scotland, 1896–1950*. Edinburgh: Edinburgh University Press

Gurney, Peter (2013) '"Intersex" and "Dirty Girls": Mass-Observation and Working-Class Sexuality in England in the 1930s', *Journal of the History of Sexuality* 8(2), 256–90.

Hamilton, Carrie (2010) 'Moving Feelings: Nationalism, Feminism and the Emotions of Politics', *Oral History*, 38(2), 85–94.

Harper, Sue and Vincent Porter (1996) 'Moved to Tears: Weeping in the Cinema in Postwar Britain', *Screen* 37(2), 152–73.

Heathorn, Stephen (2004) 'How Stiff Were Their Upper Lips? Research on Late-Victorian and Edwardian Masculinity', *History Compass* 2(1), 1–7.

Hinton, James (2013) *The Mass Observers: A History, 1937–1949*. Oxford: Oxford University Press.

James, Robert (2010) *Popular Culture and Working-Class Taste in Britain, 1930–39: A Round of Cheap Diversions?* Manchester: Manchester University Press.

Kuhn, Annette (2002) *An Everyday Magic: Cinema and Cultural Memory*. London: I. B. Tauris.

Langhamer, Claire (2016) 'Feelings, Women and Work in the Long 1950s', *Women's History Review* 26(1), 77–92.

Madge, Charles and Tom Harrisson (1937) *Mass-Observation*. London: Frederick Muller.

Maltby, Richard, Daniel Biltereyst and Philippe Meers (eds) (2011) *Explorations in New Cinema History: Approaches and Case Studies*. Malden, MA: Wiley-Blackwell.

Manning, Sam (2016) 'Post-War Cinema-Going and Working-Class Communities: A Case Study of the Holyland, Belfast, 1945–1962', *Cultural and Social History* 13(4), 539–55.

Matt, Susan J. (2011) 'Current Emotion Research in History: Or, Doing History from the Inside Out', *Emotional Review* 3(1), 117–24.

Plamper, Jan (2010) 'The History of Emotions', *History and Theory* 49(2), 237–65.
Reddy, William (1999) 'Emotional Liberty: Politics and History in the Anthropology of Emotions', *Cultural Anthropology* 14(2), 256–88.
Reddy, William (2001) *The Navigation of Feeling: A Framework for the History of Emotions*. Cambridge: Cambridge University Press.
Richards, Helen (2003) 'Memory Reclamation of Cinema Going in Bridgend, South Wales, 1930–1960', *Historical Journal of Film, Radio and Television* 23(4), 341–55.
Richards, Jeffrey (2010) *The Age of the Dream Palace: Cinema and Society in 1930s Britain*, 3rd edn. London: I. B. Tauris.
Rosenwein, Barbara (2007) *Emotional Communities in the Early Middle Ages*. Ithaca, NY: Cornell University Press.
Rosenwein, Barbara (2014) 'Modernity: A Problematic Category in the History of Emotions', *History and Theory* 53(1), 69–78.

PART III

SHAPING AUDIENCE EXPECTATIONS: CINEMA MANAGERS AND MARKETING STRATEGIES

7. 'MAKE YOUR PUBLIC CURIOUS': CINEMA MANAGEMENT, FILM ADVERTISING AND AUDIENCE TASTE IN ENGLAND, c. 1920–c. 1960

Robert James

On 26 October 1933, the cinema managers' trade journal *Kinematograph Weekly* published an article by Harry Sanders, then manager of the Lido cinema in Islington, London, in which he offered advice to his fellow managers on how to attract patrons to their cinemas (Sanders 1933). 'Make Your Public Curious', the article title advised, and in the piece Sanders suggested ways in which his fellow cinema managers across the country could entice people to see the films being exhibited at their halls. Generating curiosity was his main recommendation, hence the title of the article, but he also emphasised the importance of creating local and topical interest, with the former aspect deemed most important. Significantly, in a period during which articles in the trade press repeatedly sought to understand public taste, Sanders quite daringly argued: 'Don't worry about what the public want; see that they want what you have got' (ibid.). Sanders was, of course, as keen as any of his fellow managers to understand the vagaries of public taste. Indeed, in 1935 *The Monthly Pictorial* reported that he 'carefully studies the tastes of his patrons' and supplied the types of film they most demanded (Anon. 1935a). What Sanders was adept at, however, as intimated in his article for *Kinematograph Weekly*, was creating significant interest in the films that he had booked. He was an active film promoter who ran many, often highly flamboyant, film publicity campaigns in an attempt to attract custom to the cinemas he ran during the course of his long career in the industry. One campaign, still remembered in popular histories (Michele 2012) whenever 'Uncle Harry' – as Sanders was affectionately known – is mentioned, took place while he was managing the Granada cinema in Grantham. To promote the 1952 circus film *The Greatest Show on Earth*, Sanders took the extraordinary decision to parade a herd of elephants through the modest Lincolnshire market town, much to the amazement of onlookers.[1] Extravagant publicity campaigns like this reveal the lengths to which some cinema managers went to ensure their business was a successful and profitable one, and reveal a measure of agency that has been frequently overlooked by historians.

Indeed, despite film historians Alan Burton and Steve Chibnall calling out for more research into 'the role played by studio publicity materials and exhibitor activities' over twenty years ago (1999: 95), evaluating the actions of cinema managers is a rather neglected area of history. In the intervening years, historians investigating film and cinemagoing during the period of its greatest popularity – from the 1920s through to the mid-1950s – have focused on a broad range of areas covering a film's production, distribution and reception, but the activities of cinema managers is less well researched. Some important interventions have been made, particularly by advocates of New Cinema History (Maltby et al. 2011). For example, Kathryn H. Fuller-Seeley's 2008 edited volume on local cinemagoing in America includes a number of chapters (Fuller-Seeley, Lindvall, Midkiff DeBauche, Moray, Potamianos, Waller) that evaluate the strategies employed by itinerant showmen and cinema managers in order to attract custom.[2] The History of Moviegoing, Exhibition and Reception Network (HoMER) has, since its inception in 2004, also fostered international research into film exhibition and how it is shaped by space and place.[3] More recently, Jamie Terrill (2019: 738–61) has evaluated the activities of cinema showmen operating in rural Wales. Other scholars have also considered cinema managers' actions as part of their broader investigations into cinemagoing practices, film exhibition and promotional strategies (James 2010; Griffiths 2012; Farmer 2016; Velez-Serna 2016; Chibnall 2017; Manning 2020). Despite these welcome interventions, more research needs to be conducted into local exhibition practices, particularly those taking place in Britain, if we are to better understand the processes that came into play between a film's production and reception. Cinema managers were at the centre of that process. In undertaking their role they often shaped how the leisure activity was viewed by people outside of the trade, as well as how audiences interacted with it. By understanding the position of cinema managers in the process, then, we are better placed to appreciate the social, cultural, economic, and even political, role that this most important leisure activity of the first half of the twentieth century could play in society.

This chapter analyses the activities of cinema managers across Britain to evaluate what practices they undertook to ensure that the cinemas they ran were successful. To do this, firstly, it looks at the ways in which managers dealt with competing leisure activities and attempted to defend their trade against outside criticism, and secondly, it provides an overview of the trade's attitudes towards audience taste and evaluates the promotional activities managers undertook to attract custom. It draws heavily on the experiences of the aforementioned Harry Sanders, who managed a number of cinemas, both independent and as part of a chain, in England from the early 1920s until the mid-1960s, most notably The State cinema (later renamed Granada) in Grantham, where he served for over twenty years until his retirement in 1963. The wealth of cinema ephemera Sanders amassed – ledgers and weekly attendance sheets, press cuttings, promotional material and exhibitors' diaries – is extremely rare.[4] These types of material, particularly ledgers, attendance sheets and diaries, are generally lost over the passage of time, so there are only a few known examples left extant. I say 'known'; there must be others tucked away, hidden in a cupboard, or an attic perhaps, but at the moment the few that are available act as important documents of cinema's past. Because ledgers include attendance figures, they have been used by historians to establish which films were most popular with the public, but they can also be useful in revealing how cinema managers made choices regarding film booking, while hinting at the various determinants that influenced audience engagement. In one of Sanders's ledgers (18–23 April 1927) from when he managed the Kings cinema in Bristol, for example, he reveals that while takings over the Easter period were low because there had been 'Exceptionally fine and warm weather all week', the gambling drama *The Reckless Lady* (1926) did good business because it 'drew the ladies' (Anon. 1927d). Later in the year (7–12 November 1927), Sanders was pleased to report that despite war films 'losing the public fancy' (ibid.), he and other managers in the town booked them for Remembrance week and they all attracted good audience numbers, thus revealing that the public remained keen to commemorate the fallen.[5] These archival materials are invaluable, then, in allowing us to evaluate how Sanders responded to a range of factors that affected him as a cinema manager.

To supplement the Sanders material, this chapter also utilises evidence from cinema and film trade papers, including articles, editorials, opinion pieces and overviews of cinema managers' activities, as well as material held in local archives relating to the experiences of other cinema managers operating in England during the period under review. By using this wealth of extant material, some unmediated, some filtered through the whims of editors and local officials, we can begin to evaluate the activities cinema managers like Sanders undertook to advertise the films they booked, while also obtain an understanding of their views of the cinema trade and film audiences. It will be argued that managers like Sanders repeatedly responded to their specific patrons' demands, appreciated their film tastes – but also helped to shape them – and expended considerable energy ensuring that the cinemas they ran were a success, despite Sanders's assertion, noted earlier, that it did not really matter what the public wanted. Indeed, as Burton and Chibnall (1999: 95) note, while going to the cinema in this period has been referred to as a 'habit', the fact that distributors and managers felt the need to expend considerable sums of money on elaborate campaigns to attract custom suggests that audiences were very discerning in their tastes. The chapter thus illustrates how popular leisure activities are moulded and shaped by a range of practitioners and participants; and argues that we should accord equal status to cinema managers as we do other historical actors in the cinema industry. In doing so, it concludes that leisure participation, far from being a one-way flow from producer to consumer, is a result of a series of negotiations taking place across the whole process.

I

Going to the cinema is the result of a series of choices. In the first half of the twentieth century cinemagoers were faced with a variety of films to watch and a large number of venues in which to watch them. On top of this, consumers had a host of leisure activities competing for their free time, so going to the cinema was a conscious decision made after taking a series of choices. Cinema managers knew that if they were to be successful, they had to respond to the needs of the public. As a result, they paid close attention to their patrons' film preferences as well as ensuring that they created the right atmosphere to entice them into their cinemas. In an article in the exhibitors' journal *The Screen* in June 1914, for example, one contributor shrewdly noted (when referring to the fall off in business in the summer months):

> We can't change the weather, but we can adapt ourselves to it and that is what the alert and successful manager does [. . .] It is sometimes difficult enough to persuade the public to enter a hall in sultry weather, but having got the public inside, the obvious thing to do is put on a good class show. The hall may be hot and stuffy, but if the eye and mind are kept engaged with good films, defects of ventilation will not be noticed and the public will come again [. . .] There is always a big public to be entertained. The man with entertainment to offer must let the public know about it. But he must shout about it – all the time. And if he finds the weather and other attractions shouting out against him, he must shout louder still. (Anon. 1914b)

More than twenty years later, as the pastime grew ever more popular, a contributor to *Cinema Management*, launched in April 1937 to enable managers to have 'their own exclusive publication' (Anon. 1937), demonstrated their important role in the process by advising exhibitors:

Offer your patrons a home, the kind of home they dream about and see on the screen [. . .] A film show and a summer evening out of doors are about equally attractive. Isn't it up to you to weigh the balance in your favour? (Pirrie 1937)

These articles' references to both the weather and other attractions are significant. As the cinema was just one of a range of leisure activities available to the public, managers had to tempt potential patrons away from these other attractions and into their halls if they were to run profitable businesses; a particularly difficult task in the summer months when cinema attendance was traditionally low. Indeed, in his cinema ledgers, Harry Sanders often referred to the fall off of trade when the weather was hot. However, apart from the impact of the weather, about which Sanders or other cinema managers could do little, they had one distinct advantage over the competition: going to the cinema was chiefly viewed as a more respectable pastime when compared with other popular leisure activities, such as going to the pub, particularly for female consumers. The 'respectability' of cinemagoing was something that trade personnel used to their advantage. Time and again, the cinema hall was promoted as a more fitting location for patrons to visit than other more traditional popular leisure venues. For example, in *The Screen* one contributor described going to the cinema as 'wholesome, interesting, educative and respectable' (Anon. 1915). It was a 'cheap and healthy recreation' that kept 'many a person from the gin palace' (ibid.). Emphasising the point further, the contributor noted: 'We are in no way holding a brief against public houses as such, but no one can deny the harmful effects of intemperance. The cinema to-day stands for entertainment and enlightenment [. . .] the respectability of the cinema is unchallenged' (ibid.).

These comments were not quite accurate, for cinema was not without its detractors. In fact, part of the reason that these individuals promoted cinema's more respectable qualities was because the pastime had met with increased criticism, particularly as its popularity grew over the course of the twentieth century. In 1916, for example, a public meeting held in Exeter reported on the 'cinematograph evil', with speakers calling on regulators such as the British Board of Film Censors and local watch committees to ensure that the programmes exhibited did not include 'objectionable features' that could cause harm to those watching them (Anon. 1916a). These concerns were instigated by the supposed and real immoral activities that took place at the cinema, on-screen as well as in the auditoria. Critics were concerned that many of the films being exhibited encouraged degenerate behaviour, and a number of morality campaigns were initiated across the country, principally led by religious and purity crusaders, to protect the cinema's patrons from its perceived harmful influences (Kuhn 1988; Matthews 1994; Rapp 2002). In the early twentieth century, for example, the Public Morality Council took on the role of overseeing cinema provision across many parts of the country and forwarded its reports to the Home Office in an attempt to ensure that a 'decent standard' of film was offered (James 2010: 46). In addition, Scotland's Committee of Church and Nation compiled a report in the early 1930s concerning the types of film on offer in the country's cinemas. The report noted that cinema '[exercised] a baneful influence upon young lives, especially among adolescents', and concluded that many of the films being exhibited contained 'debased moral and spiritual values [and] suggestiveness' which, it was argued, helped to encourage 'an unhealthy sex curiosity [and] opens the door to criminals' (Anon. 1931a). Later in the twentieth century, this campaigning ethos was undertaken by the likes of Malcolm Muggeridge and Mary Whitehouse, who made regular calls for the censoring of certain types of 'immoral' film at a time when the cinema, while no longer the mass entertainment it once was, still attracted large audiences, mainly consisting of young adults who, these critics believed, would be easily persuaded to emulate the immoral behaviour they witnessed on the screen (Richards and Robertson 2009: 74).

Of course, even before a film had reached the screen it had gone through a series of filters. Censorship, for example, played a significant role in shaping what films the country's cinemagoers could see, and across the period under review here the British Board of Film Censors (BBFC) attempted to ensure that no films were released that encouraged immoral behaviour. Filmmakers were advised to send their scripts to the censorship board in order for them to be scrutinised and any inappropriate material removed.[6] However, even when the BBFC deemed a film suitable for release, local authorities could choose to override the censors' decision. Some films were thus banned by local watch committees despite being passed by the censors. In 1948, for example, the crime drama *No Orchids for Miss Blandish* was banned by many local authorities across Britain, despite the fact that it had been passed – after a third amendment to its script – as suitable for exhibition with an 'A' rating by the BBFC (Chibnall 2012: 32–3). Nothing sells like controversy, of course, so it is not surprising to find that some managers called for the decision to be overturned so that they could show the film to a public who would have been aware of its notoriety. In Portsmouth, for example, and in response to some heated discussions on the subject between managers and morality campaigners, the local Watch and Fire Committee offered to view the film at a local cinema in order to evaluate its suitability for exhibition. After the screening the Town Clerk reported that the Committee had 'raise[d] no objection to the exhibition of the film to adult audiences' (Portsmouth. Watch and Fire Committee 1948). This decision led to a flurry of letters being sent to the Committee from concerned local dignitaries who maintained that the film should not be shown in the city's cinemas. Such examples of local censorship in action reveal that cinema managers faced a series of obstacles when choosing which films to book for their patrons. Time and again, it was the effect that certain films could have on 'impressionable minds' – usually meaning the young and the working class (and in places such as the naval towns of Plymouth and Portsmouth, sailors too) – that generated most concern for the country's civic elites and morality campaigners.

On top of this, the popularity of the cinema ensured that objections to it extended from what audiences saw on the screen to the types of behaviour that took place within the cinema halls themselves. Morality campaigners, equally worried about the possibility of lewd behaviour taking place inside the darkened spaces of the cinema auditorium, worked tirelessly to ensure that the worst excesses were curbed (Hanson 2007: 28–9). In 1917, for example, the National Council of Public Morals bemoaned the apparent rise in juvenile crime and indecent behaviour (Eyles 2009: 79) caused by the opportunities afforded in these spaces, and took measures to stamp out this type of conduct. The Council established a Cinema Commission (Anon. 1917b: vi) which sought to ensure that society's use of the cinema had no ill effect on the physical health or moral standards of its patrons. These campaigns were common nationwide, but took on even greater importance in areas that were deemed strategically significant for the country's welfare. In the naval town of Plymouth in 1917, for example, long-standing concerns over prostitution and the sexualised nature of sailors led campaigners to introduce 'half-lighting of auditoriums' (Anon. 1917c) to discourage any sordid acts taking place in the towns' cinemas. Of course, at this time Britain was at war, and concerns about the physical health of the country's serving forces was uppermost in the minds of many of society's elites. Any activities that could have a negative impact on them – and on civilians on the home front too – were bound to be subject to growing scrutiny (James 2016: 179–99).

The negative associations that this popular leisure activity purportedly encouraged led to demands that members of the trade – from filmmakers through to exhibitors – step up and play their part in enhancing its reputation. In 1917, for example, the *Western Evening Herald* reported on a public meeting in which calls had been made for an improvement to the types of film being shown in the region (Anon. 1917c). It was claimed that too many films were 'unhealthily exciting', resulting in audience members emulating the immoral behaviour they had witnessed on the screen. Cinema trade personnel were reminded that they had a 'moral responsibility' to improve, not just their conduct, but that of their patrons too. Similarly, in April 1938, *Cinema Management* called for managers across the country to be more 'civic conscious' and ensure that the cinema became 'a positive instead of merely mutual force in the citadel' (Anon. 1938a). It was claimed that by doing so exhibitors would be rewarded with 'increased dividends both financially and morally'. Again, pecuniary benefits were employed as a means of persuading managers that it was in their best interests to improve cinema's reputation.

In response to the calls for the cleaning up of their trade, many cinema managers protected their industry's reputation by promoting their cinemas as 'family institutions' (Hanson 2007: 28), as well as calling attention to the fact that they were more respectable alternatives to the public house or music hall. In Plymouth, for example, Harry Harcourt, manager of the Tivoli Picture House, which was located close to the naval barracks and Royal Sailors' Rest and opposite the Military Arms public house, worked hard to ensure the cinema became known locally as a 'kind of second' home and a 'way of life with the families of Devonport' (James 2016: 191). As part of this endeavour, Harcourt instructed the cinema's staff to 'provide a cup of tea and a tea cake' to patrons attending matinee performances, held a yearly 'Anniversary Show' during which he would 'dress up as a clown and sing, tap dance and create comic ditties' (Ghillyer 1983: 109, 112), offered reduced admission prices to unemployed patrons, and gave fruit to children at Christmas and comics to those attending Saturday matinees. Harry Sanders, meanwhile, introduced 'community singing' in the cinemas he managed; an activity which, according to *Kinematograph Weekly*, was greeted with much enthusiasm among the cinemas' patrons (Anon. 1927c).[7] The use of the cinema space for these types of activity undoubtedly fostered an environment which encouraged a sense of community; one where managers could be seen as part of the cinema 'family'. Indeed, the 'Uncle' moniker given to Sanders suggests a familiarity between him and his patrons, indicating that wherever he operated he built a reputation as their friend or, at the very least, someone whose judgement could be trusted.

The use of the cinema as a communal 'family' space continued across the period under review here. Indeed, later in the century managers instigated the setting up of children's clubs as another way to bolster their reputation as respectable family institutions. In Portsmouth, for example, managers at the Plaza and Regent cinemas sent a request to council officials in 1944 calling for the granting of a licence to enable them to establish 'Junior Cinema Clubs' at their halls (Portsmouth. Report of Portsmouth's Education Officer 1946). In Grantham, meanwhile, Harry Sanders set up a children's club at the Granada cinema in 1950 (Anon. 1950). Members of the club were known as 'Granadiers' and were tasked with electing their own club 'officers' under the presidency of the 'Chief Granadier' who would organise their own programme of events. Of course, there would have been a commercial benefit in setting up children's clubs, and it was undoubtedly hoped that the result would be the establishment of a new and long-standing audience, but by demonstrating that their venues were suitable for children, the family appeal of the cinema was further enhanced.

In addition to making their cinemas more family friendly, many managers sought to promote them as charitable spaces by organising fundraising events in them. In 1927, for example, this time while managing the Beehive in Bolton, Sanders raised money for the local hospital by offering a selection of cinema tickets that came with the chance of winning £10,000 – a considerable sum of money now, let alone in the 1920s (Anon. n.d.a). Of course, because patrons had to buy tickets to stand a chance of winning the prize, this charitable endeavour would have also been a way of increasing trade. However, not all fundraising efforts came with direct pecuniary benefit for the cinema. Later in the same year, Sanders – now running the Kings cinema in Bristol – joined forces with other managers in the city and collected money from his patrons to give to the Lord Mayor's Fund (Anon. 1927b). The money was used to provide Christmas dinners for children of the city's unemployed. In 1940, upon Sanders's request, the managing director of The State cinema in Grantham gave over the hall for a community fundraising event to raise money for the local hospital (Anon. 1940).[8] The following year, Sanders organised another fundraiser at the cinema, this time to coincide with War Weapons Week, raising money for the purchase of war bonds – again for the benefit of the local hospital (Anon. 1941).

In fact, during periods of war, cinemas were employed time and again as a means of raising resources for the war effort. During World War I, for example, *The Screen* proudly announced:

> The kinematograph industry is deserving of great praise for the enthusiastic way in which it has been working on behalf of the War Loan [. . .] and has no doubt been instrumental in securing very considerable help for the fund from its patrons. (Anon. 1917d)

Film fan magazine *Pictures and the Picturegoer* likewise reported that 'The cinema theatres have given enormous help to recruiting. One exhibitor alone secured two thousand recruits, and his achievement is typical of many', adding that 'The theatres have also been placed unreservedly at the disposal of those working for charitable funds connected with the war. In the Queen's record of charitable work during the war [. . .] a high place is given to the cinema theatres' (Anon. 1916b). In World War II, Oscar Deutsch, head of the Odeon cinema chain, praised his cinemas' managers for raising 'over £10,000 for a "comfort of the troops" fund' and 'entertaining and educating [. . .] over 20,000 evacuees' in one week over the Christmas period (Deutsch 1940: 47). In fact, during World War II the Cinematograph Exhibitors' Association worked closely with the National Savings Committee to raise money for war funds as well as agreeing to provide exhibition time for the presentation of instructional and training films made by the War Office (Farmer 2016: 69). Civic-minded acts like these thus served to both strengthen cinema's place in the community as well as enhance its civic standing.[9]

As well as making their cinemas important hubs of the local community, some managers responded to demands to improve the type of films they exhibited by booking programmes that would have a more edifying influence on their patrons. In response to the increased demand to curb the exhibition of 'unsuitable' films, trade personnel attempted to reassure detractors by insisting that managers did not want to show films that could cause harm. 'I am quite sure that renters don't want to handle blood-curdling horrors', a contributor to *The Screen* noted, adding, 'neither do showmen want to present such films to their patrons' (Anon. 1917a). Local exhibitors certainly seemed to toe the line. In Plymouth, for example, the social morality tale *Damaged Goods* (1914) – in which a young man is enticed into a night of sexual debauchery with disastrous long-term consequences – was initially banned in the town because of its scandalous storyline, but the film was 'eventually permitted to be released as a *warning* to the unthinking boy and girl' (Anon. 1920, emphasis in original). Local press advertisements for the film played on its notoriety, calling it the 'sensational play on the social evil' (Anon. 1920), but it was clear from the phrasing used that audiences were intended to view the film as a lesson on how to live a moral and upstanding life. In a similar vein, and in a clear attempt to make his establishment take on a more educational role, the manager of the aforementioned Tivoli Picture House regularly booked 'important historical and classical' films and set children essays to write on them (James 2016: 191). In fact, as part of making the town's cinemas suitable for families, local officials in Plymouth suggested that managers use their halls for additional educational and social purposes; as places where singers could entertain audiences and lecturers could educate them (ibid.: 192). In a similarly educationalist drive during World War II, schoolchildren in Essex were given reduced admission prices to enable them to see the Ministry of Information-endorsed Two Cities propaganda film *Henry V* (1944) (Anon. 1945). In Portsmouth, meanwhile, managers of a cinema in its notorious 'sailortown' district repeatedly promoted patriotic dramas or films containing morality tales in an apparent attempt to counter any negative criticism (James 2013). Indeed, the films' accompanying advertising campaigns always mentioned their edifying qualities, flagging up their status as important morality tales. Elsewhere in the town, the manager of the Commodore cinema, Patrick Reed, also booked films containing moral lessons and, in doing so, clearly built up a close relationship with local civic leaders and the Admiralty. For example, after booking the film *Damaged Lives* (1933) – a powerful morality tale about an extramarital affair that resulted in a married couple catching venereal disease – Reed launched a promotional campaign that was said to have received much support from civic and naval dignitaries who had believed that the film would act as an 'invaluable help in sex education' in the town (Anon. 1934). *Kinematograph Weekly* reported that, with the support of civic and Admiralty leaders, Reed 'put over one of the biggest publicity campaigns that [had] been launched in the town' (ibid.). Not surprisingly, the film was said to have attracted 'record business' (ibid.).

The educational potential of cinema was an issue much discussed across the whole of the period under review here. In an article published in *The Screen*, aimed directly at cinema managers, it was noted that

> the value of the cinema in education is so obvious that it is remarkable that frequent use is not made of it. The omission is due, perhaps, to the fact that managers have made no overtures to the parties likely to be interested in the subject [. . .] We suggest to managers that they approach education committees with a programme of educational films and an offer of their hall and plant three or four matinees per week for a fixed sum. (Anon. 1914a: 13–14)

In 1916, a contributor to the journal made an even bolder statement, calling for all film programmes to be 'entirely made up of educational features, in the broadest sense of the word' as an economic necessity (Anon. 1916c). 'The public taste is being daily elevated', the author noted, adding, 'and if patrons to-day will go to see a second-rate programme, they will desert the theatre showing it to-morrow for the opposition show where better-class pictures can be seen' (ibid.). The author concluded by noting that 'the exhibitor who has consistently shown them will reap his just reward' (ibid.). Almost twenty years later, in June 1933, *Kinematograph Weekly* continued this long-running discussion about the educational potential of film by publishing a paper by Sir Charles Cleland which argued that 'at every point the picture house unconsciously exerts an indirect educational influence upon its patrons' (Cleland 1933). Civic leaders, not surprisingly, were also keen to promote cinema's educational role. At the opening of a new Odeon in Leeds in 1936, for example, the Lord Mayor gushingly noted: 'The development of the kinema industry has been wonderful, and has helped Britain to become a much more sober nation [. . .] Once, it was said, schools and colleges were the guiding influence. The kinemas occupied that position nowadays' (Anon. 1936a). It would seem, therefore, that the decades-long activities of trade personnel in ensuring that cinemas were seen as a force for good, not evil, had begun to reap the rewards promised to them.

In these various ways, then, cinema managers – often following the demands placed upon them by officials both within and outside the cinema trade – not only attempted to regulate how their halls were used in order for them to be seen as respectable spaces that could benefit the local community, but would also control the types of film their patrons were able to see. Indeed, in terms of the films they chose to book they could arguably help to shape their patrons' cinematic tastes. Of course, cinema's primary role is entertainment, so in order to avoid charges of being overtly didactic and puritanical, managers were careful to book films that would appeal to their patrons, and they invested significant time in trying to establish a balance between respectability and profit. Film exhibition was thus the result of a compromise between the managers and cinema audiences, with managers remaining ever vigilant regarding the tastes of their patrons. Indeed, despite Sanders's comments regarding not worrying about what his patrons wanted, he would have had to have some sense of what appealed to them in order to know how to advertise the films he had booked in a manner that would entice them in. The final section of this chapter, therefore, evaluates the cinema trade's attitudes towards audience taste, before looking at the range of ways managers touted for business. As we will see, they reveal that cinema managers, and in particular Sanders, went to great lengths to promote the films they had booked, and made sure they responded to the tastes of the people visiting their local cinemas.

II

Establishing what types of film would be popular with audiences was an ever-present pressure for film trade personnel, particularly when the leisure activity started to grow exponentially in the early years of the twentieth century. Cinemagoing was no longer viewed as just a novelty entertainment that would attract anyone, but a maturing industry whose customers could have significant cultural capital (even if, as we shall see, they were frequently disparaging of it). Popularity surveys were thus regularly conducted within the industry in order to ascertain what audiences wanted to see. One of the most prolific conductors of these surveys was the owner of the Granada cinema chain, Sidney Bernstein. During the 1920s, 1930s and 1940s, Bernstein sent out a number of questionnaires to the patrons of his cinemas requesting information regarding a range of factors, such as who were their favourite film stars and what were their all-time favourite films (James 2011: 274–6), and the results of these were published in a range of trade journals.[10] Local cinema managers also made regular forays into assessing their public's film tastes. In 1935, for example, the manager of the New Empire cinema in Ashton ran a competition in which cinemagoers won prizes if they completed a film questionnaire (Anon. 1935d). Later in the decade, the manager of the Princes Theatre in Peterborough asked patrons to air their opinions regarding the films being exhibited (Anon. 1938b).

In addition to these popularity surveys by cinema owners and managers, the film trade press also regularly reproduced its own popularity statistics. From the late 1920s, film fan magazines such as *Picturegoer* and *Film Weekly* ran features outlining the films and film stars found to be most popular with audiences nationwide. For example, *Picturegoer* published its 'Award of Merit' lists annually (James 2010: 46), detailing the most popular stars, while *Film Weekly* published lists of the 'Best British Stars' and films, as well as 'Principal Picture

Successes', which included both British and international films. From 1936, *Kinematograph Weekly* also began to publish lists of 'Box-Office Winners' (James 2006: 231) and ran regular features in which the audiences' film tastes were interpreted. Of course, many films were expected to have broad box office appeal and thus attract cinemagoers from right across the social spectrum, but even though public taste is an imprecise concept, film trade press frequently recommended to managers which films to book for particular patrons. In 1914, for example, *The Screen* ran a piece in which the tastes of the 'proletariat' were compared with those of the 'upper middle classes' (Anon. 1914c). The report concluded that films featuring the 'Wild West Cowboy breathing of the Wilds and sensationalism' should be expected to have the broadest appeal among the 'masses' (ibid.).

In *Kinematograph Weekly*, meanwhile, 'experts' were even more specific, offering managers guidance as to which films would play well in particular locations or among a specific class fraction. In 1930, for example, the American-produced *Blue Moon* was described as an 'Industrial small hall booking' because it was deemed to be 'naïve and of poor quality' (Anon. 1930a: 39, 45). A year later, the German film *A Man's Heart* was designated as a 'Quite good booking for provincial halls' (Anon. 1931b). In the same year another American production, *Why Change Your Husband*, was listed as 'Good light entertainment for the masses' (Anon. 1931c). In contrast, the American romantic comedy *Sweet Kitty Bellairs* (1930) was recommended 'for better-class halls' because it had 'a charm and fragrance' about it (Anon. 1930b). Time and again, films that contained 'rough stuff', were deemed 'broad', 'naïve', 'obvious', 'sentimental', or that contained 'ripe innuendos', were described as suitable only for the lower-class patron (James 2006: 239). Meanwhile, films that required more concentration or intelligence, such as the 1936 adaptation of Shakespeare's *As You Like It*, were deemed suitable only for the more 'intelligent audiences' of the 'better-class halls', because they would impose 'too great a strain on the masses' (Anon. 1936b).

Not all cinema managers were appreciative of the guidance offered by trade papers such as *Kinematograph Weekly*. In fact, many of them used the trade press to put across their views on their role in the booking process. They were frequently highly vocal in stressing that they knew more than most what films would play well with their audiences; after all, being closer to their patrons than other contemporaries, they were adept at understanding their customers' wants. Indeed, one manager who described himself as an 'independent small-owner' explicitly pointed out in *Kinematograph Weekly*:

> I consider I am closer to the public – my public – than any other people who are so much more articulate. Renters, producers, and the big chiefs of the circuits only know public likes and dislikes through the reports

made and results attained by men in my position [. . .] I should not be exaggerating if I said that the booker of films was always in advance of his public in matters of taste. (Anon. 1935b)

Given the importance of the 'booker of films' – the cinema manager – in this process, it will come as no surprise to find that *Kinematograph Weekly* kept abreast of their activities to see what they were doing to attract custom. In fact, so keen was the editor of the trade paper to explore this aspect of the film trade that they ran a regular feature detailing the techniques local managers employed when advertising a film. The title of the feature changed across the period, sometimes called 'What Managers are Doing', at others 'Showmanship', but it always emphasised the many activities that managers were undertaking to draw patrons to their cinemas, often awarding prizes to managers who ran the most enterprising campaigns.[11] In 1927, for example, Harry Sanders was awarded a £5 prize as recognition for the innovative campaign he organised to promote the Harry Langdon comedy vehicle *Tramp, Tramp, Tramp* (1926) (Anon. 1927g), for which he hired an unemployed Bristolian to dress up as the actor and walk from London to Bristol. According to the trade paper, the campaign generated significant interest, with newspapers across the country reporting on it.

Trade press reports on cinema managers' activities certainly reveal how innovative they could be in their never-ending quest to attract patrons. To assist them in their promotional activities, film distributors sent managers campaign books (Burton and Chibnall 1999: 90) that offered guidance on how to promote the films they were due to exhibit. Some managers chose to keep their campaigns relatively straightforward. In the early 1930s, for example, H. C. Ryder, manager of the City Picture House in Peterborough, regularly promoted films (Anon. 1932a) by having a car adorned with placards travel through the main shopping thoroughfare. However, even modest campaigns could involve a range of tactics. In Portsmouth, for example, the manager of the Gaiety cinema, F. Hilbury, was said to have put on a 'very effective and economical campaign' when promoting the circus film *The Big Cage* (Anon. 1933). The campaign involved the following tactics: four weeks before the film was due to be screened, Hilbury arranged for slides to be shown to his patrons when they visited the cinema. On top of this, display posters were erected at the front of the cinema for the attention of passers-by. In order to advertise more widely, film stills were also given to local shop-owners to place in their windows. One week before the film's screening Hilbury also arranged for 200 posters to be supplied and posted by the *Sunday Pictorial*, and these were distributed throughout the town and in the surrounding districts. In addition, 300 'throwaways' were handed out by men dressed as ring-masters to visitors on their way to the seafront. So even in a cheaply run campaign, a lot of effort was extended. It may not have been as eye-catching as parading elephants through the town or hiring someone to walk from London to Bristol, but it was clearly still very effective.

As demonstrated by these latter examples, though, other managers chose to undertake the more adventurous advertising campaigns suggested in the film distributors' campaign books. These were far more elaborate and often involved the construction of quite extensive (and expensive) displays. For example, in the run-up to exhibiting the American silent romantic comedy *Paradise for Two* in London in early 1927, Harry Sanders was reported to have 'transformed' Balham Picture House's 'vestibule into a realistic representation of "Paradise Island," complete with thatched hut, blue lagoon, palm trees, tropical forests and gorgeous flowers – not to mention a full sized monkey and cocoanuts!' (Anon. 1927e). *The Cinema* magazine remarked that the display became 'a constant source of attraction to the many thousands passing along Balham High Road', adding that 'Many motorists pulled up their cars in order to "have a good look," and it drew crowds into the vestibule' (ibid.). Most importantly, in terms of attracting custom, it was noted that 'Such a novel, artistic, and realistic display could not help but create desire on the part of everyone to see the picture' (ibid.). In a similarly impressive endeavour a few years later, the aforementioned manager of Peterborough's City Picture House, H. C. Ryder, ran a campaign to promote the British 1932 submarine drama *Men Like These* (US title: *Trapped in a Submarine*) by having what was described as a 'realistic submarine rocking in a turbulent sea' in the cinema's foyer (Anon. 1932b). In Portsmouth in 1935, meanwhile, the manager of the Commodore cinema, Patrick Reed, staged a realistic aeroplane crash when promoting the Warner Brothers action film *Devil Dogs of the Air* (Anon. 1935c). In addition to this stunt, he organised tie-ins with the local airport and over sixty shops, as well as arranging for an aeroplane to fly over the town for two hours each day that trailed a banner advertising the film and – weather permitting – spelled out the film's title in smoke.

While, as Burton and Chibnall (1999: 84) have noted, the majority of managers' promotional activities were more routine, these types of extravagant campaign were not uncommon in this period when it was largely the responsibility of individual managers to choose which advertising strategies to adopt when promoting the films they booked. Indeed, even the owners of large cinema chains who had greater control over the films being distributed, such as Bernstein at Granada, recognised that local managers knew more about their audiences' tastes than they did, and they understood that films had to be marketed with these localised tastes in mind (Farmer 2016: 169). Certainly, through the use of campaign books, film distributors would offer advice about how to market a film (James 2010: 20–4), but it was the managers themselves who chose how to organise their campaigns according to localised preferences, and it is clear that many put in a significant amount of effort when doing so. That effort was usually rewarded by commercial success, of course, but they were also rewarded by recognition among their peers and industry leaders. Indeed, some managers gathered quite a reputation for their showmanship, and became well known within the trade press by having regular reports published on their exploits.

Unsurprisingly, Harry Sanders received repeated endorsements in the trade papers for the film promotional activities he undertook. Long before receiving his 'showmanship' award from *Kinematograph Weekly* for his *Tramp, Tramp, Tramp* campaign, Sanders was praised in *The Trade Show Critic* for his 'ingenious' publicity methods (Anon. 1923). In January 1926, meanwhile, the same paper published another piece praising Sanders's advertising skills, noting: 'Though a young man, he has achieved wide renown through his enterprising publicity methods, and a shrewd study of human nature in different spheres of life has taught him a lot about the tastes and desires of the populace' (Anon. 1926a). Later the same year Sanders was awarded a prize in the European Exploitation Contest for his promotion of the Universal serial *Samson of the Circus*, which, despite being on its fifth run in Bolton, 'played to capacity houses' (Anon. 1926c) because of the public interest Sanders had created through his promotional campaign.[12] Picking up on the success of this campaign, the trade paper *Universal Exploiteer* described Sanders as a 'live-wire' when it came to advertising (Anon. 1927f), and exhibited some of his work in its museum. Nevertheless, one of the highest accolades Sanders received during his career (Anon. 1927a) came on the back of his successful campaign for *Tramp, Tramp, Tramp*, for which he was admitted to the ranks of the 'Select Circle Associates', an honour bestowed to the '100 Best Showmen in the Country' by *The Cinema* magazine.

Recognition from the trade press reveals that managers were achieving what they had set out to do as businessmen: attract attention to their activities and, most importantly for commercial success, bring patronage to their cinemas. Time and again managers were praised for the ways in which their activities helped the films they booked achieve record business.

As early as 1922, for example, a testimonial by the manager of the Beehive Picture House in Bolton, where initially Sanders served as assistant manager, noted that Sanders was so successful in attracting patrons to the cinema that 'By the end of his first twelve months [. . .] the average weekly attendance was more than doubled' (Anon. n.d.b). Two years later, Sanders was praised in *The Trade Show Critic* for increasing attendance through his energetic use of innovative campaigns, with the paper reproducing examples of the publicity material he had used to promote the comedies *Shoulder Arms* (1918) and *Alf's Button* (1920) (Anon. 1922). The aforementioned campaigns by H. C. Ryder and Patrick Reed were similarly praised for attracting increased numbers of patrons to the cinemas they managed in Peterborough and Portsmouth respectively (Anon. 1932b; Anon. 1935c).

The importance of showmanship campaigns in increasing patronage, and therefore profit, is evidenced by their continuation in World War II; a period in which severe privations were expected of the whole population. Paper rationing was introduced by the Ministry of Supply in March 1940 (Farmer 2016: 178), and the subsequent shortage of paper meant a reduction in the size and number of posters available for film promotion. However, while there was a greater reliance by managers on newspaper advertising (although newspaper length was also reduced), their film publicity campaigns continued apace. In addition, the blackout ensured that cinemas were less visible in the darkened streets (Farmer 2016: 42–7), and therefore somewhat less appealing to patrons, so managers who had relied on their window displays alone to attract patrons had to consider alternative ways to promote the films they booked. Fortunately, and again illustrating the importance of this type of external and highly visual promotional activity, managers were offered advice on how best to advertise in the straitened circumstances of wartime through *Kinematograph Weekly*'s 'Showmanship in War Time' section. As Richard Farmer has noted, many imaginative campaigns continued to be undertaken, resulting in films doing 'good business' across the war period (2016: 181–2).

What becomes clear from these promotional activities, then, is the continued importance of local cinema managers in advertising the films they exhibited at their halls. Indeed, it was not until the 1960s when, with the arrival of the multiscreen complex and national film release programming, the significance of cinema managers' individual promotional activities started to wane. As Burton and Chibnall have stated, these changes 'saw the virtual disappearance of the locally organised stunt' (1999: 94). However, from the early years of the twentieth century until the late 1950s, local cinema managers played a pivotal role in ensuring the cinemas they ran were successful, and they did this by getting to know their patrons well, advertising in ways that would entice customers in to their cinemas, protecting their trade from interference by critics from both inside and outside the film industry, and rising to the challenge of competing leisure outlets. They understood what attracted their patrons to the cinema and went out of their way to ensure that they made their venues and the films they booked as attractive as possible. It is important, therefore, to restore their activities to the historical record too if we are to better understand the complex relationships that operate between cultural provision and cultural pleasure.

Conclusion

Despite being largely overlooked within historiographies of film and cinemagoing, cinema managers held a pivotal position in the film industry during the period of that leisure pursuit's greatest popularity. Through examining the various roles that managers played, this chapter has gone some way to demonstrate how significant they were in ensuring the success of the cinema business. Their role placed them at the centre of the process between production and consumption. They were the fulcrum that helped to shape the audience's experience of the films that were made, and they were the conduits of exchange between the film industry and its detractors. Cultural critics and civic elites may have been concerned about the leisure activity's prominence in society, particularly during its earlier years, but local managers worked hard to protect their businesses from outside interference, promoting their venues as respectable places for the public to visit. In doing so, they framed the cinema as a communal space where a host of opportunities could be offered, be they for educational purposes, exercising civic duty, or simply for relaxation.

Most of all, though, cinema managers recognised that going to the cinema was about *pleasure*. To ensure that their venues fulfilled the role audiences expected of them, managers placed emphasis on the *enjoyment* of going to the cinema, and that started with staging advertising campaigns that generated curiosity and interest, enticing prospective patrons to wonder about the excitement that lay behind the doors of the cinema auditorium. In addition, managers worked hard to build a reputation as a friend to their patrons and built familial relationships that undoubtedly elicited trust from the people who visited their cinema halls. Local patrons often viewed their cinema as a 'home'; a place of familiar surroundings where they could feel comfortable. The local cinema managers' relationship with their patrons was well understood by cinema owners, be they small operators or large.

It is disappointing, then, that the importance of the cinema manager's role is still underplayed in the historiography. Burton and Chibnall's call for more research into this area has largely gone unheeded, but by viewing the cinema manager as a mediator between the screen and the audience we can better appreciate their role in shaping societies' cinemagoing experiences in this period. We know, for example, that the promotional material for the British 'New Wave' films of the 1950s and 1960s played on their controversial subject matter, leading to their being banned by some local authorities, but we know little about the ways that managers circumvented watch committee restrictions to ensure the films were exhibited and the audiences' desire for them satiated.[13] On the flip side, how would our understanding of the moral panic (Rapp 2002: 434–43) surrounding the sexually suggestive films made during World War I be modified if we took account of the part cinema managers played in policing their patrons' behaviour? Evaluating cinema managers' activities and behaviour can reveal the wider social role they played in their communities too. For example, archival records show that managers were sympathetic to their patrons' penury during the Great Depression and accepted alternative means of payment so they could still visit their halls, thus revealing a reciprocal relationship between local businesses and their communities that can enhance our understanding of social relations in the era.[14] Future research into society's cinemagoing past can surely only be enriched by scholars incorporating the activities of cinema managers into their work. They deserve greater recognition, not simply to earn their rightful place in the historical record, but to help us to better appreciate the broader social and cultural role that the leisure activity played in society. This chapter is but a small contribution to that discussion.

Notes

1. The stunt must have succeeded because Sanders notes in the cinema's 1952 ledger (28 April–2 May) that exhibiting the film resulted in a 'RECORD WEEK' (Anon. 1952, emphasis in original).
2. Research into film publicity in America has been more extensive, but is still limited when compared with research into other areas of film culture. For an example of earlier research into film publicity in America, see Staiger (1990).
3. For an example of research into film exhibition practices produced by HoMER Network participants, see 'Part IV. Exhibition, Space and Place' and 'Part V. Programming, Popularity, and Film' in Biltereyst et al. (2019). For more information on the HoMER Network, see <http://homernetwork.org/> (last accessed 17 May 2021).
4. After Sanders's death this material was donated by his son Howard to the National Science and Media Museum, Bradford, UK.
5. The ledger records that Sanders booked *The Somme*, probably referring to the 1916 documentary film *The Battle of the Somme* (Anon. 1927d).
6. For more information on how this operated over the course of the twentieth century, see Lamberti (2012).
7. The practice of community singing continued long into the century, with Richard Farmer providing numerous accounts of its taking place in wartime Britain (2016: 24, 34, 100, 226).
8. Sanders was a member of the hospital's appeals and publicity committee.
9. As Richard Farmer has noted when discussing cinemagoing in wartime Britain, managers were 'important figures within a given neighbourhood' and the cinemas they ran often functioned as a type of community centre (2016: 169, 192).
10. Bernstein conducted surveys in 1927, 1932, 1934, 1937 and 1946–7 (James 2011: 274–6).
11. See 'What Managers are Doing' (1927), where it is noted that 'The "Kine" offers £5 weekly for the best advertising stunt sent in by subscribers.'
12. The campaign included creating a 'hand-painted [. . .] striking 96-sheet poster' that was displayed 'in one of the most prominent positions of the town'. Ever the opportunist, Sanders claimed – not without hyperbole, undoubtedly – that this was 'probably the largest poster ever displayed throughout the whole country'. In

addition to creating the poster, Sanders was said to have 'distributed thousands of gag throwaways, posted several special hand-painted 18-sheets, and [displayed] numerous lobby posters' (Anon. 1926b, 1926c).
13. One humorous example of local censorship restrictions being circumvented regarding 'New Wave' films can be seen when the local authority in Warwickshire banned *Saturday Night and Sunday Morning* (1960) from being exhibited in the county, only for managers from a neighbouring county to hire coaches to take patrons across county lines to their cinemas where the film was being exhibited (Mather 1973).
14. William Woodruff, for example, when recalling his poverty-stricken childhood in Depression-era Blackburn, remembers exchanging empty jam jars for entrance to the cinema (2003: 176).

Bibliography

Anon. (n.d.a) 'The blue ballot', 2013-5343, SAN/1/1, notebook I. Harry Sanders Collection, National Science and Media Museum, Bradford, UK.

Anon. (n.d.b) 'More than doubled', 2013-5343, SAN/1/1, notebook I. Harry Sanders Collection, National Science and Media Museum, Bradford, UK.

Anon. (1914a) 'The Cinema and Education: A Suggestion to Cinema Managers', *The Screen*, 3 August, pp. 13–14.

Anon. (1914b) 'Editorial', *The Screen*, June, pp. 2–3.

Anon. (1914c) 'What Do the Public Want?', *The Screen*, July, p. 5.

Anon. (1915) 'Respectability', *The Screen*, April, pp. 1–2.

Anon. (1916a) 'Cinema Shows', *The Western Times*, 2 December, p. 3.

Anon. (1916b) 'Don't Close Our Picture Theatres', *Pictures and the Picturegoer*, 26 February, p. 494.

Anon. (1916c) 'The Film and Education', *The Screen*, 8 January, p. 6.

Anon. (1917a) 'The Censor and Crime Films', *The Screen*, 31 March, p. 10.

Anon. (1917b) *The Cinema: Its present position and future possibilities. Being the report of and chief evidence taken by the cinema commission of inquiry instituted by the National Council of Public Morals*, <https://archive.org/stream/cinemaitspresent00natirich#page/n5/mode/2up> (last accessed 18 May 2021).

Anon. (1917c) 'Films the Children Like Best; Statistics of "Regular" Cinema-Goers', *Western Evening Herald*, 27 February. 94/48, Plymouth Record Office, UK.

Anon. (1917d) 'The Triumph of the Kinema', *The Screen*, February, p. 11.

Anon. (1920) 'Advertisements and Notices', *Western Evening Herald*, 4 November, p. 2.

Anon. (1922) 'A Showman's Acknowledgements', *The Trade Show Critic*. 2013-5343, SAN/1/1, notebook I. Harry Sanders Collection, National Science and Media Museum, Bradford, UK.

Anon. (1923) 'Showmanship at Bolton', *The Trade Show Critic*, 25 May. 2013-5343, SAN/1/1, notebook I. Harry Sanders Collection, National Science and Media Museum, Bradford, UK.

Anon. (1926a) 'Ambitious Harry Sanders', *The Trade Show Critic*, 8 January. 2013-5343, SAN/1/1, notebook I. Harry Sanders Collection, National Science and Media Museum, Bradford, UK.

Anon. (1926b) 'Britain's Biggest Samson Poster', *The Trade Show Critic*, 22 January. 2013-5343, SAN/1/1, notebook I. Harry Sanders Collection, National Science and Media Museum, Bradford, UK.
Anon. (1926c) 'Samson of the Circus', *The Cinema*, January. 2013-5343, SAN/1/1, notebook I. Harry Sanders Collection, National Science and Media Museum, Bradford, UK.
Anon. (1927a) '100 Guinea Cup Enthusiasm Rising to its Peak', *The Cinema*, 21 July. 2013-5343, SAN/1/1, notebook I. Harry Sanders Collection, National Science and Media Museum, Bradford, UK.
Anon. (1927b) 'Bristol Mayor's Fund', *Kinematograph Weekly*, 15 December. 2013-5343, SAN/1/1, notebook I. Harry Sanders Collection, National Science and Media Museum, Bradford, UK.
Anon. (1927c) 'Community Singing at Bristol', *Kinematograph Weekly*, 14 April. 2013-5343, SAN/1/1, notebook I. Harry Sanders Collection, National Science and Media Museum, Bradford, UK.
Anon. (1927d) 'Kings cinema ledger', 2013-5343, SAN/4/1/5. Harry Sanders Collection, National Science and Media Museum, Bradford, UK.
Anon. (1927e) '"Paradise" in Balham', *The Cinema*, 17 March. 2013-5343, SAN/1/1, notebook I. Harry Sanders Collection, National Science and Media Museum, Bradford, UK.
Anon. (1927f) 'A Prize-Winning Showman', *Universal Exploiteer*, March. 2013-5343, SAN/1/1, notebook I. Harry Sanders Collection, National Science and Media Museum, Bradford, UK.
Anon. (1927g) 'What Managers are Doing', *Kinematograph Weekly*, 19 May. 2013-5343, SAN/1/1, notebook I. Harry Sanders Collection, National Science and Media Museum, Bradford, UK.
Anon. (1930a) 'New Films at a Glance', *Kinematograph Weekly*, 13 February, pp. 39, 45.
Anon. (1930b) 'New Films at a Glance', *Kinematograph Weekly*, 25 September, p. 38.
Anon. (1931a) 'Censorship Inadequate: Church of Scotland's Attack. Demand for Government Enquiry', *Kinematograph Weekly*, 21 May, p. 48.
Anon. (1931b) 'New Films at a Glance', *Kinematograph Weekly*, 2 April, p. 42.
Anon. (1931c) 'New Films at a Glance', *Kinematograph Weekly*, 9 July, p. 47.
Anon. (1932a) 'What Managers are Doing', *Kinematograph Weekly*, 7 January, p. 144.
Anon. (1932b) 'What Managers are Doing', *Kinematograph Weekly*, 21 January, p. 48.
Anon. (1933) 'Showmanship (what Managers Do)', *Kinematograph Weekly*, 17 August, p. 33.
Anon. (1934) 'Showmanship', *Kinematograph Weekly*, 22 February, p. 38.
Anon. (1935a) 'Islington's Perfect Talkie Theatre', *The Monthly Pictorial*, February, p. 13.
Anon. (1935b) 'Must We be Prigs? A Few Words on "Audience Reaction" by an Independent', *Kinematograph Weekly*, 25 July, p. 4.
Anon. (1935c) 'Showmanship', *Kinematograph Weekly*, 17 October, p. 64.
Anon. (1935d) 'Testing Public Taste', *Kinematograph Weekly*, 26 September, p. 48.
Anon. (1936a) 'Kinema's Part in Education. Tremendous Onus on Proprietors, Says Mayor at Leeds Opening', *Kinematograph Weekly*, 1 October, p. 5.
Anon. (1936b) 'New Films at a Glance', *Kinematograph Weekly*, 10 September, p. 30.
Anon. (1937) 'Editorial', *Cinema Management*, April, p. 3.

Anon. (1938a) 'Cinemas Should be More Civic', *Cinema Management*, April, p. 5.
Anon. (1938b) 'What Managers are Doing', *Kinematograph Weekly*, 7 July, p. 34.
Anon. (1940) 'Full house at State Sunday show', 2013-5343, SAN/1/1, notebook I. Harry Sanders Collection, National Science and Media Museum, Bradford, UK.
Anon. (1941) '£100 from State concert', 2013-5343, SAN/1/1, notebook I. Harry Sanders Collection, National Science and Media Museum, Bradford, UK.
Anon. (1945) 'Film Praise from Educationists', *Essex Newsman*, 24 July, p. 3.
Anon. (1950) 'The "State" becomes the "Granada"', 2013-5343, SAN/1/1, notebook L. Harry Sanders Collection, National Science and Media Museum, Bradford, UK.
Anon. (1952) 'Granada cinema ledger', 2013-5343, SAN/2/1/5/10-15, SAN/2/1/5/14. Harry Sanders Collection, National Science and Media Museum, Bradford, UK.
Biltereyst, Daniel, Richard Maltby and Philippe Meers (eds) (2019) *The Routledge Companion to New Cinema History*. London and New York: Routledge.
Burton, Alan and Steve Chibnall (1999) 'Promotional Activities and Showmanship in British Film Exhibition', *Journal of Popular British Cinema* 2, 83–99.
Chibnall, Steve (2012) 'From *The Snake Pit* to the *Garden of Eden*: A Time of Temptation for the Board', in Edward Lamberti (ed.), *Behind the Scenes at the BBFC: Film Classification from the Silent Screen to the Digital Age*. London: Palgrave Macmillan, pp. 29–52.
Chibnall, Steve (2017) 'Banging the Gong: The Promotion Strategies of Britain's J. Arthur Rank Organisation in the 1950s', *Historical Journal of Film, Radio and Television* 37(2), 242–71.
Cleland, Sir Charles (1933) 'Widening the Appeal of the Kinema', *Kinematograph Weekly*, 29 June, p. 6.
Deutsch, O. (1940) 'Proceedings of the Society. Twelfth Ordinary Meeting', *The Journal of the Royal Society of Arts*, 5 April, 466–81.
Eyles, Allen (2009) 'Exhibition and the Cinemagoing Experience', in Robert Murphy (ed.), *The British Cinema Book*, 3rd edn. London: Bloomsbury, pp. 78–84.
Farmer, Richard (2016) *Cinemas and Cinemagoing in Wartime Britain, 1939–45: The Utility Dream Palace*. Manchester: Manchester University Press.
Fuller-Seeley, Kathryn H. (ed.) (2008) *Hollywood in the Neighborhood: Historical Case Studies of Local Moviegoing*. Berkeley: University of California Press.
Ghillyer, P. F. (1983) 'The Tivoli Picture House: Home of My Childhood Dreams and Fantasies', in W. S. Power (ed.), *Plymouth Theatres and Cinemas*. Plymouth: Publisher unknown, pp. 107–24.
Griffiths, Trevor (2012) *The Cinema and Cinema-Going in Scotland, 1896–1950*. Edinburgh: Edinburgh University Press.
Hanson, Stuart (2007) *From Silent Screen to Multi-screen: A History of Cinema Exhibition in Britain since 1896*. Manchester: Manchester University Press.
James, Robert (2006) *Kinematograph Weekly* in the 1930s: Trade Attitudes towards Audience Taste', *Journal of British Cinema and Television* 3(2), 229–43.
James, Robert (2010) *Popular Culture and Working-Class Taste in Britain, 1930–39: A Round of Cheap Diversions?* Manchester: Manchester University Press.
James, Robert (2011) 'Popular Film-Going in Britain in the Early 1930s', *Journal of Contemporary History* 46(2), 271–87.

James, Robert (2013) 'Cinema-Going in a Port Town, 1914–1951: Film Booking Patterns at the Queens Cinema, Portsmouth', *Urban History* 40(2), 315–35.

James, Robert (2016) '"If there's one man that I admire, that man's a British tar": Leisure and Cultural Nation-Building in a Naval Port Town, c. 1850–1928', in Brad Beaven, Karl Bell and Robert James (eds), *Port Towns and Urban Cultures: International Histories of the Waterfront c. 1850–2000*. Basingstoke: Palgrave Macmillan, pp. 179–99.

Kuhn, Annette (1988) *Cinema, Censorship and Sexuality 1909–1925*. London: Routledge.

Lamberti, Edward (ed.) (2012) *Behind the Scenes at the BBFC: Film Classification from the Silent Screen to the Digital Age*. London: Palgrave Macmillan

Maltby, Richard, Daniel Biltereyst and Philippe Meers (eds) (2011) *Explorations in New Cinema History: Approaches and Case Studies*. Malden, MA: Wiley-Blackwell.

Manning, Sam (2020) *Cinemas and Cinema-Going in the United Kingdom: Decades of Decline, 1945–1965*. London: University of London Press.

Mather, I. (1973) 'Why the Film Censor is in Big Trouble', *Daily Mail*, 25 September, p. 6.

Matthews, Tom Dewe (1994) *Censored: The Story of Film Censorship in Britain*. London: Chatto and Windus.

Michele (2012) 'Uncle Harry Put the Fun into Grantham', *Grantham Matters.co.uk*, 22 July. <https://www.granthammatters.co.uk/sanders-harry-uncle-harry-put-the-fun-into-grantham/> (last accessed 18 May 2021).

Pirrie, G. (1937) 'Make Your Patrons Your Guest', *Cinema Management*, July, p. 16.

Portsmouth. Report of Portsmouth's Education Officer (1946) *Children's Cinema Clubs*, 2 April. DC14/40, Portsmouth Local History Centre, Norris Central Library, Portsmouth, UK.

Portsmouth. Watch and Fire Committee (1948) *No Orchids for Miss Blandish*. DC14/43, Portsmouth Local History Centre, Norris Central Library, Portsmouth, UK.

Rapp, D. (2002) 'Sex in the Cinema: War, Moral Panic, and the British Film Industry, 1906–1918', *Albion* 34(3), 422–51.

Richards, Jeffrey and James C. Robertson (2009) 'British Film Censorship', in Robert Murphy (ed.), *The British Cinema Book*, 3rd edn. London: Bloomsbury, pp. 67–77.

Sanders, H. (n.d.) 'Weekly attendances sheet', 2013-5343, SAN/4/1/6. Harry Sanders Collection, National Science and Media Museum.

Sanders, H. (1933) 'Make Your Public Curious: The Way to Big Box-Office Business'. *Kinematograph Weekly*, 26 October, p. 52.

Staiger, Janet (1990) 'Announcing Wares, Winning Patrons, Voicing Ideals: Thinking about the History and Theory of Film Advertising', *Cinema Journal* 29(3), 3–31.

Terrill, Jamie (2019) 'More to the UK than England: Exploring Wales' Cinemagoing History through its Showmen', *Participations* 16(1), 738–61.

Velez-Serna, M. A. (2016) 'Preview Screenings and the Spaces of an Emerging Local Cinema Trade in Scotland', *Historical Journal of Film, Radio and Television* 36(3), 285–304.

Woodruff, William (2003) *The Road to Nab End: An Extraordinary Northern Childhood*, 2nd edn. London: Abacus.

8. HARRY SANDERS: REMEMBERING A LIFE IN CINEMA MANAGEMENT

Robert Shail

Our true intent is all for your delight.
– Harry Sanders, Grantham, December 1937[1]

Harry Sanders was a cinema showman. He spent fifty years working in the film business from 1913 to 1963, and even when he retired he continued to take a keen interest in the medium to which he had given so much of his life. He was not a movie star, a producer, or a director. He never wrote a screenplay or composed a musical score. He did not make a single film himself and yet his role, like many others who shared his vocation, helped to shape the cinemagoing experience of literally millions of people in Britain, generation after generation. Harry Sanders was a cinema manager. His job took him to picture palaces all over the UK during an era when cinema was the nation's most popular leisure activity outside of the home. This was a time when the cinema manager had a level of autonomy rarely seen today. Not only did he choose the films to be shown, he was responsible personally for the publicity materials which would, hopefully, bring in a paying audience. It was the latter which was Harry Sanders's real passion and which he took particular care over.

Harry's other grand obsession was collecting the materials that he had created, and over the years the boxes of paper and artefacts accumulated to become an archive of the cinema showman's trade. These yellowing, fragile pages eventually found their way via his son, Howard Sanders, to the archives of the National Science and Media Museum, Bradford, UK. The Harry Sanders

Archive constitutes six large boxes of material, with some additions made more recently from his son's personal collection. The materials include a detailed career outline with dates of his tenure at each cinema, scripts for public talks he occasionally gave, diaries, cinema programmes, albums of press cuttings, letters, financial records (including booking diaries which show audience figures and costings), a collection of photos, and a number of examples of handbills, posters and other publicity materials either made by Sanders or commissioned by him from various local printers. There are even cassette recordings of his recollections, including interviews with local radio stations in Lincolnshire. These materials are largely in excellent condition and well organised, providing a clear narrative line through his career. They are also remarkably varied, providing an interlocking mosaic of his life and work. An interview with his son provided additional evidence of his activities to fill in the gaps. Sanders's careful collection and preservation of these materials clearly attests to the value and importance he placed on the cinema business and cinemagoing, as well as to the personal pleasure it provided him to work in this field.

Methodological Context

Hermione Lee, in her book *Body Parts: Essays on Life-Writing*, borrowing from the work of Boswell and Carlyle, suggests that writing about a person's life should be driven by 'the feeling for detail, the evocation of personality, and the commitment to truth-telling' (2005: 1). But above all it should be guided by sympathy. In 'the rescuing of lives, however obscure, from oblivion', she argues for the personal engagement of the researcher with their subject and with the valuing of evidence in all its forms, even apparently trivial or contested material such as anecdotes (ibid.: 2). She suggests that the role of anyone undertaking life-writing is to 'track' the materials that are available and present them with sympathy. For Lee, the minutiae of a life, as evidenced in the mundane and the everyday, can provide as much insight to the meanings inherent in that experience as the more dramatic episodes as seen from the outside. This is highly appropriate in considering an archive as idiosyncratic as that of Harry Sanders, where we are presented with musings, doodles and marginalia which nonetheless give an evocative sense of his daily experience as a cinema manager and pioneer of film promotion. Sympathy here is part of a recognition of the connection with our own lived experience, similarly constructed from such liminal material.

The fact that the picture is incomplete is a reflection of the contested nature of life experience itself; the picture is never complete, it is always in flux. The work of the historian inevitably involves 'a messy, contradictory, mixture of approaches' (ibid.: 3). Without apologies, this is the picture presented here regarding the life of Harry Sanders. The materials in the Harry Sanders Archive are a mosaic. They form a fragmented pattern, a collection of jigsaw pieces which when taken together provide an extraordinary picture of a working life in cinema management and promotion. Lee's definition of life-writing has led to the development of an academic approach to utilising personal archives (and a wide variety of other anecdotal materials) to piece together such fragmented portraits: the website of the Oxford Centre for Life-Writing (n.d.) suggests that 'life-writing involves, and goes beyond, biography. It encompasses everything from the complete life to the day-in-the-life ... it embraces the lives of objects and institutions as well as the lives of individuals, families and groups.' The memory work invited by the Harry Sanders Archive specifically provides a priceless doorway into the relationship between cinemas and their audiences in Britain.

In adopting this methodology, this chapter builds on a small but growing body of work within the field of film studies which seeks to expand the types of documentary evidence used in charting the medium's history. In her essay 'Film History Terminable and Interminable: Recovering the Past in Reception Studies' (1997), Barbara Klinger suggests the value of combining textual film analysis, the traditional starting point for much film studies scholarship, with approaches taken from reception studies in the pursuit of a more 'complete' understanding of the past. Similarly, Sarah Street, in *British Cinema in Documents*, argues for the use of a multiplicity of documentary sources in the writing of film history, or any history/ies, foregrounding the need for historians to 'research and write creatively about a subject' (2000: 9). Both authors acknowledge the impossibility of true 'completeness' in historical accounts and emphasise the need to situate the researcher within the processes of investigation but, nonetheless, champion the continuing expansion of possible source materials.

Similarly, Sue Harper's work in the *Historical Journal of Film, Radio and Television*, analysing Portsmouth cinema ledgers, charts changing patterns in audience preferences and the impact of the weather on cinema attendance, an issue which played heavily on the mind of Harry Sanders (Harper 2004, 2006). Jamie Terrill's recent article in *Participations* (2019) features discussions of the Welsh pioneer Arthur Cheetham, seen as a similar kind of manager, civic leader and local celebrity, while María Vélez-Serna's two chapters in *Early Cinema in Scotland* (2018a, 2018b) – 'Travelling Bioscopes and Borrowed Places' and 'Fixed-Site Cinemas and the First Film Renters' – use archival sources to explore the rise and fall of touring showmen. This essay also offers a complementary narrative to Robert James's chapter in this collection, '"Make Your Public Curious": Cinema Management, Film Advertising and Audience Taste in England, c. 1920–c. 1960'. James's work utilises the same Harry Sanders collection in Bradford, among other materials, but, whilst this essay offers a form of micro-history, referencing a mosaic of documents from the archive to trace Sanders's career and his impact on specific audiences, James adopts a more macro approach that explores Sanders's role in comparison with his contemporaries.

What remains unique about the Harry Sanders collection is the light it sheds on the role of a cinema manager outside of cinema's earlier period, providing fresh perspectives on cinemagoing itself and on the promotion of films. This chapter considers and exemplifies how a personal archive such as that of Harry Sanders can be used effectively to chart the popular success of the cinema with British audiences and to illustrate the ever-shifting correspondence between the cinema manager and the audience as they address each other in a developing dialogue.

Chronology

Harry Sanders was born in Maesteg, South Wales, on 16 September 1898, just three years after the Lumière Brothers had given the first public screening of moving images in Paris. Like his father, and most of the male population of the town, on leaving school he went to work in the local coal mine where he was apprenticed as an engine driver. He might have stayed there if it had not been for his attendance at a film screening which so impressed the fifteen-year-old that he decided to try for a part-time evening job in this nascent entertainment business. According to his own meticulously collated timeline, he quickly graduated from rewind boy at the Gem (part of the Poole circuit) to part-time assistant projectionist at the Cosy Cinema (owned by Richard Dooner's Enterprises). By 1917 he was their chief operator, meaning that he had overall responsibility for projecting the films. In 1920 he and his friend Robert Fisher moved to Penrhyndeudraeth in North Wales where they established their own cinema management business, Fisher and Sanders, and presided over three venues in Porthmadoc, Criccieth and Penrhyndeudraeth.[2] He had first met Robert Fisher in Maesteg where Fisher worked as a projectionist; when Fisher was demobbed following World War I they set up in business together.

Harry Sanders's responsibilities included managing the venues and staff, organising the publicity, and booking films for the weekly programme. The latter included investing £4 on *The Sheik* (1921), featuring Rudolph Valentino, for a week's run in Criccieth.[3] He had already developed an entrepreneurial streak: his diaries record how he took a 'terrific gamble' by paying an unprecedented £40 to book *The Kid*, featuring Charlie Chaplin, for a six-day run in 1921. His eye for publicity was also already well developed. Aware that the prime minister, Lloyd George, was visiting the area, he wrote to his secretary extending an invitation to visit his cinema at the Parish Hall, Criccieth; unfortunately, the prime minister had another engagement. The reply from 10 Downing Street became one of the earliest items in his personal archive. When he moved on from North Wales he organised his own benefit screening at Snowden Street,

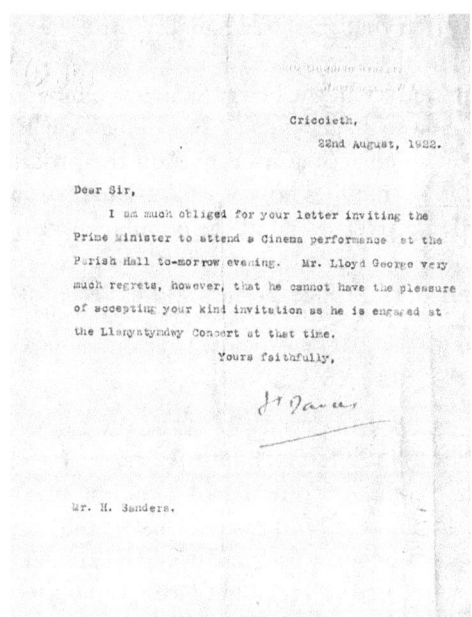

Figure 8.1 The Prime Minister is not available. (Source: The Harry Sanders Archive at the National Science and Media Museum, Bradford, UK.)

Porthmadoc, featuring D. W. Griffith's *True Heart Susie* (1919) and Charlie Chaplin in *The Fireman* (1916), which he described in his diary as 'a scream. Two reels. Nuff said.' Admission was five pence, nine pence, or one shilling.

His abilities as a manager were soon recognised among his peers in the developing cinema business: by January 1923 he had parted from his business partner and was working for the cinema owner E. Gratton Milley, overseeing both the Co-op Picture House in Kirkham and the Beehive, Bolton. Next was the Palace, Walkden where he staged a chrysanthemum show in the cinema auditorium, attracting a good deal of press coverage (Anon. 1926b). Then came the Picture House, Balham; both this and the Palace were managed for the exhibitor Ernesto Carreras whose son, James, would later go on to lead Britain's premier horror producer, Hammer. By March 1927 he was running one of the largest cinemas in the West Country, the Kings in the Old Market district of Bristol. Daily numbers at the Kings could be as much as 4,000. Here he began to shape the venue's publicity materials, overseeing or creating the posters, flyers and newspaper advertisements for its weekly programmes, and even starting to stage the publicity stunts which became his speciality. A playbill he designed from November 1926 showcasing the release of *Camille*, starring Norma Talmadge, indicates his taste for hyperbole: 'Wonderful clothes!

Luxurious Settings! Peerless acting!"[4] Although, he still thought it necessary to point out to his audience that this version of Dumas's classic was 'not a costume story but a drama of modern life with up-to-date dresses and settings'. He was beginning to garner recognition from his peers for his work in cinema 'exploitation', as it was named in the trade, and was awarded Third Prize in the Silver Challenge Cup from the trade magazine *The Cinema* for his promotion of the Harry Langdon comedy *Tramp, Tramp, Tramp* (1926). His reward was the not insignificant amount of 100 guineas. In its issue of 10 November 1927 he was named one of the '100 Best Showmen in the Country' (Anon. 1927a).

The Kings had also been a variety hall, and Sanders took full advantage of the opportunity to stage other attractions around the film programme. This included booking the Anglo-Australian musical-comedy duo Mr Flotsam and Mr Jetsam (real names Bentley Collingwood Hilliam and Malcolm McEachern) at a fee of £125, and organising a live broadcast from the cinema to mark Bristol Radio Week. The latter consisted of a short performance by the cinema's own symphony orchestra under the direction of Alfred A. Freeman. Harry meticulously recorded all of his activities, building up a roster of artists whom he could call upon for performances, from vocalists like Signor Silvio Sideli to jazz ensembles such as Wingate's Temperance Band. He also began to make notes of all the films he screened and their comparative popularity with audiences. A disappointed entry from 3 October 1927 records that a film version of *Faust* proved 'too highbrow for Bristol' with a return of only £623, three shillings and sixpence. Occasionally he raged at authority, wondering 'will wireless soon be the cause of all the trouble? Thus giving the cinema a well-deserved rest from magisterial and ministerial blame.' The usual British obsession with the weather took on a particular interest for cinema managers like Harry, when sunshine became something to dread as it kept the customers out of his darkened auditorium. The phrase 'exceptionally fine and warm weather all week' was not a happy one.

By 1928 Harry had arrived, by way of the Coliseum and the Canton in Cardiff, at one of the new breed of 'super cinemas' being opened by the Carreras circuit: The Lido, Upper Street, in Islington. In 1929 it even installed the latest technological breakthrough, sound. The Lido was an art deco palace and Sanders created a monthly programme booklet to match, complete with an elegantly stylised cover promoting 'the perfect talkie theatre'. By now he was a master of the art of cinema exploitation and could turn any film screening into an opportunity for an extravagant promotional 'wheeze', the more imaginative the better. For *The Ring* (1927), directed by Alfred Hitchcock, he created a campaign that implied that an actual boxing contest between the film's two stars, Carl Brisson and Ian Hunter, was going to take place in his auditorium. He could not resist the chance to incorporate as much wordplay as possible with references to how the film would 'stand up to the world's best' and 'give

Figure 8.2 Sanders's art deco programme design for The Lido, Islington. (Source: The Harry Sanders Archive at the National Science and Media Museum, Bradford, UK.)

the knock-out to ninety-nine per cent of its rivals'. On the opening night he rigged up the corner of a boxing ring in the cinema foyer complete with sponge, water and gloves at a cost of six shillings.

While previously at the Beehive, Harry developed a penchant for mildly racy campaigns that appealed to the male and female sections of his audience in different ways. For the film *Treat 'Em Rough* (also known as *Brothers Under the Skin*, 1922) he issued two flyers. The first asked in large print 'Should wives be beaten?', while a second one warned wives not to let their husbands see the film without them as it might cause 'poor henpecked, dish-washing, baby-minding, floor-scrubbing, husbands' to rise up in rebellion. These small cards were typically distributed to cafés, bars, libraries and other public areas around the town or city where he was working and left for patrons to discover for themselves. The strategy was always to disguise that they related to a film screening and catch the attention with an outrageous narrative. Only on closer inspection was the title of a film revealed and the true purpose of the calling card uncovered. A fine example is his campaign for *The Letter* (1940), starring Bette Davies, when he distributed what appeared to be a personal letter from a frustrated housewife in the throes of a passionate affair around various venues in Grantham: 'My husband will be away for the night . . . I am desperate, and

A LIFE IN CINEMA MANAGEMENT

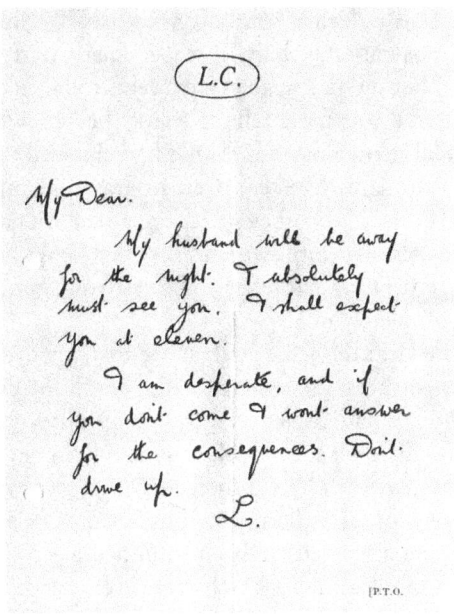

Figure 8.3 A typical promotional 'wheeze' designed by Harry Sanders for *The Letter* (1940). (Source: The Harry Sanders Archive at the National Science and Media Museum, Bradford, UK.)

if you don't come I won't answer to the consequences.' Only on turning over the apparently mislaid letter did the reader discover it was promoting the latest Bette Davies vehicle. Another simply had the phrase 'A confession' on one side of the paper. Turning over, we discover 'I confess that I have failed. I have struggled with my thoughts and my vocabulary and I cannot find words to adequately describe the remarkable acting of Emil Jennings in the picture of his career, *The Way of all Flesh*.'

When The Lido in Islington passed from the Carreras chain to the Ben Rose circuit, and then was swallowed up as part of the major Odeon network, Harry decided to move on, noting in his diary that he was 'an independent sort of guy'. Over the next two years he restlessly passed through the Regal at Uxbridge, the Central and the Playhouse at Folkstone, and the Ritz at Aldershot, which he described as a 'dismal garrison town'. He was distinctly unimpressed with his then employers, Union Cinemas; he noted that they were 'about the craziest circuit in the business', although he does not specify why. After six months he resigned. There was a brief stay at the Picture House, Oldbury (Emery circuit), before he finally arrived at The State, Grantham in December 1937. This cinema would be his happy home for the rest of his career in cinema management; another diary entry records that 'it was indeed a very happy Christmas'. In 1941 it became the Granada and joined this national chain (it was formerly part of the much smaller E. L. Manches chain) but by that stage Harry seems to have lost something of his defiant individualism and was more willing to toe the line with the tighter managerial structures of a large organisation. Times had changed too and cinema managers were not given the same free rein over programming and publicity that he had previously experienced. Nonetheless, he remained in charge at the Granada for another twenty-two years until his retirement in 1963; he then continued to work in stock management in their television sales wing, going part-time in 1970 and finally retiring completely in 1977.

However, even in Grantham he had never lost his eye for the chance to generate publicity or to keep his cinema at the centre of public discussion. In 1947 the local authority had considered the possibility of closing cinemas on Sundays. Harry immediately set to work on a campaign against this action. A public vote was organised by the Council to gauge local opinion, and Harry bombarded the citizens of Grantham with posters urging them to vote to keep cinema doors open. He appealed to 'broad-minded electors' to vote in favour of Sunday opening and, in a move which seems remarkably contemporary, he targeted the young, as those between sixteen and twenty-one years of age were

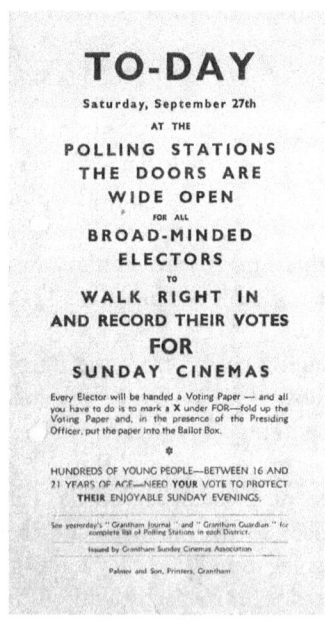

Figure 8.4   Sanders campaigns (successfully) to keep the Granada open on Sundays. (Source: The Harry Sanders Archive at the National Science and Media Museum, Bradford, UK.)

permitted to take part in the vote. He urged them to 'protect their enjoyable Sunday evenings' from Council interference. The motion to keep cinemas open on Sundays was safely passed by a vote of 4,129 to 859.

The Archive: Marketing the Cinema of Attractions

Throughout his career, Harry Sanders kept careful, detailed notes of his plans and ideas for publicity stunts or 'wheezes'. These included gloriously surreal drawings for costumes or exhibits which he might place around the streets of any town where he was working. In neat, clearly defined line drawings he depicts curious metal vehicles such as his 'steel stunt' which might be pushed around town to publicise the day's screenings. Another illustration shows a costume in the shape of a question mark to be worn by one of his hawkers, along with a large arrow on a stick which they could carry to point the way to the cinema. His spare moments seem to have been taken up with thinking of ever more ingenious ways of catching the attention of the public. If visual devices did not work, then he would put into play catchphrases or elaborate puns for his signage. He called these 'Eye-catchers' and collected them in his notebooks. The phrases often had little to do with the film in question but

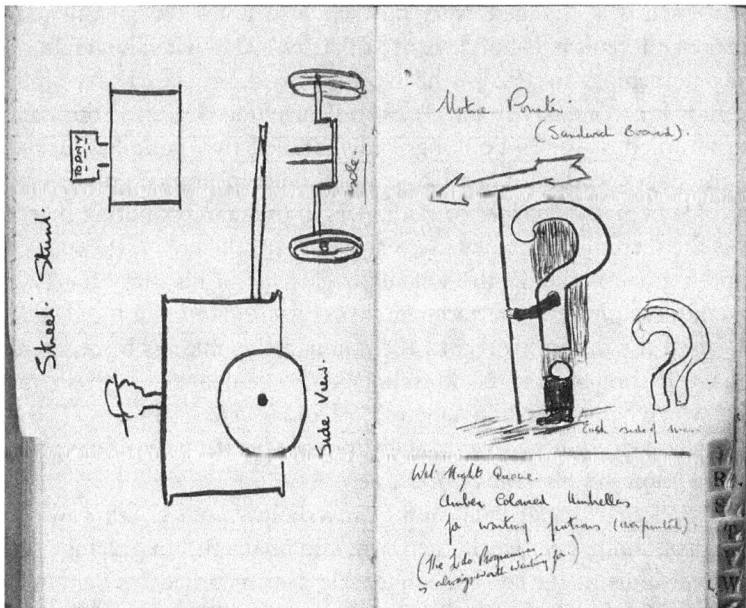

Figure 8.5   Typical notebook designs for a publicity campaign. (Source: The Harry Sanders Archive at the National Science and Media Museum, Bradford, UK.)

were selected for maximum impact: 'All people should stop making love ... after they're 80 years old' proclaimed one announcement, while another simply instructed passers-by to 'Marry the girl!' He also used the notebooks to record aphorisms and mottoes designed to remind him of the motivations that always underpinned his activities. Some are sentimental or lean towards cliché but they clearly held personal significance for him, whether it was a copy of Kipling's poem 'If' or statements like 'All things I thought I knew; but now confess, The more I know I know, I know the less.' There is a touching, almost childlike delight in the way he would print his name at the top of a page to claim authorship or meticulously record the dates of each location in which he worked. The essence of his personality is there in his entry in Grantham in 1937: 'Our true intent is all for your delight.' For Harry, cinema was a magical medium capable of bringing joy to the people and he was its chief magician.

He kept diaries of his film bookings which provide a fascinating week-by-week history of changing cinematic styles and public tastes from the silent period to the early 1950s, by which time cinema managers typically no longer booked films themselves but accepted a programme dictated by head office. These small volumes, written in a meticulous hand, record the film's title, the rental company from which it was hired, its length in feet (a nicety in film exhibition observed to this day in the magazine *Sight and Sound*), and the price he had paid for the rental. His booking diaries from the 1930s show that the film being screened was changed every day. He also notes special calendar dates such as the children's half-holidays or St Patrick's Day when he might organise a themed screening. In 1923–4 he typically paid between thirty shillings to two pounds for a one-day rental. Back in Penrhyndeudraeth at the start of the decade he noted a week's bookings only totalled two pounds. Tucked away within the pages we find items like his buildings insurance policy. He would also scribble occasional asides or reminders in the margins noting that 'combination is the secret of efficiency in every game' or 'the only difference between a rut and a grave is the depth'. On the back page of his diary for 1924–5 he wrote 'a modern pirate – entertainment tax collection or income tax collection'. He also used the diaries to record the comparative takings of different films. For the week commencing 28 March 1927 he bemoaned the 'very mediocre features' which had netted him a mere £597 and fourteen shillings. The weather was a constant cause for concern as it directly affected box office takings; one exasperated note simply reads 'total gale'.

The diaries chart the gradual shift from a daily change of film towards three different programmes per week, then two, and finally just one change per week; high-interest films might run for longer. He also recorded his income and his outgoings, which provide a testament to both gradual inflation and to the pressure cinema managers began to experience in the 1950s as audiences declined. A list for 1930 records the following costs:

National Screen Service	£1 per week
Film Transport	£1 per week
Youngers Publicity	£50 (London)
Rateable Value	£717
Music and Dance Licence/Cinematograph Licence – costs not recorded	
Refuse Removal	£2 10/-

Similarly, he recorded the gradual increase in ticket prices over the years, so that in 1940 he was charging two shillings for the best seats in the stalls and three shillings for the equivalent in the balcony. By 1951 he was charging an additional seven pence for the best seats at the back of the stalls and the equivalent in the balcony had risen to three shillings and eleven pence. At the same date he noted that a full house, including ninety-six standing in the stalls, could net him five pounds, thirteen shillings and six pence. One of the most striking entries is on 9 January 1941 at The State, Grantham, when he records a cost of four pounds, seventeen shillings and six pence needed to repair four holes in the theatre roof caused by bomb damage.

There was also a sense of camaraderie, and gentle competition, between rival cinema managers in the era of independence; Sanders always maintained his membership of the *Kinematograph Weekly* Company of Showmen. The life of an itinerant cinema manager could be a lonely one, with many geographic moves and changing employers. The hours were also long. His son, Howard, testified to the strain this placed on his father (Sanders 2017). Among Harry's possessions was a booklet entitled *Read This and Weep! (For Cinema Managers)* by W. L. Pember (n.d.), 'one of them'. This slender volume contains a series of comic anecdotes charting some of the wilder publicity stunts contrived by cinema managers in pursuit of the elusive audience. Sanders's job, with its unusual hours and daily pressure, obviously involved an element of isolation, and publications like this, as well as the in-house magazines published by chains like Granada for their staff, helped to foster a sense of community. Harry's efforts were often recognised with coverage in these publications and occasionally with more formal acknowledgement in the way of prizes. A letter from the European Motion Picture Co. Ltd. dated 11 January 1926, while Harry was still manager at the Beehive, Bolton, commends him for his ability to exploit the potential of the 'wonderful serial' *Samson of the Circus* and rewards him with a cheque for £10.

In his later years in semi-retirement – Harry never seemed to really retire – he spent a good deal of time in nostalgic contemplation of the golden age of cinemagoing, giving interviews to local radio and to the press about his exploits. He was never slow in talking to anyone who would listen about his career, always spurred on by his endless enthusiasm for the medium. In June 1981 he was contacted by the *Cambrian News*, a newspaper still operating to this day in West Wales, who wanted to commemorate his links with the area and to celebrate this 'showman, publicist, exploiter and administrator in the cinema' (Anon. 1981). He kept his press cuttings, carefully preserving the articles that recognised him as 'a man of the cinema' and 'master publicist' (Martin n.d.). One diary entry records the number of times he had appeared in the letters page of the in-house publication of the Granada chain, which totalled twenty-nine between July 1950 and September 1963. These press cuttings provide a rich panorama of changing audiences, as Harry charted his successes and recorded his various 'wheezes' for the pleasure of his peers. *The Trade Show Critic*, as early as 8 January 1926, devoted an article to his exploits headlined 'Ambitious Harry Sanders' (Anon. 1926a). It reported how he had established a 'wide renown through his enterprising publicity methods'. These included producing a ninety-six-sheet poster for the film serial *Samson of the Circus* (1926), which was reported as the biggest ever for a serial. The trade paper *Kine Weekly* reported, on 16 September 1926, how he had hired two men, whom he dressed in morning coats and top hats, to walk the streets of Balham holding a card inscribed 'Ask me for a tonic!' When passers-by took them up on this offer they were told to go and see Harold Lloyd in *For Heaven's Sake* at Harry's cinema (Anon. 1926c). In 1952 the *Granada Newsletter* responded to one of his publicity activities with the comment: 'if the ghost of Barnum had been in the neighbourhood of Grantham last week, it would have doffed its spectral hat to a worthy disciple in Harry Sanders, who pulled off one of the most spectacular stunts of recent years' (Anon. 1952).

He kept many of the handmade playbills that he produced throughout his career. He had a particular fondness for mildly suggestive teasing of his audience or sensationalism. His playbill for *Love Burglar* (1920) informed the 'young men of Penrhyn in need of wives' that they should not miss the picture. For *Czar of Broadway* (1931) his handbill looked like a sensational news announcement, proclaiming 'King of the underworld shot by rival gangsters.' Subsequently, the Director of Publicity at Universal Pictures wrote to compliment him on his promotion of the film. When he screened Fritz Lang's *Metropolis* (1927) at the Kings in Bristol he commissioned a local artist to produce a poster depicting what the city's tramways centre might look like 100 years in the future. Little did he know that it would not even exist and its place would be taken first by a traffic island and then by a water feature. When the film *Canton Girl* (1928) arrived at his cinema in the Canton district of Cardiff he could not resist creating a poster that claimed 'Should be seen by every Canton girl', although the film's subject had no real connection with the city. The importance of posters for him was reflected by this diary entry: 'the poster is the window of the cinema. It must hit you. It must convey its meaning at a glance . . . so be brief, be concise, and arrive at your point in bold face type.' He also produced his own monthly programme magazines for The State in Grantham with an editorial feature called 'Manager's Chat'. One notice

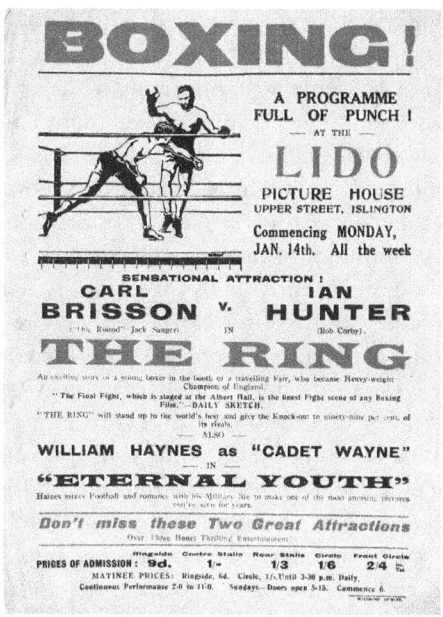

Figure 8.6 One of Harry Sanders's characteristically inventive playbills. (Source: The Harry Sanders Archive at the National Science and Media Museum, Bradford, UK.)

in the magazine draws customers' attention to the cinema café, which served 'delightful dainty teas' which could be brought to your seat by an usherette, an innovation recently reintroduced in some 'boutique' cinemas.

Musical entertainments designed to enliven a programme were another favourite and brought out Harry's strong sense of the important place of cinema in the community. At the Kings in Bristol he introduced audience sing-alongs before each performance which proved immensely popular. The *Bristol Times and Reporter* recorded that the Lord Mayor and Lady Mayoress had attended so that they could join in on 13 April 1927 (Anon. 1927b). On 12 May 1927 he organised 'A Musical World Tour' which consisted of a slide show of images from exotic locations with musical accompaniment from the cinema orchestra; the tour started and ended in Bristol. Before screenings of *Spanish Passions* (1927) he created an entertainment entitled 'Spanish Prologue' which consisted of a tableau, a dancer and then songs – all with a Spanish theme. Harry always remained keen to supplement film programmes with other forms of entertainment or by star appearances. One of his greatest coups during the war period was to host Glen Miller and his orchestra. Gracie Fields also made an appearance at his Grantham cinema on 31 August 1943. The auditorium was packed with 2,000 factory workers who had been given the afternoon off from work so that they could attend, and the streets were crammed with 8,000 more spectators on St Peter's Hill. In the early 1960s Harry arranged for a succession of popular entertainers to appear at The State including many of the first wave of British rock and roll stars such as Tommy Steele, Billy Fury, Adam Faith, Lonnie Donegan and Cliff Richard, as well as American imports like Gene Vincent. However, the only one who could fill the 1,500-seater auditorium for both performances of his one-night stand was the more mainstream entertainer Max Bygraves. For Harry Sanders, it was always about knowing your audience.

Another notable coup from early in his career was to feature the future child star Freddie Bartholomew as part of a variety bill at The Lido. Bartholomew, who gave a recitation, went on to feature in the Hollywood version of *David Copperfield* (1935). Despite the fact that Bartholomew's star waned rapidly in adulthood, Harry never ceased to play on his distant association with him, sometimes billing himself as the man 'who gave boy star his chance' or as 'friend of Bartholomew'. He even wrote to him on 7 November 1978 during a period when he seems to have been nostalgically revisiting his career by trying to contact people who had figured in its success; he never received a reply. When between jobs and looking for a position, Sanders advertised in trade magazines as the man who had discovered Freddie Bartholomew. He was never out of work for long.

In the 1950s he started The Granadiers as part of the national circuit of Saturday morning children's clubs that covered the UK and which were affiliated to the Children's Film Foundation (CFF). A diary entry for Saturday, 16 February 1952 lists a typical programme for a children's matinee with a Woody Woodpecker cartoon followed by a Laurel and Hardy short, then episode eight of a Batman and Robin serial, before a full screening of Robert Flaherty's *Nanook of the North* (1922); the fact that this feature was being shown to children thirty years after its original release is an unfortunate testament to the tendency of cinema managers to view children's screenings as requiring little thought, a trend that had led to the creation of the CFF in the first place. Harry's affection for The Granadiers seems to have grown during the 1950s and he increasingly devoted his energies to their activities, perhaps frustrated by the fact that the cinema manager's role was being increasingly subsumed within the corporate structures of large organisations like Granada. He even created his own song for the club sung to the tune of 'The British Grenadiers'. The Granadiers seems to have given him the chance to bring his marketing skills to the fore once more. It was clearly a success as he records weekly audiences of 1,000 in the first half of the 1950s.

The core of his approach to marketing, however, always lay in the 'wheezes' which he took such delight in executing. These fired his creative imagination and often combined the literal with the surreal, as when he advertised *The Cat and the Canary* (1927) by wheeling a giant cut-out of a canary in a cage on board a wagon around the streets of Bristol. For *Jailbirds* (1931) he had actors dressed as convicts marching up and down under guard outside The Lido, Islington, while *Murders in the Rue Morgue* (1932) led inevitably to a man in a gorilla suit being walked by his keeper around Islington's streets. There were wax models in the foyer for *The Mystery of the Wax Museum* (1933) and skeletons for *The House of Doom* (1934), while a paper-thin man was made from wooden battens for *The Thin Man* (1934). For Ealing's chilling *Dead of Night* (1946) he organised an 11p.m. screening which could be attended by written application only and which was followed by an apparently serious discussion of the meaning of dreams. Any occurrence in nearby streets could be turned into an advertising opportunity, so that the road works in Islington High Street soon had an improvised sign above them reading 'Paving the way for *King Kong*'.

One of his most outrageous stunts was to place an advert in the local Islington newspapers stating that 1,000 shorthand typists were needed – applicants were asked to report to The Lido. When they arrived in their hordes they discovered that they had been conned into attending a screening of *After Office Hours* (1935); he did not record their reaction. For *Five of a Kind* (1939) he even managed to find seventeen sets of twins whom he invited to a tea party at The State, attracting huge press coverage. Later again, he made 500 handwritten holiday postcards captioned 'Having a wonderful time' which were delivered to addresses around Grantham to promote *Summer Holiday* (1963), starring Cliff Richard; his diary records the week's takings as £1,681 net for six days. In his later career in Grantham he tended to focus on a more regular pattern of talent shows, beauty contests and fundraising charity events, often for the town's hospital.

Perhaps his most concerted campaign of all was the one for the Harry Langdon comedy *Tramp, Tramp, Tramp* (1926) at the Kings in 1927. He began by distributing 5,000 flyers in the streets offering a chance to win free tickets. Then a poster campaign informed Bristolians that 'Harry's coming'. Four hundred wanted posters were put up two weeks before the first night and then the winners of the free tickets were announced in the press. Finally, he employed a local youth, Harry Rousseau, to walk all the way from London to Bristol in a pair of Lennard's boots (a well-known shoe shop in central Bristol). He kept photos of the queues outside the cinema when the film opened.

A Philosopher of Cinemagoing

In his own way Harry Sanders was a philosopher of cinema entertainment, building a clear sense of what he felt worked or did not based on his immense experience of cinema audiences. At a talk for the Rotary Club in Grantham on 14 August 1950 he told them that cinema is 'the cheapest and most significant form of entertainment' available.[5] Its accessibility to the masses was always a key feature in its importance for him, as it provided 'comfort and luxury at a such a reasonable rate'. Technical innovations and improvements in facilities were to be welcomed, so he was delighted first by the arrival of sound and then by the appearance of colour films and widescreen. He believed that silent films had required more engagement from audiences as they needed to imagine the dialogue for themselves, whereas sound meant 'far less demand on one's powers of concentration'. Patrons should be rewarded for parting with their hard-earned money by a sumptuous environment in which they could forget their everyday boredom and frustration. The exemplar of this, for him, was The Lido in London, which 'had all the luxury trimmings – sponge rubber upholstered seats, beautiful thick carpet in the foyer and gangways, the most up-to-date air conditioning plant, perfect projection equipment, smartly uniformed attendants'. He saw cinema as a social leveller, lifting the aspirations of his poorest customers and giving them a glimpse of a better life: 'the roughs and toughs started to dress up, put on collar and ties and their Sunday best suits'.

He had his views on the kind of films which the public preferred as well. For Harry Sanders there had to be a point of identification rooted in their own lived experiences: 'the most successful are those with a strong factual background . . . reflections of reality, whatever the genre, it has to feel like a real life situation'. Even a fantasy film or a western had to contain this seed of reality if it was to succeed with audiences. At the same time, there needed to be heightened emotions to take the audience away from their lives: 'somewhere to go, to forget their worries for a couple of hours, to escape the daily gloom and to relax'. Nonetheless, he was aware of the potential social impact of cinema; his playbill for *Love on the Dole* (1941) was captioned 'It carries a vital message whilst it also offers first rate entertainment.' He also noted how audiences tended to copy styles of clothing from the films they watched. It is interesting to speculate on what he would have made of the cinemagoing decline in Britain of the 1970s and 1980s when fading picture palaces were often unsympathetically converted into multiscreen venues, frequently with poor projection and sound. He might have been more impressed by the subsequent rise of the multiplex with its return to escapism, as well as those thick carpets and comfortable seats.

His greatest irritation was caused by professional critics who seemed more concerned with their own views rather than considering the needs of the audience: 'surely their job is to state whether the film is worth the individual one-and-ninepences which will be paid by millions of ordinary folk'. His conception of cinema was based on an escape from everyday life for the common people. If correct, what this tells us about the possible quality of life he witnessed around him over those sixty years is a less cheerful consideration. He often liked to talk directly to his audience, creating newsletters or writing a manager's column in his programme guides. His programme booklet for The Lido included 'Our

Monthly Chat' where he pondered such questions as whether the stars or the story were more important; he decided it was the stars (Sanders 1935). His son, Howard, remembered that at the end of his career his father remained optimistic for the return of popular filmgoing: 'he thought cinema would come back for socialising, escapism, comfort and spectacle' (Sanders 2017).

The Final Curtain

In 1981 Mrs Frances Ciano of Penrhyn wrote to the *Grantham Weekly Shopper* having seen an article about Harry Sanders:

> He was the first person to show silent films over sixty years ago in this small village situated in the foothills of the Snowdonia mountains. At the time I was eleven (I am now seventy-one) and I remember Mr Sanders as a young man opening what he called the 'living pictures'. There was no electricity or gas in the village, so the projector was worked by turning a handle. (Ciano 1981)

Harry Sanders's life at the pictures provides a narrative charting the growth of the twentieth century's most popular form of public entertainment. In his dedication to attracting audiences he was a pioneer of marketing and publicity that predates the activities of the viral campaigners on today's internet. In compiling his personal archives, he charted six decades of social change, recording, for example, the night in 1940 when he had to stop a screening of Charles Chaplin's *The Great Dictator* because of an air raid; on his retirement, the *Granada Newsletter* suggested that 'Harry Sanders' career sounds like a history of the cinema' (Anon. 1963). At a talk for the King's School Film Society in Grantham, 9 September 1962, he recalled playing synchronised records in the auditorium during early experiments at establishing sound films, as well as the technical challenges of the later introduction of colour and widescreen. He described for his young audience his ideal cinema: '1600 seater with rising floor, heating and ventilation kit, huge screen, no fancy fittings to distract, a stage for occasional events'. He speculated for them what the attraction of cinema was: 'Numerous factors, relaxation, romance, laughter, excitement, the herd instinct, getting away from the blinking telly.' By that time cinema managers no longer booked their films or organised publicity. The golden age of filmgoing had ended and with it the careers of pioneers like Harry Sanders, men and women who had helped to make it a viable medium in the first place.

The last film screening at the Granada, Grantham was *Tales of Beatrix Potter* (1971) on 8 April 1972. It continued as a bingo hall before being demolished in March 1988. Harry Sanders died in 1987 and was spared the pain of seeing its final curtain. What remains particularly striking from the materials in his archive is the sense of an intimate relationship between the cinema manager and the audience. All of Harry Sanders's publicity materials speak to that audience in a direct voice, sometimes teasing, always conveying a shared excitement for the medium of cinema. Throughout, there is personable dialogue which seems a distinctive feature of the period and which has largely vanished from the corporate communication of contemporary cinema chains, albeit that it is still to be found in the independent sector.

Acknowledgements

This chapter is drawn substantially from primary materials held by the National Science and Media Museum, Bradford in the Harry Sanders Archive. I would like to extend my thanks to them and in particular to their curator, Toni Booth. I am also immensely grateful to Harry's son, Howard Sanders, whom I interviewed and who provided additional materials used in compiling this chapter.

Notes

1. Direct quotes from Harry Sanders and autobiographical references are taken from his notebooks and diaries which form part of the Harry Sanders Archive at the National Science and Media Museum, Bradford, UK.
2. The records of the *London Gazette*, the official journal of record for British government, contain statutory notices from 1921 showing Henry Ewart Sanders and Robert George Fisher as co-partners in Fisher and Sanders, initially registered as a business at the Town Hall, Penrhyndeudraeth, and then at their apartments at The Gables. The anglicised spelling of Welsh place names – Porthmadoc rather than Porthmadog, for example – has been adopted here as these are the spellings used by Sanders himself in his papers as well as being commonplace during his lifetime.
3. Harry Sanders kept detailed records of the rental cost of the films he screened, as well as audience figures.
4. All publicity materials created by Harry Sanders are from the National Science and Media Museum, Bradford, UK.
5. The script for his public address is held at the National Science and Media Museum, Bradford, UK.

Bibliography

Anon. (1926a) 'Ambitious Harry Sanders', *The Trade Show Critic*, 8 January.
Anon. (1926b) 'Flower Show in Cinema', *Kine Weekly*, 4 November.
Anon. (1926c) Untitled report, *Kine Weekly*, 16 September.
Anon. (1927a) '100 Best Showmen in the Country', *The Cinema*, 10 November.
Anon. (1927b) Untitled report, *Bristol Times and Reporter*, 13 April.
Anon. (1952) Untitled report, *Granada Newsletter*, May.
Anon. (1963) 'Harry Sanders Retirement', *Granada Newsletter*, Christmas edn.

Anon. (1981) 'Harry Sanders', *Cambrian News*, 5 June.
Ciano, Frances (1981) 'Letters to the Editor', *Grantham Weekly Shopper*, 19 May.
Harper, Sue (2004) 'A Lower Middle-Class Taste Community in the 1930s: Admissions Figures at the Regent Cinema, Portsmouth, UK', *Historical Journal of Film, Radio and Television* 24(3), 565–88.
Harper, Sue (2006) 'Fragmentation and Crisis: 1940s Admissions Figures at the Regent Cinema, Portsmouth, UK', *Historical Journal of Film, Radio and Television* 26(3), 361–94.
Klinger, Barbara (1997) 'Film History Terminable and Interminable: Recovering the Past in Reception Studies', *Screen* 38(2), 107–28.
Lee, Hermione (2005) *Body Parts: Essays on Life-Writing*. London: Vintage.
Martin, Brian (n.d., probably early 1980s) 'Harry's Screened it All', unidentified newspaper cutting from the Harry Sanders Archive, National Science and Media Museum, Bradford, UK.
Oxford Centre for Life-Writing (n.d.) 'What is Life-Writing? Oxford Centre for Life-Writing. <https://oxlifewriting.wordpress.com/what-is-life-writing/> (last accessed 8 April 2019).
Pember, W. L. (n.d.) *Read This and Weep! (For Cinema Managers)*. Marlow: White Hill Press.
Sanders, Harry (1935) 'Our Monthly Chat', *The Lido Programme*, November.
Sanders, Howard (2017) Interview by the author, 24 March.
Street, Sarah (2000) *British Cinema in Documents*. London: Routledge.
Terrill, Jamie (2019) 'More to the UK than England: Exploring Rural Wales' Cinemagoing History through its Showmen', *Participations* 16(1), 738–61.
Vélez-Serna, María A. (2018a) 'Travelling Bioscopes and Borrowed Spaces', in John Caughie, Trevor Griffiths and María A. Vélez-Serna (eds), *Early Cinema in Scotland*. Edinburgh: Edinburgh University Press, pp. 14–32.
Vélez-Serna, María A. (2018b) 'Fixed-Site Cinemas and the First Film Renters', in John Caughie, Trevor Griffiths and María A. Vélez-Serna (eds), *Early Cinema in Scotland*. Edinburgh: Edinburgh University Press, pp. 33–51.

9. *THE YELLOW TEDDYBEARS:* EXPLOITATION AS EDUCATION

Adrian Smith

The Yellow Teddybears (Hartford-Davies, 1963) was an 'X'-rated depiction of a contemporary scandalous news story about British schoolgirls having sex and then wearing a badge to make sure their friends knew they were no longer virgins. Trading on the idea that this is 'Every parent's worst nightmare', this was the first time a mainstream British film had dealt explicitly with the concept of underage sex and the resultant unwanted pregnancies and social shame. *The Yellow Teddybears* pushed the limits of what the censors would allow.

This chapter uses new interviews alongside censorship records, newspaper articles, and archival material related to the promotion of the film as a tool for positive discussion and education. It contrasts this with evidence of a more salacious advertising campaign based on the titilatory promise of both the subject and its 'X' certificate. My methodology has been developed through marrying together my twin obsessions of exploring dusty (digital and physical) archives and employing detective-like skills to track people down who made films over fifty years ago and have often long since left the business behind. It is, of course, entirely valid to solely make conclusions from archival research, but if it is also possible to draw on the recollections of people who were actually there then as a historian I feel obliged to do so. Eye-witness testimony can bring the research to life, and it also provides the vital function of preserving an oral history that will otherwise be lost.

Mazdon and Wheatley described the dichotomy or opposition between European arthouse film texts and their British distribution as adult entertainment in the 1960s as the 'sex/art binary' (2013: 113). Dozens of European films, celebrated elsewhere for their artistic achievement, were repackaged for

British audiences with an emphasis on the 'ooh-la-la factor' (Sarris 1999). One particularly striking example of this was the British distributor Gala's retitling of the Italian drama *Adua e la compagne* (Pietrangeli, 1960) as *Hungry for Love*, a punning title given that the film is about former prostitutes who open a restaurant.

For the purposes of this chapter I have borrowed and adapted Mazdon and Wheatley's concept and will be using the term 'sex/altruism binary' to connect this research to theirs, and to demonstrate the conflict at the heart of this case study between the desire to promote public welfare and the commercial intentions of filmmakers and distributors. Whereas their focus was on European films in British cinemas, *The Yellow Teddybears* is British from beginning to end, but it builds on an audience awareness of changes in what was permissible onscreen. This had, in part, been fuelled by the aforementioned increase in European arthouse cinema. As far as I am aware, this film and its place in the developing post-war youth culture has not been explored from this vantage point. However, as will be discussed later, the idea of a film with a proposed educational remit being exploited for its adult content was tried and tested decades earlier in the USA. The lack of a legally enforced country-wide censorship there meant that almost anything could be screened by an exhibitor brave enough to do so. This kind of cinematic ballyhoo was never really possible in the UK because of legally enforced certification requirements. Once the BBFC strictures slowly began to loosen, following the introduction of the 'X' certificate in 1951, more explicit material gradually found its way onto screens, often with some sort of educational dressing. Nudist camp documentaries were particularly popular.[1]

The Yellow Teddybears was an early production for Compton Films, formed by Tony Tenser and Michael Klinger in early 1960. Tenser had worked for the independent distributor Miracle Films, whilst Michael Klinger ran a variety of successful clubs around Soho. Together they started a private cinema club on Old Compton Street which could screen films that did not require a certificate from the British Board of Film Censors (BBFC). Membership was ten shillings per year and gave members access to the films of a more adult nature which were becoming more prevalent in European and American cinema. Whereas these films were often cut for public exhibition at the request of the BBFC or the Local Authority, at the Compton Cinema Club they could be screened completely uncut. The opening night saw a screening of *Private Property* (Stevens, 1960),[2] which had already been refused a certificate by the BBFC. Other early printed adverts for the club list films such as an uncut print of the naturist documentary *Travelling Light* (Keatering, 1960), which had been cut to receive an 'A' certificate for general release, and *Striptease de Paris* (also known as *Mademoiselle Strip-tease*, Foucaud, 1957), which was eventually cut in 1962 to also receive an 'A' for UK distribution.[3]

It was not long before Klinger and Tenser realised that they could make a lot more money by distributing films to other cinemas, and could also make their own films in order to ensure a constant supply of new product. Compton Film Distributors began initially to circulate the cut versions of films which had already been screened in their cinema club. Compton-Cameo was formed in October 1960 to start making films ('The Career', Michael Klinger Papers 2010), which initially mimicked some of the European and American exploitation films they were already familiar with. Their first production was the nudist film *Naked – As Nature Intended* (Marks, 1961), a faux-documentary extolling the health benefits of nudism, starring glamour model Pamela Green. Wishing to make slightly more mainstream films, Compton-Tekli[4] was then formed, through which they produced their first fully-fledged feature film *That Kind of Girl* (O'Hara, 1963). It was a warning to young women about the dangers of venereal disease and featured lengthy scenes of medical professionals explaining the disastrous results of casual relationships. These first two films produced by Klinger and Tenser relied on the tried and tested formula of dressing up exploitation themes as education; methods which, as documented by Eric Schaefer (1999), were being used in America twenty years earlier for films such as *Mom and Dad* (Beaudine, 1945) and *Child Bride* (Revier, 1938). This formula would be heavily leant on again for their next production, *The Yellow Teddybears*.

The writer of *That Kind of Girl*, Robert Hartford-Davis, was promoted to director-producer for this next film, from a story suggestion from Tony Tenser. Initially titled 'The Yellow Golliwog', it was based on an account in the national press of schoolgirls who took to wearing yellow metal 'Gollywog' badges (of the type that customers could collect by saving labels from jars of Robertson's jam) to signify that they had lost their virginity. This news story came from comments made at a meeting of the British Medical Council in July 1961, and was reported to have occurred at a school in the West Country. It was greeted with an element of outrage in some newspapers. The *Daily Mirror* headline read, 'Their Badge of Shame', and quoted Dr Ronald Gibson of the British Medical Association as admitting collective responsibility as well as calling for harsher punishment:

> The loss of moral discipline sweeping the country is something for which we, as doctors and as responsible members of the community, must take our share of blame. What we need now is a little intelligent psychiatry and a lot of common sense. We want to return to the rod, the pole and the birch – properly administered. (Gibson 1961a: 20)

When questioned later by the press he gave his opinion: 'I believe that most girls do not want intercourse outside marriage', and that children should be taught about sex from the age of eleven (Gibson 1961a: 20).

Other newspapers treated the story as more of a curiosity: *The Times* quoted the opinions of real school pupils originally printed in *Sixth Form Opinion*, a magazine reportedly edited by a seventeen-year-old girl from Bedales School in Hampshire. One girl had written: 'Yellow golliwogs do not necessarily mean that the wearer has had an affair; only that, not wishing to seem different, the wearer wished other people to believe them unchaste.' One boy added, with a surprisingly mature outlook:

> A girl's virginity is hers to bestow on whom she chooses and there should be no moral standard interfering with her liberty of choice . . . A man should, if anything, be flattered that an unchaste girl should finally choose to spend the rest of her days with him. He should not be jealous of her past lovers for, if a couple are in love, intercourse is the height and climax of mutual understanding. ('Sixth Form' 1963: 5)

These views were simply described by *The Times* as 'Outspoken' (ibid.: 5).

Although no evidence was ever found to support the veracity of the original story, the concept of the 'Yellow Golliwogs' resonated with wider public fears around pre-marital sex and teenage behaviour. Together with pop music, 'X'-rated films and the availability of the contraceptive pill, there was a great deal of concern about the morality of the younger generation. In 1961, a seventy-three-year-old judge stated at a trial involving two nineteen-year-old men and two girls of fourteen that 'Young people seem to attach as much importance to the act of sexual intercourse as they do to ordering an iced lolly' ('Sex' 1961: 7). The idea of schoolgirls openly wearing their sexual experience on their uniforms with pride was a gift to any filmmaker who might be brave enough to accept it.

The news story was developed into a script by Derek and Donald Ford,[5] and follows a schoolgirl called Linda (Annette Whiteley) who has recently discovered she is pregnant by the school window cleaner and part-time singer, Kinky (Iain Gregory). He tries unsuccessfully to find some pills she may be able to take, and when that does not work she finds help from an older woman, June (Jill Adams), who is actually a prostitute. Linda will have to pay for her abortion by becoming a prostitute herself. Her father (Victor Brooks) catches her in June's flat before the abortion is carried out and is furious when he learns the truth. His main reaction is one of concern for his own public reputation rather than for the welfare of his daughter. Indeed, the reaction of most of the older generation depicted in the film is similarly unfair towards the girls, who think of their parents as 'Squares'. Teacher Miss Mason (Jacqueline Ellis) is the only one who is prepared to see things from their point of view, and because of this she is at odds with the school governors and is forced to resign. Linda meanwhile runs away from home and hitches a lift to London with a lorry driver, to an uncertain future. Before leaving with him she is warned by an older woman: 'Do you think you can lose yourself in London? Listen baby, THEY lose you. Go home. I wish to God I had.'

The script is generally sympathetic in tone to the viewpoint of the schoolgirls, and condemns the outdated attitudes of parents and authority figures, the latter represented by the school governors. It contains dialogue which contributes to the notion that the filmmakers are genuinely attempting to address a social problem, most notably when Miss Mason confronts the girls, having learned the awful truth about the badges:

> Linda – It's our parents. They don't understand us. Squares.
> Miss Mason – I suppose by your definition I'm square. I knew what I was doing. I wasn't sixteen. I didn't have to pin a badge on afterwards to prove it really happened. You see, it meant something to me.
> Linda – You're just like the rest of them. When you do it it's alright, but if we do it, it's dirty!

Miss Mason becomes involved in discussions with the school board about the problem, but when they find out that she has been talking to the girls about her own sex life she is fired. Her pleas for understanding towards this young generation fall on old deaf ears.

When the story outline was first submitted to the BBFC, as was common practice at that time, there were concerns, even then, over the use of the word 'Golliwog' in the title. Tony Tenser recalled that he was called in to see John Trevelyan:

> Trevelyan was a nice guy and we got on very well but he said he was not happy with the title. He thought it could be racist . . . so I said what if we change it to 'The Yellow Teddybears', which is even better than Golliwogs anyway, and he said it was fine. (Hamilton 2005: 25)

Another letter exists in the BBFC file from John Trevelyan to the director Robert Hartford-Davies, where he writes, 'I was much reassured by our conversation yesterday. Please bear in mind the point that I made about the title. There is no immediate hurry to settle this.'[6] Another note states that on 25 March BBFC President Baron Morison of Lambeth joined a discussion with John Trevelyan, Tony Tenser, Michael Klinger and Lord Kimberley on the 'Yellow Golliwog' title: 'After some discussion Mr. Tenser agreed that the title be changed to "The Yellow Teddy Bear".'[7] Lord Kimberley appears to have been involved through his PR company, and he then wrote the following proposed press statement which allowed Compton-Tekli to take credit for the name change:

> The Producers of Tekli Animated Motion Picture production 'THE YELLOW GOLLIWOG' announce that the title has been changed to 'THE YELLOW TEDDYBEARS'. The reason is that they do not wish to embarrass anybody associated with the B.M.A. disclosures in July 1961 that certain schoolgirls were proudly displaying a yellow golliwog badge on their jackets to show they had lost their virginity.[8]

A handwritten message written on the back of the BBFC document goes on to state: 'The film, which will show the dangers of such practices, is not based on any actual incident.'[9]

This apparent contradiction in the archival material suggests that the title change was on the insistence of the BBFC, something which Compton-Tekli were not publicly willing to admit. Despite the title change a self-referential line of dialogue was retained in the script where two teachers in the showers at a swimming gala joke about the yellow teddybears, and one says, 'Girls will start wearing golliwogs next, and it could even get in the papers!'

The script had been submitted to the BBFC prior to production, and one of the notes reads that regarding the girls:

> They are described as 'about sixteen'. Nothing in the script indicates that any of the 'golliwogs' are under the age of consent, but they had better not look it, either. We have enough on our plate here, without that sort of criminal offence.[10]

Annette Whiteley, who played Linda, the pregnant schoolgirl at the heart of the drama, was seventeen at the time:

> I don't know why I was cast like this, [a promiscuous schoolgirl] because I was totally innocent. I was the right age. I was big-busted and [had] a tiny little waist. They had to bind my boobs, I remember that! They didn't want me to be quite as busty as I was. They bound my boobs and put the school shirt on.[11]

It may have alarmed the BBFC to know that although Annette Whiteley was seventeen, one of the uncredited schoolgirls in the classroom scenes, Gaynor Martine, confirmed to me that she was only fifteen.[12] It is possible that others were under sixteen too. The first examiner to read the script noted that, 'I think this important script (from the point of view of precedent) should be read by a number of people if time allows. It is bound to cause a good deal of head-scratching, and better now than later.'[13] Consequently it was reviewed by several others.

The script was also sent by Derek Ford to The National Council for the Unmarried Mother and Child,[14] who responded enthusiastically:

> We think it presents a true and vivid picture of the circumstances that lie behind many of the cases in which our help is sought. No doubt the story will shock a great many people who are unaware that some young people can and do behave like this. [The film] underlines the necessity for action if the next generation of school girls and school boys are to acquire a balanced view of sexual behaviour.[15]

Sir Ronald Gould, General Secretary of the National Union of Teachers, also read it and reported: 'I feel that this script represents an entirely laudable attempt to present in vivid dramatic terms a problem of very great social importance, and one about which the Union itself has, at least indirectly, expressed very great concern.'[16] He closes the letter with one note of concern: 'My view is that the effect would have been greatly improved if the presentation had been a little less sensational.'[17] He does not elaborate as to which elements he was referring to.

The script went through several changes following the detailed feedback from the BBFC. The original contained a scene in a brothel and made it very clear that Linda, the schoolgirl at the heart of the drama, becomes a prostitute to earn the money to pay for the costs of her abortion, and this was too specific for the BBFC who preferred that just a suggestion of this inevitable outcome remain. Other details regarding this important element of the story were highlighted as problematic before the script was finally approved. As Trevelyan explained to Robert Hartford-Davies:

> We are very worried about the party scenes . . . it should not turn into a debauch, there should not be any strip games, and there should not be any monetary transactions with June Wilson which pin-point the gathering as a recruiting ground for professional prostitutes. I am still nervous that the 'sensational' elements in this story may be over done. I am sure that if they are, you will run into trouble with us, and I think it most unlikely that any film with this kind of thing in it, whatever its good intentions, will meet with approval, and therefore the support of the National Union of Teachers and British Medical Council, etc.[18]

The script was adjusted as requested, and the finished film received an 'X' certificate following further requests. Specific cuts were required to dialogue ('The rhyme recited by Kinky is unacceptable') and visuals ('At the opening of the scene in the shower baths at the swimming pool the girls' bodies are clearly visible through the slightly obscured glass'), although the real issues were with the lengthy party scenes:

> Virtually the whole of the party sequences should be removed. The most that we can allow is to see the people concerned sitting around the place and drinking . . . The party games should entirely be removed and the total effect of the party can be no more than one of necking and drinking.[19]

Trevelyan justifies their excision with the point that this material 'is of a "sensational" nature which is liable to destroy any claim that this film deals seriously with an important medical problem'.[20] As will be seen later, Compton further damaged this credibility at the film's premiere.

The schoolgirls involved in the sexually charged scenes at the party do look older than their sixth form status would suggest.[21] Promotional imagery does suggest that a 'hotter' version of the party scene was shot, most likely for export but possibly for showing in the Compton Cinema Club. Stills used in the press book, and on the poster itself, feature the character Carol (Caron Gardner) first wearing a blindfold surrounded by eager-looking men, and then stripped down to her bra during a party game. In the film itself we see that she has already removed clothing, but this is only shot from the shoulders up. Later in the party whilst Pat (Georgina Patterson) is helping her boyfriend Mike (Doug Sheldon) after he has passed out in a bedroom, a couple burst in. In the film the girl is fully dressed, but a still which was used in the press book features the same couple, only this time she is semi-naked. Annette Whiteley also recalled a scene which was not in the final version:

> There was a scene of me in a slip when I first know I'm pregnant, and I'm in the bedroom and my parents are downstairs. I'm alone in my bedroom and I'm lit, I was completely covered, it was a full-length slip, but I'm standing in front of the mirror and I'm holding the slip down to see, I'm looking at my pregnant self, but the censors wouldn't have it because I was in a slip.[22]

If this scene was shot there is no mention of it in the BBFC documentation, suggesting that Hartford-Davies removed it himself before submission, or that it was also intended only for an overseas version.

It was common practice then to shoot sequences that would not pass the BBFC's requirements but would enable a wider distribution. Another example of this practice can be found in the Compton-Tekli production of *The Pleasure Girls* (O'Hara, 1965), in a party scene where a woman poses topless at an artist's party. In the UK version she is holding a sheet over herself, whereas in the export version she is topless. Betraying the low-budget limitations, the soundtrack is identical in both, revealing that the UK version was shot with picture only.

When the final revisions had been made and the film was viewed at the BBFC, it was decided that 'The sensationalism has been largely, if not wholly, removed.'²³ John Trevelyan wrote to the director again, this time to 'Express my appreciation of the skilful way in which you have made these cuts. We all felt that the removal of this material has greatly improved the film.'²⁴ Not entirely satisfied, however, he went on to request that further cuts might be made to make Linda's father seem less concerned about his own reputation than his daughter's well-being. 'This might give thoughtless teenagers the idea that parents in general do not want to help their children when they are in difficulties, and that parents are responsible for any folly that the young commit.'²⁵ Hartford-Davies immediately replied to explain:

> These parents are not typical, but in the realms of the story are necessary to show the difference between the parents of children who are needed and those who are unloved and who want the feeling of security. Therefore, they gather round them other youngsters to do the same type of offence, so that there is a sense of belonging in the gang.²⁶

This justification seemed to satisfy the BBFC and the film received the 'X' certificate without further interference.

Although the film was made to exploit the 'ripped from the headlines' 'X'-rated potential the story held, Compton initially marketed *The Yellow Teddybears* as something which could help encourage a healthy public discussion of teenage sexuality. This is where the aforementioned sex/altruism binary becomes particularly relevant. Producer Michael Klinger explained to the press that 'This is a serious problem among adolescents. We made the film with complete integrity and are glad that it may be used as a valuable lesson for young people' (Klinger 1963: 1). The national release was planned for December 1963, and prior to this, screenings of *The Yellow Teddybears* were held with health and family planning experts, alongside star Annette Whiteley, which naturally received national publicity.

Dr Alford, former medial officer for the Ministry of Education, congratulated the filmmakers after a screening in London and stated:

> The trouble these days is that emotional development does not take place at the same time as physiological development. The average age of maturity of girls these days is about 13. I believe the average parent is unable to face up to this problem. I think this film is too late, dealing with the problems of 16-year-old girls. Sex information should start at home at the age of 10. ('Teach Sex' 1963: 3)

At this same screening, which included a discussion panel, Annette Whiteley commented that 'One of the main problems is getting teenagers and adults to talk freely in the same room about these problems' (Whiteley 1963: 15).

A retired headmistress explained that 'The 13- and 14-year-olds are far more anxious about this because they are worried about not being in the swim. They may think that promiscuity is the done thing' ('Other Areas' 1963: 7). Others at the screening were slightly concerned that the film was being advertised with 'Misleading posters' and, in an uncanny prediction, '[It] was likely to be shown with other, less reputable "X" certificate films' (ibid.)

Following the publicity generated by this event a group of around eighty sixth form girls from six different Birmingham schools were invited to see the film at the Jacey-owned Cinephone on Bristol Street in the centre of Birmingham. Having been vetted by a headmistress, biology teachers and a Health Education doctor, the film was ruled suitable for the girls to see ('X Film' 1963: 1). Reported in the press as a social experiment, the screening was widely covered in both the local and national newspapers in a positive light. *The Birmingham Post* quoted the cinema owners, most likely someone from the Jacey group, as stating, 'The feeling of the teachers earlier this week seemed in favour of the film being seen by older pupils as a ground for discussion' ('Schoolgirls' 1963: 5).

As well as watching *The Yellow Teddybears*, the sixth form girls were invited to talk about such issues with a doctor, a marriage guidance counsellor, a vicar, a headmistress and Annette Whiteley, who now admits that the girls were more interested to talk to her about what it was like to be in films than to talk about sex.[27] As reported in the *Daily Mirror*, the girls were first asked to raise their hands if they had been horrified or shocked by what they had seen, and no hands were raised. Echoing the sentiment offered by one of the schoolgirls in the film, girls were quoted as stating that their own parents did not know how to talk to them about sex: 'They can't express themselves in the right language and therefore they leave the situation alone.' One girl stated that 'Boys should be made to see films like this so it can be driven home to them how easy it is to get a girl into trouble, and what a terrible thing it is for the girl.' Another said, 'Parents and teachers should realise that they should never tell us NOT to do something, because it only gives us an incentive to do it.' At the end of the discussion an unnamed doctor told the audience, 'Go back to your schools and discuss this experiment with your teachers. Talk to your parents about it too. We hope it will make things easier for you' (Hill 1963:7). A Jacey spokesman was quoted as suggesting that local welfare and education services would be approached around the country, wherever the film was playing ('Other Areas' 1963: 7).

The day after the screening in Birmingham both local and national newspapers had a field day with their headlines:

> 'SHOCKED? NOT US, SAY GIRLS: Sixth-formers see the Teddy Bear sex badge film' (Hill 1963: 7)
> 'GIVE TALKS ON SEX TO THE UNDER TENS: Why not? asks a top doctor' ('Give Talks' 1963: 5)

'GIRLS TOLD "SEE THIS SEX FILM"'[28]
'X FILM SHOW FOR THE SIXTH FORM GIRLS' ('X Film' 1963: 1)
'SCHOOLGIRLS HAVE X-FILM LESSON AT CINEMA'[29]

In Birmingham, the doctor who had arranged the screening told reporters: 'In discussions [the schoolgirls] had revealed a very moral attitude to sexual problems, and standards more Victorian than most of their elders.' He also thought that 'Young people who were deviant were more likely to be impressed by these standards if they heard them expressed by others of their own age than by adults whom they suspected of being critical.'[30] The BBFC's John Trevelyan sought a report from the *Birmingham Evening Mail*, so the editor sent a copy of the article and commented, 'It turned out very well and may have been unique – it might be useful for you to refer to on some future occasion.'[31]

Before these special screenings had occurred an official premiere of *The Yellow Teddybears* had been held on Thursday, 11 July 1963 at the Jacey-owned Cinephone on Oxford Street. John Cohen, grandson of the founder of the Jacey group, worked with Tony Tenser to create all the displays and attended the event to represent the Jacey company.[32] Also representing them was Aisha Ahmed, otherwise known as Miss Jacey, who had formerly been employed in

Figure 9.1 Displays at the premiere of *The Yellow Teddybears* at the Cinephone on Oxford Street, London, 11 July 1963. (Source: Used with the permission of Annette Conder-Prill.)

the company's Birmingham head office. Crowds gathered outside to see the stars of the movie, including the pop band David and the Embers who featured in the film and were playing in the foyer. Perhaps the main surprise of the night was the appearance of Robert Hartford-Davies's personal friend Robert Mitchum, who was in the UK shooting *Man in the Middle* (Hamilton, 1964) at Elstree Studios. That a Hollywood A-lister would be at the premiere of a low-budget exploitation film attests to the showmanship powers of Compton, and as the photos from the night show, the opportunity to meet pretty girls and enjoy free drinks was surely an attractive proposition for Mitchum ('Yellow' 1963: 11). When he asked for a scotch and soda, Miss Jacey had to break the news that they were out of soda, to which he replied, 'Just spit in it doll.'[33]

The premiere clearly represented the other side of the sex/altruism binary, where the emphasis was about as far from the serious social problem angle as possible. True to form Compton acquired dancers, most likely through Michael Klinger's contacts in the Soho club scene, and dressed them as schoolgirls to add some illicit sex appeal to the evening. Klinger would often secure the services of dancing girls and strippers to liven up Compton's film premieres. At the gala screening of *London in the Raw* (Miller, 1964) the following year he paid Windmill Girls Valerie and Marion Mitchell to appear in topless dresses outside the cinema, where they were promptly arrested.[34]

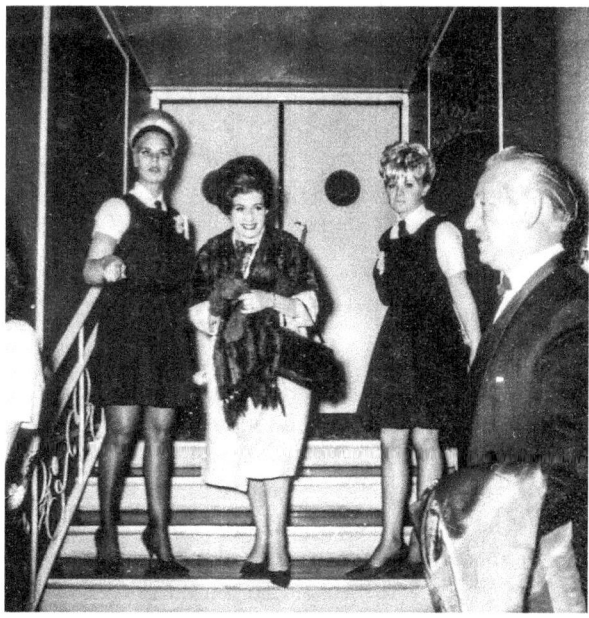

Figure 9.2 Dancers dressed as schoolgirls at the premiere of *The Yellow Teddybears*, 11 July 1963. (Source: Used with the permission of Annette Conder-Prill.)

The Yellow Teddybears was a commercial success for Compton when it was finally released in public cinemas in December 1963, despite critics describing the film as 'Inadequate' (Wilson 1963: 3), and 'Silly, sordid and splendidly ludicrous' ('Review' 1963: 122), with 'the direction hit[ting] a new low' (ibid.). The financial returns demonstrated to Compton that low-budget 'X' certificate films with an exploitative angle could make a healthy profit, and this encouraged them to focus even more on production. Earlier concerns about the film being shown with other, less reputable 'X' certificate films proved to be well founded, however. *The Yellow Teddybears* went out on a double bill with the Compton-produced Sherlock Holmes meets Jack the Ripper thriller *A Study in Terror* (Hill, 1964), and was still showing two years later in London and Birmingham, amongst other places, on a bill with *London in the Raw* or the Italian necrophilia drama *The Terror of Dr. Hichcock* (Freda, 1962).

In April 1964 a full-page ad was taken out in the trade publication *Daily Cinema* in the style of a letter. The headline reads: '*The Yellow Teddybears* Speaks for Itself 1000 Times!' In this open letter to Brian Millwood, Director of Sales Tony Tenser wrote:

> As Producer of 'THE YELLOW TEDDYBEARS', I am delighted to see on my desk the ONE THOUSANDTH contract for this film. This is an unprecedented achievement in the annals of film distribution in the United Kingdom for a film which has been sold as a completely Independent release, and it is a pattern of selling of which every Producer would be proud. (Tenser 1964)

Referencing upcoming films *Saturday Night Out* (Hartford-Davies, 1964), *London in the Raw* and *The Black Torment* (Hartford-Davies, 1964), he closes: 'You will, I know, be pleased to convey this news to your 1000 happy and satisfied customers who have adopted the slogan COUNT ON COMPTON!' (ibid.).

The by-line, 'Play it again while it's still very hot!' (ibid.), is another reminder that the 'altruism' element of the sex/altruism binary had been completely forgotten by this point. This aspect is rammed home further when one regards the advertising campaign in America, where the film was retitled *The Thrill Seekers* by the Topaz Film Corporation (the same company who handled *Fire Maidens from Outer Space*, Enfield, 1956).[35] The main poster image is a half-dressed Carol Gardner, with the tagline 'Teenage school dolls . . . what they learned isn't on any report card!'

As per Eric Schaefer's history of exploitation cinema in America, this idea of claiming films as performing a public service is nothing new, but this is one of the only examples of the sex/altruism binary at work in Britain to this extent. Despite the claim by the Jacey spokesman that health and education services would be contacted wherever the film was playing, I have not found any evidence to support that happening again beyond the two screenings documented here. Therefore, the screening of *The Yellow Teddybears* to Birmingham schoolgirls represents something of a unique event in the history of British cinema audiences, and demonstrates the marketing skills that independent production companies like Compton would employ to stay well ahead of the competition in the 1960s.

As the decade progressed, the desire to project an element of public service in their filmmaking slipped away as censorship standards adjusted and their product became more focused on sex and horror. In 1966 Tony Tenser and Michael Klinger went their separate ways, the latter to produce and the former to develop Tigon, a production company that would continue to push at the boundaries of acceptability. Occasionally Tenser did still operate under the guise of the sex/altruism binary when producing or distributing material such as the documentary *Love in Our Time* (Allan, 1968) or the educational film *Sex, Love and Marriage* (Grant, 1972), with one eye on profits and the other on making sure the public was being kept fully abreast of the ever-changing sexual climate of the UK.

The methodology employed in this chapter has demonstrated that combining interviews with archival research offers new understanding, even if it also shows that sometimes history can be contradictory. Memory is a slippery thing, yet its inclusion adds colour in a way that can be sorely lacking in archival research alone. Speaking to people who were there can raise questions, present unique insight, and in some cases prove a long-held suspicion; for instance, I had heard the legend that nightclub dancers were dressed as schoolgirls at the premiere for *The Yellow Teddybears*, but a visit to Annette Whiteley's home to look at old photos provided concrete evidence. Access to the archive of John Cohen of the Jacey cinema chain came about through interviewing him as part of a bigger project, and this was vital in providing access to newspaper clippings kept in a family scrapbook that could have otherwise been very difficult to find in commercially available archives. His memories of the premiere of *The Yellow Teddybears*, plus being able to put me in touch with Miss Jacey, provided additional evidence which was able to support my argument of this film being located in this sex/altruism binary position. I feel that in this particular case study, my methodology has enabled a unique look at an otherwise neglected exploitation film yet to be reclaimed and granted cultural relevance by the gatekeepers of British film history, whilst also providing additional insight into the attitudes held by the public and the establishment towards teenagers and sexual relationships in the culturally turbulent early years of the 1960s.

Notes

1. *Isle of Levant* (*Lockender Süden*, 1957, Werner Kunz, Switzerland: Werner Kunz) is an early example. It was distributed by Miracle Films and received an 'A' certificate from the BBFC in 1958 following cuts.
2. As detailed in an undated Compton Cinema ad (Hamilton 2005: 13).

3. Undated Compton Cinema ad, ibid.: 12. Certificate information from BBFC database.
4. Tekli being a contraction of Tenser and Klinger.
5. Brothers who wrote together many times, including other films for Compton in the 1960s. Derek went on to direct in the 1970s, mostly sex comedies. Tony Tenser claimed to John Trevelyan that Donald Ford was an ex-Chairman of the Children's Committee of the London County Council (BBFC Archive, *The Yellow Teddybears* file, letter dated 29 January 1963).
6. BBFC Archive, *The Yellow Teddybears* file, letter to Robert Hartford-Davies from John Trevelyan, 8 March 1963.
7. BBFC Archive, *The Yellow Teddybears* file, 'Note – The Yellow Teddy Bear', 25 March 1963. It appears that originally 'Teddy Bear' was to be two separate words, and it is referred to as such in many of the BBFC documents.
8. BBFC Archive, *The Yellow Teddybears* file, Statement Proposal by Company, 26 March 1963.
9. Ibid.
10. BBFC Archive, *The Yellow Teddybears* file, script reader's report, 6 February 1963.
11. Interview with Annette Whiteley by the author, 7 November 2016.
12. Email correspondence with Gaynor Martine, 14 May 2019. She recalls nothing about the film other than being in love with Iain Gregory. Given its 'X' certificate, she did not see the film on its release.
13. BBFC Archive, *The Yellow Teddybears* file, script reader's report, 31 January 1963.
14. Founded in 1918, now better known as *Gingerbread*.
15. BBFC Archive, *The Yellow Teddybears* file, letter to Derek Ford from Margaret Bramall, 25 March 1963.
16. BBFC Archive, *The Yellow Teddybears* file, undated letter.
17. Ibid.
18. BBFC Archive, *The Yellow Teddybears* file, letter to Robert Hartford-Davies from John Trevelyan, 11 March 1963.
19. All extracts taken from BBFC Archive, *The Yellow Teddybears* file, letter to Robert Hartford-Davies (Dear Bob) from John Trevelyan, undated.
20. Ibid.
21. In personal correspondence with Caron Gardner, 12 October 2016, she confirmed that she was twenty-one at the time of filming. She told me that most of the girls came from the Corona Stage School, and Caron was a little older than the others so only appeared in the party scene, and not in the school. Despite this her character appears to know the other girls, suggesting that she is a former pupil. As previously mentioned, Gaynor Martine was fifteen at the time of shooting, but it is not clear if she is in the party scene.
22. Interview with Annette Whiteley by the author, 7 November 2016.
23. BBFC Archive, *The Yellow Teddybears* file, censor note, 4 June 1963.
24. BBFC Archive, *The Yellow Teddybears* file, letter to Robert Hartford-Davies from John Trevelyan, 2 July 1963.
25. Ibid.
26. BBFC Archive, *The Yellow Teddybears* file, letter to John Trevelyan from Robert Hartford-Davies, 3 July 1963.
27. Interview with Annette Whiteley by the author, 7 November 2016.

28. Source unknown, taken from clipping in the Jacey family archive, available at <https://www.jncohen.net> (last accessed 19 May 2021).
29. Source unknown, taken from clipping in Jacey family archive, available at <https://www.jncohen.net> (last accessed 19 May 2021).
30. Ibid.
31. BBFC Archive, *The Yellow Teddybears* file, letter from Anthony Steele to John Trevelyan, 20 November 1963.
32. Interview with John Cohen by the author, 18 July 2015.
33. Interview with Aisha Wills née Ahmed by the author, 22 July 2015.
34. Marion Mitchell became better known as Janie Jones, and enjoyed a brief pop career before serving a lengthy prison sentence for prostitution offences, where she befriended Myra Hindley.
35. The film was also known in some territories as *Gutter Girls*.

BIBLIOGRAPHY

'The Career of Michael Klinger – an Overview' (2010), University of the West of England. <http://michaelklingerpapers.uwe.ac.uk/biography.htm> (last accessed 19 May 2021).
'The One Topic for Bad Girls Says Women Remand Home Chief' (1961), *Daily Mirror*, 1 November, p. 7.
Review: *The Yellow Teddybears*' (1963), *Monthly Film Bulletin*, August, p. 122.
'Other Areas May Copy Teenage Sex Film Experiment' (1963), *Birmingham Post*, 13 December, p. 7.
'Schoolgirls to See "X" Film' (1963), *Birmingham Post*, 14 November, p. 5.
'Sixth Form Views on Chastity' (1963), *The Times*, 18 February, p. 5.
'Teach Sex Facts at Ten Says Doctor' (1963), *Daily Mail*, 13 December, p. 3.
'"Yellow Teddybears" Premiere' (1963), *Kinematograph Weekly*, 18 July, p. 11.
Gibson, Ronald (1961b), in 'Sex and the Teenagers', *Daily Mirror*, 1 November, p. 7.
Gibson, Ronald (1961a), in 'Their Badge of Shame', *Daily Mirror*, 18 July, p. 20.
Hamilton, John (2005), *Beasts in the Cellar: The Exploitation Film Career of Tony Tenser*. Godalming: FAB Press.
Hill, Ray (1963), 'Shocked? Not Us, Say Girls', Ray Hill, *Daily Mirror*, 16 November, p. 7.
Klinger, Michael (1963), in 'X Film Show for the Sixth Form Girls', *Daily Mail*, 14 November, p. 1.
Mazdon, Lucy and Catherine Wheatley (2013), *French Film in Britain: Sex, Art and Cinephilia*. Oxford: Berghahn.
Sarris, Andrew (1999), 'Summer Films: International; Why the Foreign Film Has Lost its Cachet', *New York Times*, 2 May.
Schaefer, Eric (1999), *Bold! Daring! Shocking! True! A History of Exploitation Films, 1919–1959*. Durham, NC: Duke University Press.
Tenser, Tony (1964), in '*The Yellow Teddybears* Speaks for Itself 1000 TIMES!', *Daily Cinema*, 1 April.
Whiteley, Annette (1963), in 'Give Talks on Sex to the Under Tens', *Daily Mirror*, 13 December, p. 15.
Wilson, Cecil (1963), 'Film', *Daily Mail*, 10 July, p. 3.

PART IV

HOME VIEWING CONTEXTS AND AUDIENCE MEMORIES

10. ARCHIVES, SOURCES AND MEMORIES FOR A HISTORY OF EARLY ITALIAN TV AUDIENCES

Damiano Garofalo and Cecilia Penati

This chapter aims to reflect the historical research on early Italian television, with a specific focus on the audience's point of view.[1] With the term 'early' we refer here to the first decade following the beginning of regular programming, in January 1954 (Grasso 2004). This chapter stems from extensive research on Italian early audiences carried out independently by the two authors, who afterwards detected many intersections and common aspects. The issue of archives and audiences' memories will be approached from two different perspectives: on the one hand, the social and historical trajectories of early TV domestication (Silverstone 1994); on the other hand, the political configuration of the first viewers, especially in the working and middle classes. Two main methodologies were used by the authors to investigate early Italian audiences and represent the framework of this chapter. Firstly, oral history and ethnography as crucial tools to collect private memories of the first TV viewers. Secondly, the analysis of printed sources: both private accounts of viewers' experiences during that first stage (outlined in diaries and letters), and representations of spectatorship in the popular press and advertisements. With this methodology, the chapter discusses images and practices of the early TV audience in Italy in the mid-1950s.

This chapter presents the empirical research carried out by the two authors as a means of highlighting some methodological issues related to TV history and some characteristics of the Italian TV studies landscape. Our common premise was the urge to fill a gap: for a long time, the Italian academic debate largely neglected a history of early TV audiences, their practices, and the meanings conferred on the medium in its early stage. As opposed to historiographies on other media, in particular regarding cinema where a history of audiences, spectators and media-goers has always been a crucial field of study and research, for Italian television this area of inquiry is quite a recent development (Monteleone 2003; Anania 2004; Grasso 2013; Penati 2013; Piazzoni 2014).

In a recent account of the history of Italian methodologies in television studies, Massimo Scaglioni (2017) has pointed out how a nation-specific approach to this tradition of studies, originally established in the British context, has actually existed since the 1980s and has revolved around various areas of interest spread through various branches. Specifically, since the establishment and the international diffusion of the 'school' of *audience studies* in the 1990s, much research has been conducted in Italy on contemporary audiences, and their behaviours and habits, carried out using various field techniques (starting from the pioneering research led by Francesco Casetti, *L'ospite fisso*, 1995). But when we look back at the time when this old media was new, few and sporadic contributions stand out. Moreover, a television studies-specific approach to early TV audiences is new: crossovers with other disciplines, interestingly, have been much more common. Specifically, this includes studies of contemporary history and general sociology (Foot 2015; Forgacs and Gundle 2007), which have largely shaped our knowledge about the first audiences of the medium. Also, the first proper study on the Italian TV audience stemmed from a 'social experiment' conducted in the 1950s by psychologist Lidia De Rita among the rural population of Lucania (Basilicata), in southern Italy, and its reception of television (De Rita 1964).

In Italy, the historiography of early and Italian television *tout court* (a still limited field, with lots of research paths in need of development) has mainly revolved around two branches, barely focusing on audiences with specific studies. The first branch has considered TV as an 'institution', with some key studies dating back to the 1970s and 1990s and focusing on the governance of RAI (the Italian public service broadcaster that held a monopoly in the 1950s) (Chiarenza 2002). This was a result of the specificity of the Italian television system: the strong, and sometimes twisted, connection between television and politics, peculiar to the southern European television systems (Bourdon 2011), has pushed historiography towards a focus on researching the management, political affiliations, policies and legislation, and so on, of television as an institution.

For this research path, archival, printed documents – what we can call *traditional sources*, such as legal documents, internal publications, surveys, reports on ratings, memos – were the almost exclusive tools of research. We have to point out that, as opposed to other countries (such as France, with the INA), Italy does not have a proper national, systematic archive devoted to public television which is fully accessible to researchers. Documents are preserved quite randomly in various corporate offices and buildings; even a valuable treasure such as the surveys of Servizio Opinioni has been scarcely considered by academic debate due to a lack of access to the documents. Servizio Opinioni was Rai's internal department committed to tracking viewers' feedback and opinions on its programming, schedules, genres and TV personalities. Lacking a system of audience measurement, Servizio Opinioni was the first attempt to probe audience tastes with a quantitative approach based mainly on interviews and surveys.

Progressively, Italian TV historiography has started to take into account programmes, genres and TV personalities while struggling with the very poor state of preservation of the early RAI programmes. This poor state of preservation stems from two principal issues: the first is that most of the early programmes were broadcast live and before Ampex recording technology was widely available; thus, they were never recorded on a physical intermediary (Barra and Penati 2013). The second matter relates to the specificity of TV archival practices in Italy: lacking a national 'independent' audiovisual archive, Teche Rai, which is the PBS in-house audiovisual archive, has always been used more as an industrial tool (a gold mine of precious footage, very useful for producing TV programmes such as documentaries and even variety shows) than as an instrument open to researchers. Very few examples of early television programmes have been saved and it took a while before academic historiography started to take them into account, relying on 'secondary' sources (reviews and articles in national journals) to piece together a history of genres and styles.

Unconventional Archives

According to the most recent direction in international television studies, however, growing importance has been attached to television as a complex object whose history cannot be confined within the borders of institutional organisations or within the limits of audiovisual texts. According to Amanda Lotz and Jonathan Gray, one has to consider its broader context, including production and audiences, to better contribute to building a 'cultural history of the medium' (2012: 121). In order to do this, the material conditions of writing history have undoubtedly changed, and a methodological rethink of what is admissible as a historical source is nowadays more and more mandatory. Also necessary is a change in the conceptualisation of *what is* the history of television, so a change in how we think about archives is needed. By extending the traditional Italian way of using archives mainly as sources for industry, we think that is possible to shed more light on how early Italian television was consumed, beyond the fixed and somehow stereotyped model of 'paleo-television'. This definition was proposed by Umberto Eco (1983) to summarise RAI's main features during the age of its monopoly, such as the pedagogic mission, the scarcity of programming, and the paternalistic approach of the first executives towards the broadly illiterate TV audience.

The use of more unconventional archives represents a key resource to help shed light on the social and cultural history of the first years of television in Italy. The word 'unconventional' is used here to mark a strong difference from some traditional 'top-down' archives which preserve only videos and printed documents. How can we piece together this unconventional archive? What are the main issues at stake? What types of source can be used to shape this unconventional archive in order to deal with the archaeological phase of the medium? In addition to traditional sources (corporate documents, TV shows), two other types of source that are more 'bottom-up' and deal with the audience's perspective must be considered. This is a major methodological shift in the historical research of the medium which raises a number of issues. How can these sources be properly collected and preserved? How do they challenge the classical idea of an archive as a space (material or immaterial) with specific boundaries, implementing instead the idea of a 'diffused archive'? How can they have a dialogue with other archives (private collections, funds, and so on)? How can singular stories be treated as representative of a 'general', common history?

The Role of Popular Media

The first type of unconventional source deals with the role of *popular culture* as a sort of diffused archive that collects, also unintentionally, the ways of interpreting and conceptualising television, crystallised in the paratexts (Gray 2010) of the television medium produced by other popular media (for example, in film, women's magazines and advertisements). Studying the arrival of television in the home in the 1950s, one begins to understand the valuable role of other popular media in collecting evidence on how television was interpreted and described and also in providing instructions to the audience on how to interact with television (Spigel 1992). For example, gender was a crucial issue in addressing the process of incorporating television into the home: in weekly women's magazines (*Grazia* and *Annabella*)[2] the first contact between women and the TV set is presented as a matter of incorporating it very carefully in the home, principally as a piece of furniture, or even as a phenomenon that gave rise to new social protocols and rituals that they had to deal with and properly perform.

Columns with experts giving advice on how to deal with the TV as a piece of furniture or as a social promoter flourished. At the beginning, the relationship between women and the new medium was represented mainly as a problematic issue, as we can see from examples from mid-1950s advertising: a competition over attention and the male gaze, a complicated and unsolvable matter of technology, a mere strategy to 'keep the husband at home', away from the threats of social life. It is interesting to note how some promotional campaigns launched by RAI in this early stage were based on this idea as well: in 1960, the public broadcaster distributed a pamphlet, *Invito alla televisione*, explaining how to arrange the receiver set in the domestic space. A whole section of the pamphlet is dedicated to guidelines on the proper handling of the new technological device, and its advice to women is that

> The TV set must be handled with the special care reserved for fragile objects. In particular, the inner parts must only be cleaned by specialist technicians, and not by the inexpert hands of the good housekeeper. Better a little dust than the risk of damaging expensive technology.[3]

Conversely, when masculinity was discussed in relation to the advent of TV in the home, it had more to do with issues of familiarising oneself with fairly complicated technology and with consuming the first TV programmes and content.

Personal Accounts and Oral Sources

The second kind of source that needs to be included in an unconventional archive on the development of television is *personal accounts*: personal memories of the first viewers of the medium represent a key asset in constructing a cultural history of television. These memories are crystallised both in printed sources (letters and memoirs preserved in private archives) and in oral sources that need to be generated through interviews by researchers. In many of the most significant studies about the introduction of television into the home, early viewers' personal memories have proved to be a crucial source in outlining the historical course of the integration of the TV set into the domestic space, shedding light on aspects that have been largely neglected by the historiography rooted in printed sources, and will be discussed below. For example, the different models of TV adoption that characterised inhabitants of big cities as opposed to small rural villages, or the part that gender and family roles played in the incorporation of the TV set in the domestic environment.

After the seminal work by Shaun Moores (1988) on the arrival of radio in British homes, other studies have shed light on media in the home as both a historical process and a phenomenon of everyday life, relying on the collection of individual recollections to theorise a broader and general pattern of incorporation and illuminating a collective memory on the medium, both as a material object and as a 'cultural form' (Williams 1974). A slow acceptance of oral testimonies as historical sources has also been observed in film studies (Taylor 1989; Kuhn 2002).

In the Italian context, a case in point of this kind of empirical research is the study conducted by Cecilia Penati and outlined in the volume *Il focolare elettronico* (2013). This research was developed through a qualitative methodology based on a corpus of twenty in-depth interviews with 'ordinary witnesses', which followed the technique that Jerome Bourdon and other scholars have defined as 'limited life story' (Bourdon 2004): the interviews did not aim to cover the whole life span of the respondent, but were focused on the period relevant to the research. Media consumption was framed in the life experience of the respondent, as in the classic model of life story interviews. All the interviews followed a semi-structured discussion guide, developed to investigate different issues concerning the adoption of the medium, such as the ideal and economic circumstances which led to purchasing the television set, how it was incorporated into the domestic space, different family members' roles before and after the arrival of television in the home, the meanings that different family members attributed to the new medium, and the viewing habits that developed around it. During the interviews, all these issues explored the personal life story of each storyteller to understand the social and cultural backgrounds in which their viewpoints were rooted.

All the twenty interviewees selected were frequent visitors to five main Senior Community Centres in Milan, located in different neighbourhoods, in both the city centre and the suburbs, in order to cover different social and cultural backgrounds. The first criterion used to select the panel of potential interviewees was age: all of them were born before 1940, so that in 1954 they would at least have been in their teens. Secondly, the group contained equal numbers of men and women, and it was balanced (albeit less precisely) between 'early and late adopters' (themselves or their families) of the television set in the 1950s and early 1960s. Their memories shed light on how the process of adopting television in Italy was shaped in different ways depending on a multilayered set of factors (for example, age, gender and geographical origin).

The collection of the interviewees' personal stories and experiences has revealed very different ways of imagining television and distinct ways of conferring meanings on the new medium. For instance, people who experienced the arrival of television in rural villages tended to emphasise a perception of 'magic' and 'miracle', and they were more likely to have experienced forms of collective viewing in the private domestic space of the few families that owned a set in those early years. In contrast, the urban citizens tended to stress more the link between their desire for modernity and having a television in their private homes.

When one of us first arrived in Milan, living in the city centre, even there, in the beginning, very few people owned a TV set, even though there were more TV sets in the centre than in the suburbs, and more in Milan than in the south of Italy. Before that move to Milan, in Bari (Puglia), no one owned a receiver except a lottery winner who spent the entire prize on a TV set and hosted TV nights for all the neighbours at his place (M 1).[4]

As already pointed out above when discussing popular media as historical sources, gender was crucial in determining the first approaches and interactions of viewers with the television set:

> The TV set was so big: it occupied half the lounge. It was huge and very deep; I still remember the brand: it was a Philips. I put it in a corner of the lounge, on a mobile dolly, a piece of furniture with a space to hold drinks. And we use to cover the TV set with a lace cloth or a little ornament. (W 2)

> When people came over to watch TV, I used to make coffee for everyone. There were more than twenty of them; I even had to buy some more cups and spoons. And then I had to tidy up after them. (W 3)[5]

As for the content of this first period of television programming, bottom-up histories using audiences' testimonies challenged and belied the simplism of the widely held assumption as to the principal mission of the Italian 'paleo-television', quite often described merely as an instrument of education for the masses by both academics and important 'above-the-line' RAI managers of the time. As in most other European countries, Italian television was indeed characterised by the 'public-service' institutional model: until the mid-1970s, RAI operated as a monopoly broadcaster, shaping its mission around the traditional public values of education and entertainment established by the BBC. However, in the memories of early Italian TV viewers, only a few programmes stand out, and curiously they all belong to the popular entertainment genre, so often accused in the public debate of corroding the public-service ideal and largely responsible for the medium's initial and subsequent poor critical reputation. As confirmed also by the early research led by psychologist Lidia De Rita, the most prominent programme of the time was undoubtedly *Lascia o Raddoppia?*, a quiz show based on French and US models, hosted on RAI from 1955 by popular host Mike Bongiorno. Alongside *Lascia o Raddoppia?*, just a few other programmes capable of becoming 'television events' emerge: children's television, *Carosello* (an anthology of commercials aired from 1957 after the evening news) and *Il Musichiere*, a televised musical contest inspired by famous US show *Name That Tune* and hosted by popular radio talent Mario Riva. Both *Il Musichiere* and *Lascia o Raddoppia?* have deeply shaped the collective memory of early Italian television, as confirmed also by the various articles in the principal daily newspapers of that period, such as *Corriere d'Informazione*, which dedicated much attention to the shows.

Memories, Diaries and Autobiographies

An important type of personal source is diaries written by members of the working class during the 1950s and 1960s – or soon afterwards, in the form of memoirs and autobiographies. As part of our research, we looked at hundreds of diaries collected by the National Diary Archive, based in Pieve Santo Stefano, a little town in the north of Tuscany (Garofalo 2018). Here, we found references on television consumption in almost fifty diaries and memoirs written by working-class people, both factory and agricultural workers. In all these references, differences were identified based upon the varying geographical backgrounds and gender identities of early TV audiences. As well as in the previous findings on oral sources, most of the memories of the arrival of television are characterised by a sort of 'magical' and 'miraculous' narrative. As Daniela Antonello, an agricultural worker born in northern Italy, observes in her diary:

> The arrival of television at our home was, for us as for adults, an event that changed our lives and habits. When that mysterious 'box' arrived, one evening at the nightfall, we were all coming in to welcome it, as one welcomes a special guest. It was an astonishing discovery that brings with it an aura of magic.[6]

In recalling their memories, most of the audiences seemed to be more interested in remembering sociability and forms of collective spectatorship, rather than specific programmes or television stars. This memory refers directly to the arrival of television at home within the walls, but the bar seems to be the place where almost all of the 'first time' stories are set in front of the small screen. This is the case for Irene Cattini, who has worked for a rubber manufacturer since the age of fifteen:

> Then in some bars in the town the first TV sets were installed; in the evening everyone, adults and children alike, found themselves punctual in a spacious room, in the dark, their eyes glued to the video and they all drank. Those were the years of the first broadcasts of *Lascia o Raddoppia?* presented by Mike Bongiorno. With how much enthusiasm, I followed the transmission and I cheered for the competitors! Mom was not happy that we girls went to watch TV at the bar and reluctantly gave us permission. For me it was a real pain not to go down even for one night.[7]

In this case, the memory of the advent of television is associated with the bar, and is also connected with the programme *Lascia o Raddoppia?*, with which the memory of all the early Italian television audiences is often identified. The appearance of television is also associated with sports programmes, in particular with the great heroes of cycling or with great football matches, which were also consumed in the collective dimension of the bar, often only among men, as in the case of Giampaolo Massani, a son of two farmers from Urbania (a town in Marche region), who remembers the arrival of the television when he was a child:

> The people of the town could go and see those magic boxes, in which the images of *Lascia o Raddoppia?* were screened in the central bar of the town or at the bar *Massimin*, located at the end of via Garibaldi, on the corner of piazza San Cristoforo. It is with a certain emotion that Mario (my brother, eight years older than me) told me when in the *Massimin*, full of people, the TV broadcasted the images slightly dotted and strictly in black and white of legendary football player Schiaffino in a wonderful final (29 May '59) of the Champions League, lost by Milan 3–2 after extra time against the invincible army of the great Real Madrid. Or that time when, together with Rubolini and two or three other friends, he was a 'cathodic witness' of Ercole Baldini's victory at the cycling world championships of 1960 in front of the parish hall television.[8]

The 'cathodic' testimonies of the sporting events, experienced by his brother in a bar full of people, like a football stadium, entered indirectly into the television memories of Giampaolo, influenced since childhood by the contemplation of what he also calls the 'magic box'. The role of the parish hall as an alternative to bars and public places is also crucial, especially if written in contrast to the communist counterpart, the so-called *case del popolo*. This is present in many other testimonies collected, even if produced after the fact. On the other hand, in fact, several testimonies written in the 1980s or the 1990s remember early Italian television in a 'corrupted' way. Massimo Degl'Innocenti notes in his diary how:

> The infernal machine gradually shaped us, we changed our way of thinking and of carrying ourself. We began to travel remaining seated, to study without books or blackboards. It changed also the speed of life and of thoughts. The squares become empty and, to the contrary, bars, clubs, rooms started to be crowded.[9]

The idea of television replacing books and traditional culture, going beyond the scholastic duties, is connected to one of empty squares in favour of bars and public places – places *par excellence* of early television. The social bewilderment felt with the advent of the new medium is summarised in several testimonies: some gripped, others surprised, most still not ready yet in the face of the advent of modernity. This is probably because of the influence of the advent of commercial television in the late 1970s – and this is all the more true in reference to the more politicised factory workers (as Degl'Innocenti was). For this reason, it seems impossible to us to look at television audiences without considering their leisure habits and their change in terms of cultural consumption in the long run.

The public advent of television was not limited to the bar or the parish hall. Again, Irene Cattini remembers the exact day when what she calls the 'big glass' appeared:

> I remember the day when, in the only shop in the town that sold radio equipment, appeared the first television. The programs were few and started at 9 pm. [. . .] I ate dinner quickly, tidied up the kitchen, and with Aurora, Franca and Mauro we ran in front of the window of the radio shop. There were already about a hundred people, still waiting, with their necks drawn towards the large glass behind which the luminous apparatus was beautifully displayed. The owner, for advertising purposes, switched on the device and let us enjoy the programs. There was a movie almost every night; sometimes comic; sometimes romantic. 'Hey, move a little please! I don't see it!'. 'Now I don't see it!' I had already heard of television, but seeing it was a source of great wonder to me. 'But how is it possible?' I wondered 'It is extraordinary!'. 'Lucky [are] the owners of such a marvel!'.[10]

This memory highlights the aspect more properly linked to the magical dimension of the television. It also recalls a small reality in which hundreds of people meet one another, after dinner, in front of the window of a store, to watch television shows without audio. In order to understand the social dimension of TV consumption, it is crucial to underline the invasion in the public space of the 'new' medium: television overcame not only domestic walls, but also those of bars, clubs, parish halls, public places, closed environments, bringing spectators on the street.

Readers' Columns and Public Opinion

A third type of source is a kind of a mixture between popular media and private sources. Here, we would like to talk briefly about the readers' columns of *rotocalchi* (weekly illustrated magazines very popular in Italy between the 1930s and 1960s), which offer a unique opportunity to observe at a distance public debates directly carried out by audiences, which often took their inspiration from television programmes and current affairs. Italian historiography has at least partially analysed the attitude of *rotocalchi* with respect to the advent of the consumer society, but the role played by the readers' columns in these publications has received little attention. A good measuring stick to estimate the philosophical disparity between intellectual and political leaders and audiences regarding television is the readers' columns of the two leading *rotocalchi* of the time. These were *Famiglia Cristiana*, a direct production of the Christian Democrat culture, and *Vie Nuove*, the cultural periodical of the Italian Communist Party (PCI). Both publications had columns reserved for the readers' editorials in which, on a weekly basis, clarifications, questions and protests on the most variable topics were presented. Here, analysing the changes of writers' attitudes in these columns is crucial to understanding how popular public opinion was also changing regarding the television programmes produced by RAI.

For example, this letter written by a reader of *Famiglia Cristiana* in 1956 stated how television was seen as a 'revolver', a weapon to be kept in a safe place, for fear that it could harm people who do not know how to use it:

> Maybe it's just my impression, and maybe I'm wrong here, but it seems to me that, from our part, that is, from the Catholics' point of view, we complain but we don't do very much to resolve the moral problem of television. Television is an attractive, but dangerous, toy. It's attractive because it fascinates us all, both children and grown-ups . . . As a first step, I think that parents and educators should be convinced that the TV, like the medicine cabinet and the revolver, should be kept in a safe place. Before turning it on in front of children, one has to be completely certain that the program will be designed for them. Because of this, we need to train our kids to understand that not everything that the TV presents can be seen by them. (Anon. 1956a)

The necessity of being *educated* in the use of the TV, in order to render oneself immune to its *poison*, is strictly connected to the necessity of moralising modern life. This Catholic reader's impressions take their inspiration from the premise that the television, as it is closely linked to daily life, also reflects all of society's problems. On the other hand, the perception of an undesirable 'outside', where the improbable occurs, and an 'inside', where one can feel oneself safe and secure, remained constant. The television, in this sense, was viewed as a window which, if left open, risked granting access to elements which were hostile to the family unit – precisely the element of life which people felt was menaced by modernity.

Again in 1956, a mother wrote to Father Atanasio, the curator of one of the *Famiglia Cristiana* readers' columns:

> This television is nice, Father Atanasio, but the programs aren't always acceptable. At 5:00 pm, for example, there are puppets which are nice and instructive, even comic. But there aren't always puppets. Sometimes there's a film, and everything is in there. There are people who rob, bandits who kill with their famous impunity and all sorts of evil that would be unimaginable for children. You can imagine the frenzy of the children

> after the show: nobody is able to keep them under control any more, and then they do the things that they have seen outside. My children are acting like the bandits from the cinema here at home. [. . .] Have we become so uncivilized as to simply take whatever is given to us? What sort of education is this? I think if my father could see us now, he'd beat us all with a shoe. (Anon. 1956b)

And television itself might have even remained acceptable, but real worries began to emerge when films, as well as television programmes, began to be broadcast.[11] There was no need, in fact, to continue to go to the cinema when the TV could bring movies directly into the home. In the same period, the first communist protests against television began. According to the readers of *Vie Nuove*, television was guilty of not spreading objective information, but of feeding the pretentious propaganda of the Americans and the Christian Democrats:

> I recently saw a film on the TV which was little other than a partisan propaganda campaign. It happens ever more frequently on the radio, too, that one must listen to transmissions that seem to have no other purpose than to satisfy the political demands of the dominant party. Can it really be possible that citizens should have to pay the registration fee, only to listen to propaganda? Don't you believe, dear *Vie Nuove*, that this represents an abuse? Is there no way to force RAI to be impartial? (Anon. 1956c)

This call to action, whether or not it was completely true, gave the green light to Luciano Malaspina, a documentary film director and communist journalist, to publish an article lambasting the partisanship of RAI's programming, in which he summarised the methods that the Christian Democrats had adopted in order to influence public opinion. Among RAI's sins, Malaspina listed 'omission and deformation of the news regarding the initiatives and activities of the Left; a slur campaign against the parties of the Left and continuous propaganda in favour of the Christian Democrats and the government'. He concluded:

> If hundreds of thousands lined up in ranks against RAI, it would be possible to force this entity to come back to the rule of law, and put itself to the service not just of one party, but of the entire Italian population. (Anon. 1956c)

This response from Malaspina reflects the position of *Vie Nuove* regarding television, as compared with the official attitude of the PCI. If, in fact, the PCI held the television to be a naturally reactionary medium, *Vie Nuove* left it some breathing room for its potential to be used as a communist communication device. If this position can be considered instrumental in the direction of RAI by the Christian Democrats, *Vie Nuove*'s timid attempt at confronting the problem created some discontinuity in the communist field. Entering into this ideological confusion, it is not surprising that, during the magazine's subscription drive of 1957, *Vie Nuove* offered twenty television sets as well as hundreds of other prizes for the readers who managed to collect the most magazine subscriptions among their friends (Anon. 1957c).

As the 1950s came to an end, the complaints against the propagandistic nature of Italian television did not diminish. In 1957, a Roman factory worker employed by the Stefer company denounced in a letter to *Vie Nuove* 'one of the many embarrassments that abide in our Republic: RAI-TV':

> The TV and the radio are without a doubt the most important means of diffusion of culture, and should not be government propaganda. Our television and radio network, whose actions mostly depend on the IRI, must be an instrument of the state, and not of the party. The listener's or watcher's intelligence is offended by what the TV makes us see on the news, and hear from the 'millionaire' voices of Ugo Zatterin and Gianni Granzotto (who, according to *L'Unità* makes 450,000 lire per month). Furthermore, I know that the director of TV programming is one Sergio Pugliese, ex-federal secretary of the defunct PNF [National Fascist Party] who was already expelled from radio, and who has now been set up in a well-paid position by the clerical government. This makes one think that culture in Italy must still come to terms with the fascists. I am sure that in the columns of your publication you are going to denounce the people who direct this important state-owned entity. I am also sure that you will want to denounce the billions which it earns annually and which can and must be put to the service of all opinions, and also to lighten the evening after a long day of work. (Anon. 1957a)

The response of the editors clearly invited the readers to write in protest directly to RAI, calling for all of the 'unjustly indignant citizens' to threaten to unregister their televisions. This was to be 'a warning, that if it should become a mass movement, would be particularly beneficial, considering the arrival of the next election' (Anon. 1957a). With these protests, the concerns over television broadcasting threatened to become the linchpin of the political contest. However, the editors of the communist magazine would, for the moment, exclude an open call for more space on the small screen. They were still too preoccupied with demonising a communicative device which, by its very nature, was still considered incompatible with the revolution of the workers. Regardless of the standing orders to the leaders of the PCI sections not to acquire television sets, some directors of local PCI sections took advantage of the columns 'Your Lawyer' and 'A Lawyer Responds' to ask for information about television advertising rates put in place by the government. (Anon. 1957b)

At first glance, it is possible to see in the readers' columns of the two magazines that the attitude of the viewers of early Italian television was fairly similar in both political camps, in terms of style, but differentiated according to content. On the Catholic side, there was a fear of a moral crisis, threatened by the 'society of sin' spread by the television, and acting on the youngest members of society. From the communist side, there was fitful attention paid to the partisanship and propaganda intention of the programmes, mixed with a natural diffidence regarding a product of consumer society (Garofalo 2016).

Conclusion

In conclusion, examining our different but related research, we have noticed several recurring issues that we would like to share in the form of a few findings. First of all, both popular and private sources have proved the need to partially rethink the practical effect of the pedagogical aim of Italian public television service. This is because in the majority of audiences' memories we found a strong centrality of entertainment programmes, rather than educational ones. At the same time, we both noticed some specificities of early Italian television spectatorship, such as political background and gender identity (but we can consider geographical and generational differences as well). As we have partially seen, if the communist complaints feature a primarily political content fuelled by an anti-Catholic and anti-American prejudice, the Catholic complaints differed from these because they assumed an aesthetically self-righteous, formally religious and moralist framework. Regarding other matters, gender was a crucial issue in addressing the process of domestication of television as well, with women who were at the same time represented and discussed as weak subjects in need of protection from the new technology but also core engines who activated the first social shaping of the new medium, with its new rituals and interactions.

Considering the social and geographical differences of early television audiences could help us to more broadly interpret the years of the so-called economic miracle. This term designates a period of strong economic growth in Italy after World War II to the late 1960s, and in particular the years from 1958 to 1963 (Forgacs and Gundle 2007). These are the years, not by chance, when early television started to spread, in different forms, all over the country. As a consequence, analysing historical change and audiences' attitudes in the long run could help us to better define the contexts and the periodisation of our research. Paying attention to consumption rather than production, we can talk of a 'long miracle' that has its own origin – and also its main development

– during the 1950s, that begins with Italian television's origins in 1954 and finishes with the complete adoption of the medium (which more or less occurred at the end of the 1960s) in the house. The idea is to adhere to a vision of a 'long miracle' as has been described by Italian historian Silvio Lanaro. Lanaro observes, in fact, that

> what breaks against Italy during the years 1958–1963 is a series of phenomena which were developed over time and connected via a causal relationship (though not always a linear one) which changed the structure of the country from top to bottom. Notwithstanding the 1964–1965 recession, these phenomena continued to exert their effects until 1970. (Lanaro 1992: 239)

This means also reconsidering the traditional chronology of Italian television 'from below', proposing therefore a social history of Italian television.

A lot of work still has to be done. Here, we would like to end by proposing some paths to be followed in order to apply our research findings. First of all, we strongly believe that it is necessary to adopt a systemic approach to these sources: we think that television audience analysis should be integrated within a broader history of media and cultural consumption. This also means encouraging an interdisciplinary methodology, taking into consideration research and approaches from other disciplines, such as film studies, cultural sociology and social history (to name but a few). In this sense, comparing the practices of oral history with work on letters and diaries could be helpful. The difficulties in approaching personal stories lie in the attempt to integrate biographies from different worlds, contexts and periods, while still maintaining the specificity of these ego-documents (Nora 1987, 2001). As Danilo Montaldi has noted, autobiographies and life stories reveal their usefulness when their relativity, the inevitable and interesting 'partiality', is recognised (1961: 40–1). What we tried to do was to combine the cultural imaginary constructed by witnesses (oral sources, interviews, autobiographies and memories) with different subjective perceptions of the same event (diaries and letters), starting from a similar social condition. The subjective identification with a popular and subordinate condition, perceived above all in a dimension of 'otherness', seems to strongly affect a class relationship with the medium as a symbolic object of consumption linked to a dimension of visible well-being.

To better analyse the last types of source that have been addressed in this chapter, we must also remember that all of the letters we mentioned passed through the filter of magazine editors. There have been people who have even doubted the veracity of these letters, suggesting that some of them could have been written directly by members of the editing staff, in order to promote guided debate. Unfortunately, as none of the original letters has been preserved, it is not possible to verify their origins. If some of the letters were, in fact, false, this fact would still say something about the cultural vision of the two weeklies and about how they interpreted the situation of their own readers. Furthermore, one cannot assume that, although *Famiglia Cristiana* and *Vie Nuove* had an affirmed readership among the working class, they limited themselves exclusively to this subset of the population. All these remarks suggest we should rethink the traditional rigidity of social structures, and even consider these types of source as inspirational material to be integrated with various sets of other documents. We firmly believe that only by following these paths will we be able to expand further the boundaries of our 'extended' and 'unconventional' television archive.

Notes

1. Though we contributed equally to this work, conceiving and discussing the entire essay jointly, Cecilia worked on the introduction and the sections on popular media and oral sources, while Damiano worked on the sections on diaries, memories, letters, and the conclusion.
2. This storytelling is broadly adopted in the issues of the two weekly magazines throughout 1955 and 1956.
3. *Invito alla televisione*, RAI – ERI, 1960.
4. Male interviewee; see Penati (2013: 171) for the full account.
5. Female interviewees; see Penati (2013: 81) for the full accounts.
6. Daniela Antonello (San Martino di Lupari, PD, 1952), *La casa dei giochi*, 1996, Archivio diaristico nazionale, MP/99, p. 4. Some portions of her diaries have already been published in *La casa dei zoghi* (Padua: L'Espresso, 2014).
7. Irene Cattini (Massa Carrara, 1941), *Se mai di me qualcuno ricorderà, 1996–1997*, Archivio diaristico nazionale, MP/07, p. 21.
8. Giampaolo Massani (Urbania, 1952), *Quel munuel*, 2008–9, Archivio diaristico nazionale, MP/10, p. 6.
9. Massimo Degl'Innocenti (Arezzo, 1948), *Anni sessanta e dintorni*, 1994, Archivio diaristico nazionale, MP/07, p. 27.
10. Irene Cattini (Massa Carrara, 1941), *Se mai di me qualcuno ricorderà, 1996–1997*, Archivio diaristico nazionale, MP/07, p. 21.
11. The post-war period represented a decisive moment in the relationship between cinema and morality in Italy. A new film law was introduced by Giulio Andreotti in 1949, which transformed censorship into a form of prior checking under the ideological control of the Catholic establishment. Through the surveillance of state film censorship, the Catholic Church tried to promote a moralised cinema nationally. As a consequence, the possibility to broadcast films on television raised a whole set of additional moral questions for the Christian Democratic government. For a detailed discussion on this topic, see Della Maggiore and Subini (2018).

Bibliography

Anania, Francesca (2004) *Breve storia della radio e della televisione italiana*. Rome: Carocci.
Anon. (1956a) 'La televisione', *Famiglia Cristiana*, 3 January, p. 5.
Anon. (1956b) 'Programmi televisivi', *Famiglia Cristiana*, 29 January, p. 4.
Anon. (1956c) 'Propaganda radiofonica', *Vie Nuove*, 29 September, p. 2.
Anon. (1957a) 'Abusi televisivi', *Vie Nuove*, 21 December, p. 2.
Anon. (1957b) 'La tassa per la TV', *Vie Nuove*, 13 April, p. 38.
Anon. (1957c) *Vie Nuove*, 2 March, p. 20.
Barra, Luca and Cecilia Penati (2013) 'Catch-up with archives. La télévision numérique terrestre et le patrimoine audiovisuel du service public en Italie', in Valentine Frey and Matteo Treleani (eds), *Vers un nouvel archive numérique*. Paris: L'Harmattan, pp. 133–42.
Bourdon, Jerome (2004) 'Old and New Ghosts: Public Service Television and the Popular, a History', *European Journal of Cultural Studies* 7(3), 283–304.
Bourdon, Jerome (2011) *Du service public à la téléréalité. Une histoire culturelle des télévisions européennes 1950–2010*. Paris: INA Éditions.
Casetti, Francesco (ed.) (1995) *L'ospite fisso. Televisione e mass media nelle famiglie italiane*. Turin: San Paolo.
Chiarenza, Franco (2002) *Il cavallo morente. Storia della Rai*. Milan: Franco Angeli.
De Rita, Lidia (1964) *I contadini e la televisione. Studio sull'influenza degli spettacoli televisivi in un gruppo di contadini lucani*. Bologna: il Mulino.
Della Maggiore, Gianluca and Tomaso Subini (2018) *Catholicism and Cinema: Modernization and Modernity*. Milan: Mimesis International.
Eco, Umberto (1983) *Sette anni di desiderio*. Milan: Bompiani.
Foot, John (2015) *Milano dopo il miracolo. Biografia di una città*. Milan: Feltrinelli.
Forgacs, David and Stephen Gundle (2007) *Mass Culture and Italian Society from Fascism to the Cold War*. Bloomington: Indiana University Press.
Garofalo, Damiano (2016) *Political Audiences: A Reception History of Early Italian Television*. Milan: Mimesis International.
Garofalo, Damiano (2018) *Storia sociale della televisione in Italia, 1954–1969*. Venice: Marsilio.
Grasso, Aldo (2004) *Storia della televisione italiana*. Milan: Garzanti.
Grasso, Aldo (ed.) (2013) *Storie e culture della televisione italiana*. Milan: Mondadori.
Gray, Jonathan (2010) *Show Sold Separately: Promos, Spoilers, and other Media Paratexts*. New York: New York University Press.
Kuhn, Annette (2002) *An Everyday Magic: Cinema and Cultural Memory*. London: I. B. Tauris.
Lanaro, Silvio (1992) *Storia dell'Italia repubblicana*. Padua: Marsilio.
Lotz, Amanda and Jonathan Gray (2012) *Television Studies*. London: Polity Press.
Montaldi, Danilo (1961) *Autobiografie della leggera*. Turin: Einaudi.
Monteleone, Franco (2003) *Storia della radio e della televisione in Italia*. Venice: Marsilio.
Moores, Shaun (1988) 'The Box on the Dresser: Memories of Early Radio and Everyday Life', *Media, Culture and Society* 10(1), 23–40.
Nora, Pierre (1987) *Essais d'ego-histoire*. Paris: Gallimard.

Nora, Pierre (2001) 'L'ego-histoire est-elle possible?', *Historein* 3, 19–26.
Penati, Cecilia (2013) *Il focolare elettronico. Televisione italiana delle origini e culture di visione*. Milan: Vita e pensiero.
Piazzoni, Irene (2014) *Storia delle televisioni in Italia. Dagli esordi alle web tv*. Rome: Carocci.
Scaglioni, Massimo (2017) 'Television Studies: genealogia e prospettive nazionali', in Aldo Grasso (ed.), *Storia della comunicazione e dello spettacolo in Italia*, vol. III. Milan: Vita e pensiero, pp. 301–7.
Silverstone, Roger (1994) *Television and Everyday Life*. London: Routledge.
Spigel, Lynn (1992) *Make Room for TV: Television and the Family Ideal in Postwar America*. Chicago: University of Chicago Press.
Taylor, Helen (1989) *Scarlett's Women: Gone With the Wind and Its Female Fans*. New Brunswick, NJ: Rutgers University Press.
Williams, Raymond (1974) *Television: Technology and Cultural Form*. London: Collins.

11. THE EXORCIST IN THE HOME: REMEMBERING PARENTAL REGULATION

Martin Ian Smith

'Tis the eye of childhood
That fears a painted devil

– William Shakespeare, *Macbeth* (II.ii)

Robert Allen states that no serious history of film could exist without an account of its audiences (1990: 348). Narratives focusing on exhibition and consumption in the New Cinema History tradition have redressed the previous film-centric bias and within the subfield of 'cinema memory' studies it has been observed, and become widely accepted, that individual films matter little to audiences (Kuhn 2002: 100; Kuhn 2011: 93; Stokes and Jones 2017: 84). Annette Kuhn (with Biltereyst and Meers) questions whether this finding is an artefact of a research process in studies such as her 1930s cinemagoing project, in which the line of questioning lends itself only to accounts of cinemagoing as a social habit (2017: 10). The acceptance of this finding in such projects has, nevertheless, led to histories of the cinema without *films*. The focus of this chapter is my study of memories of *The Exorcist* (1973), which sought to realign histories of audiences with histories of films while offering a new approach to doing film history. The aim of this chapter, then, is to demonstrate the value of using a single film, rather than a specific period, as the organising principle of inquiry. Studies of *Alien* (Barker et al. 2016) and *Gone With the Wind* (Taylor 1989) have already revealed much about fandom and family viewing. Trends in New Cinema History have rightly brought audiences to the forefront, but at the cost of understanding audiences' relationships with films: one bias has been exchanged for another.

The Exorcist (1973) was selected for this study because of its phenomenal success, censorship history, and folklore concerning extreme audience responses. The film was breaking box office records and being nominated for ten Oscars (winning two) while it faced down bans from British councils at the cinema and reports circulated about audiences fainting, vomiting and even dying (Klemesrud 1974; Anon. 1974). In Britain, *The Exorcist* was withdrawn from sale on home video after the implementation of the Video Recordings Act 1984 (VRA); *The Exorcist*'s status as a censored text defined many audiences' experiences with the film over the years. These experiences are the focus of this chapter.

Data was generated using a grounded theory methodology (after Kathy Charmaz 2014), using a globally distributed, English-language survey (746 responses) and interviews (thirty-three participants). A grounded audience studies approach allowed research questions to be generated from initial survey findings and these were further developed with participants in interviews. At its core, a grounded audience study amounts to simultaneous data generation and analysis phases and the use of theoretical sampling to follow up common themes deemed important to participants. A key tenet of grounded theory, and therefore grounded audience studies, is the rejection of existing concepts or theories. Old ideas or positions from other studies of audiences, such as 'the effects tradition' and 'interpretive communities', were not brought into this study for testing.

Stanley Fish's (1980) concept of interpretive communities has become a mainstay in much audience studies work and was cited as the future of audience studies by Martin Barker (2006: 129). The concept relates to the idea that audiences with similar backgrounds have at their disposal the same interpretive tool set and will, as a result, often interpret texts in a group-defined way. This has led to a focus on differences in audiences' interpretations of popular texts based on nationality, language, gender and fandom, and a trend towards international, survey-based projects (Barker et al. 2008; Barker 2016; Hirsjärvi et al. 2016; Veenstra et al. 2016). That Barker's (2006: 128–30) stated aim to make such communities measurable and testable has not been achieved in the field in the subsequent fourteen years since his 2006 article testifies to the concept's unsuitability for purpose in explaining audience processes. The results of studies which have failed to find such interpretive communities where explicitly sought (Hirsjärvi et al. 2016; Veenstra et al. 2016) have also not prompted challenges within the field to the wide acceptance of this still unverifiable concept, which was transposed wholesale from an anecdotal account – Fish's (1980) original work is not an empirical study – from literary studies. The use of grounded theory allowed for the discarding of such academic baggage and a fresh start, taking only participants' words as the raw materials for theory-building.

The emphasis here was entirely on an inductive, explorative research process which used participants to guide its direction and only participants' data to produce new theories. This process started with broad concerns – including how audiences remembered controversial films and how relationships with films may change over the years and through repeated viewings – and as data was generated from the survey and interviews the key concerns of the project were allowed to emerge from participants' accounts. In this way, censorship and parental regulation of viewing came to the forefront as research concerns; these matters were important to participants, rather than arbitrarily chosen for study by the researcher. (This methodology is outlined in detail – and argued for quite enthusiastically – in Smith 2019a.) Participants are identified only by their first names in this chapter which, as a result of this collaborative process, examines the importance and meaning of censorship, particularly in the form of parental regulation of children's viewing in the home, as it emerged from participants' accounts. I offer a new model for thinking about censorship, one which, for the first time, addresses the stakes for audiences, particularly child audiences.

The Censorship Studies Paradigm

Due to the near-exclusive focus on national censor boards, *The Exorcist*, passed uncut by both the British Board of Film Censors, now Classification (BBFC) and Motion Picture Association of America (MPAA), has received minimal attention in the field of censorship studies. This focus on the BBFC and MPAA follows the 'prohibitions/institutions' model of inquiry, presenting narratives of a series of actions taken by institutions with the remit to censor (Kuhn 1988: 11). Kuhn's revised model treats censorship as a fluid process and describes a wide range of relationships between a number of parties with their own influence, including the media and politicians (ibid.: 8): 'There is more to censorship than cuts, bans and boards of censors', Kuhn states (ibid.: 126). In using either the former or the latter model, however, questions are still restricted to an industrial context. The concern is, in both instances, about understanding how censorship *happens*, and it is therefore only understood in terms of what happens to the film itself. A crucial question of censorship remains unasked: what does censorship *mean*?

Audiences have been overlooked in historical censorship studies and the spectre of the 'effects tradition' looms over much contemporary work, obfuscating our understanding of everyday experiences. The 'effects tradition', the study of the tabloid-favourite 'common sense' theory that violent media encourages violence in its audiences, directs most research into controversial and violent media, most notably Annette Hill's (1997) studies of adult audiences of violent cinema and Barker et al.'s (2001) investigation of audience responses to *Crash* (1996). The latter study is of direct responses to the film and it seeks to function, at its core, as a rebuttal of the 'effects' model offered by the *Daily Mail* (Barker et al. 2001: 3). The narrative of the *Mail*'s censorship campaign, a textbook example of the 'effects' model as described in the reception study chapters of the book, is that *Crash*, a story about a subculture of people who fetishise car crashes, would inspire copycat crimes of reckless driving and ram-raiding by young men (ibid.: 14). The aim of the audience research by Barker et al. (2001) is to complicate this, to look at the ways in which people, affected by its reputation, *really* approached the film. In this way, the *Mail*'s narrative drove the design of this research. This framing is all too common in studies of violent media. Our understanding of such media, as they pertain to audiences' experiences, is therefore restricted to direct audience responses to a text with little of the context of everyday places or relationships. The academic research, however rigorously conducted, is in such cases structured by non-academic folk theories propagated in tabloid newspapers. That no participants discussed 'effects' in this study, even in discussions of other horror films as they arose, is telling of how far removed from audiences' lived experiences are audience studies driven by anti-'effects' priorities. The gap in our understanding of audiences' experiences of censorship has been highlighted by Daniela Treveri Gennari and Silvia Dibeltulo (2017) in their investigations into Italian cinemagoing in the 1950s. Their participants' experiences are of being denied films, of being aware of films which were repressed by Catholic and State censorship (ibid.: 240). So, there is little talk of *viewings* of censored films. Kuhn's (2002) chapter on childhood memories of horrific moments in the cinema provides understanding of horror cinema (if not censorship). Her analysis of the language and structure of such memories – particularly as 'bodily memories' which are centred on the self (ibid.: 68) – provides a basis for understanding experiences of younger audiences of *The Exorcist*. Censorship was discussed exclusively here in the context of childhood viewing, so it is clear that to reach any understanding of the impact of censorship one must understand childhood viewing practices. David Buckingham's (1996) insightful work on child audiences emphasises the role of parents in these practices and is a useful point of comparison for this study of *The Exorcist*; however, it is framed within talk of government policy on media education and is designed, as is Hill's (1997) work, to be a challenge to the 'effects tradition'.

Work on fans and cult audiences does provide insights into the appeal and practices of audiences of censored films beyond discussion of 'effects'. Emma Pett (2017) examines the appeal, for cult film fans, of 'extreme' Asian cinema from the distributor Tartan. She describes the importance of 'transgressive desires' (ibid.: 45), which certainly speaks to the appeal of censored films as evidenced in data here, even if censorship does not feature in her discussion. However, Pett's focus is on interpretations of the brand, Tartan, rather than audience experiences within the context of their homes and their lives. Other studies which concentrate only on interpretations of acts of censorship and moments of controversy miss this context of everyday experiences (for example, Barker 2005; Barker et al. 2001; Weir and Dunne 2014). These studies provide useful understandings of individuals' viewing strategies, but they do lack this grounding in the everyday; participants discuss their responses to scenes and moments and there is a conceptual film-to-viewer path for the film's meaning, with little room for everyday interruptions, motivations or relationships. Kate Egan's (2007) work on fan practices concerning censored films grounds audiences' experiences, through analysis of fan sites, collecting and trading, within a nexus of fans, and it is the project of this chapter to do the same with the family, to move away from examining an individual person's response, by discussing film-viewing practices in the environment in which they actually occur. A large part of this concerns the fact that studies of censorship are largely of adult viewers. With the most effective form of censorship being parental regulation, being censored, in data here, is an exclusive feature of childhood viewing habits. Studies of censored films focusing exclusively on adult audiences miss much of the overall picture by neglecting child audiences. This study finds that children are those most affected by acts of censorship in a number of concrete ways and, as such, the implications of censorship on meaning-making cannot be truly understood in discussions which exclude children.

This study of *The Exorcist* theorises what censorship means for audiences who were denied a single film, in whole or in part, and who, importantly, *circumvented* that censorship. It offers an understanding of experiences of censored films within the context of the home and the family, moving away from anti-'effects' dogma to understand, rather than argue, what encounters with films like *The Exorcist* mean for child audiences. And, crucially, this study examines what censorship comes to mean to these audiences as time passes and introduces audiences into historical narratives of censorship.

Parental Regulation

There is more to censorship than industry, artistry and the law; censorship changes audiences' experiences. Parental regulation, in particular, shaped many experiences participants in this study had with *The Exorcist* and how they remembered it. That parental regulation is the most effective and everyday form of censorship has been noted by both Buckingham (1996: 253), in the most thorough exploration of childhood viewing habits so far, and Sarah Smith (2005: 123), in her study of children's cinemagoing habits in the 1930s. This certainly proved to be the case in this study, with the BBFC and MPAA hardly warranting mention, and it is censorship on this personal level which forms the focus of this chapter.

Sixty-two participants were told they could not watch *The Exorcist* as children under the age of sixteen. (There are no accounts of parental regulation for those over sixteen, so this seems a reasonable cut-off point for describing 'children'.) This group does not account for a large percentage of the overall data set, but the topic of censorship proved crucial for these participants in how censorship changed how they initially viewed and now remember the film. The potential for parental regulation in terms of the effect on meaning and on the development of tastes in childhood film-viewing is enormous – including children rebelling against their parents' wishes to perform identity work and being denied part of the film itself due to having to watch surreptitiously – and such censorship defines many recollections. The importance of censorship is clear also from the pleasure evident in talk of regulation of childhood viewing practices. Participants, as a rule, enjoyed discussing restrictions on their behaviour as children, marking it as an important part of their lived experience. Parental regulation was an important theme of the data set which, as a whole, emphasised the importance of familial relationships in film experiences. Inter-family 'gifting' of the film (after Barker et al. 2016), from parent to child, was another important process. Analysis of this process is beyond the scope of this chapter, but can nevertheless be seen as the flipside of parental regulation.

Regulators

Any instance of censorship includes two actors, the person doing the censoring and the person who is denied the text: the *regulator* and the *regulatee*. That censorship is not *caused* by a single actor is understood thanks to Kuhn's (1988) insightful model, but this study argues that it is *enforced* by a single actor. From the accounts provided by participants, it is clear there are three varieties of regulator. A regulator may be direct, potential or indirect:

1. *Direct regulators* are those people who *enforce* regulation, such as parents, siblings, teachers, and workers at video stores and cinemas. Parents have, by some way, the most power and desire to regulate.
2. *Potential regulators* include anyone in the above list who is circumvented by a regulatee's actions. Children watching *The Exorcist* in secret, knowing their parents would not allow it, were acting within the domain of the potential regulator. Potential regulators have the *potential* to enforce regulation, if given the chance.
3. *Indirect regulators* have no direct contact with the regulatee and the regulatee's actions have no bearing on these individuals or groups. The BBFC and MPAA are indirect regulators; official censors have only as

much power as they are given by direct regulators. Other indirect regulators include organisations or people who have either expressed disapproval of the film or who the regulatee imagines would disapprove of their act of watching the film.

These three kinds of regulator have three different kinds of influence over viewing strategies and processes of interpretation. Potential and indirect regulators are closely linked and were used by participants as discursive constructs in their recollections. First, let us discuss the direct regulators, chief among whom are parents.

Motives

Protectionist censorship, keeping children free from distress, was the overriding theme of parental concerns regarding *The Exorcist*. Kieran (focus group 1) described his first encounter with horror in full at eleven or twelve years old, how it was terrifying even though he felt himself 'ready', and contrasted this with an account of how his parents saved him from potential nightmares prior to that introduction:

> Kieran: Even like sneaking horror films as a kid, I went out and watched it round a friend's house, and thought it was great. *Halloween 4* was the first one I watched. And it was great. And I come back to my house and I'm in bed that night and I was terrified. So, I'm definitely glad they didn't show me any horror until I was like eleven or twelve.
> Interviewer: You're glad they weren't just sitting you down in front of *Silence of the Lambs* as a kid?
> Kieran: Well, that's actually one of the ones. When I was like ten, we were at a Christmas fair and I bought it, and my mum was like, 'Here, you can watch that one.' I put it on for ten minutes and it was the first-person Buffalo Bill kills and my dad went over and hit the eject button and said, 'Ah, we'll put that one away for a while.'

Kieran's parents' actions are remembered as protectionist, and necessary. His dad's postponement of the film was not remembered as a judgement of the film, but of Kieran's readiness. Jan (interview, UK), a grandmother now, expressed no fears of children learning untoward language or behaviours, or of their learning of any sexual details – 'effects' in this sense were not a concern for any participants – stating, 'Certainly I wouldn't have let a child of mine watch it. I have four grandchildren now and I don't think any of them would cope with it.' Courtney (interview, UK) was told to hide her eyes for gorier scenes: 'I have fond memories of my family sitting round to watch films like *Final Destination* [. . .] and I'd constantly have to miss all the "good" bits in case I'd get nightmares!'

Nightmares were the most common consideration where parents censored films for their children. Courtney's parents relented as she got older and allowed her to indulge in her curiosity about *The Texas Chain Saw Massacre* (1974), *Friday the 13th* (1980) and other infamous horror films, and her mum 'changed her standpoint to "I won't stop you, but if you get nightmares that's on you!"' These protectionist motives echo Buckingham's findings that preventing upset is the primary goal of parental regulation (1996: 305). Regulation did occur due to conflicting tastes between parents and children, but this was rare. The link between anti-fandom and pro-censorship sentiment has been established (see Jones 2015; Gray 2003; Smith 2018, 2019b) and may be a mitigating factor, but its rarity here suggests that to always link censorship to anti-fandom would be a mistake. The most oft-cited reason ascribed to parents for their regulation was that the participant was 'not old enough' (#378, survey, UK). Also in line with Buckingham's (1996: 262) findings, there were no patterns in who was deemed in need of protecting; it was more tailored to each child. The concerns of parents were tied to the character of their children and defined by the extent to which they felt their children needed protecting.

Concerns of parents did not always ally themselves with those of the censors, as evidenced in Jeff's (interview, USA) account of his religious upbringing. Some parents used the classifications of the MPAA and BBFC as a guide for when regulation may have been necessary – age ratings were rarely taken at face value, but they did inspire more caution – but in Jeff's home this was not enough. Jeff's parents did not trust that the MPAA had a person's spiritual well-being as their foremost concern. They deferred the decision to a religious authority to safeguard his religious development. Jeff was told that he could only watch *The Exorcist* if he obtained permission from Father Valentine, the family's local priest. (Permission was granted, the experience was terrifying, and Jeff said, 'I would never trust a priest again.') It is clear that most parents suspect that censors are too conservative and underestimate a child's ability to cope with violent imagery, but Jeff's experience demonstrates that there exist other factors which prompt parents to stop their child watching a film. For *The Exorcist*, these factors may have been spiritual. For other films, they may be related to politics, to taste (as discussed above), or even to more concrete factors such as the cinema one attends and the company one keeps, where reasons may be related to the social activity rather than the film.

Strategies

The effect of parental regulation upon meanings, of the film and of memories of the experience, is changeable based on strategies of regulation and strategies of circumventing it. There are four ongoing strategies of parental regulation evidenced in this study:

1. The child was permitted free rein to watch anything.
2. The viewing of films was restricted based on established criteria, such as genre or age rating.
3. Parents viewed a film and then decided whether it was suitable for the child in a more case-by-case process.
4. Parents viewed the film with the child, prepared to censor the film by fast-forwarding or telling the child to look away.

There was a variation from the four standard strategies where there was an *anything-but-The-Exorcist* rule as an addition to the usual procedure. Six participants describe how this was the case for them. For some, this approach manifested even in a complete refusal to have a copy of the film present in the house. For other parents who did allow the film in the house for themselves, the VHS was treated like a firearm and locked away out of sight. These exceptions made for *The Exorcist* demonstrate the dynamic nature of systems of regulation. They are changeable over time and based on the films or viewing circumstances in question, and as the child grows older they are discarded. Buckingham found that most parents felt that by the age of thirteen, children were mature enough to regulate their own viewing (1996: 315). With the average of participants here watching *The Exorcist* at the age of thirteen, Buckingham's findings tally with this study. Even though a large proportion of children watched the film without parental consent, that many children chose to watch the film at about this age would suggest they were coming into their own. Though, the age at which parents eventually allow their child free rein is variable, since parents judge based on past experiences and their child's general character.

In accounts of parental censorship, an unexpected pattern emerged concerning the parents: there were considerably more mentions of mothers restricting viewing activities. From the sixty-two mentions of parental censorship, twenty-seven stated it was both parents or did not specify and three stated their father forbade it, but twenty-eight described how their mother did not allow them to watch *The Exorcist*. Sarah Smith made this same discovery regarding parents of the 1930s: 'Where parental authority is mentioned [. . .] it is nearly always maternal authority; indeed, many respondents recall their mother's authority as a powerful influence in the regulation of their behaviour' (2005: 121). Buckingham came to a similar conclusion: 'In the vast majority of cases, it was the mother who was identified as the parent most likely to take responsibility for regulating children's viewing. Insofar as fathers made an appearance in these discussions at all, they were almost exclusively seen to be simply imposing their own tastes' (1993: 118). Although quantitative trends in survey responses show that mothers were more censorious of *The Exorcist*, they were also much more likely to sit down with their child and share the film with them, and particularly with their daughters. That this finding contradicts those of Barker et al. (2016) and Egan (2020) – they found that fathers were more likely to share their love of *Alien* and Monty Python with their children – hints that there is something about *The Exorcist* that particularly connects with mothers. Sadly, there is no scope here to seek answers about this, but it is clear, from this study and from those of *Alien* and Monty Python, that there are features of specific kinds of texts which make them more or less likely to be regulated and shared by parents. This speaks to the importance of the character of individual texts: memories of film-viewing cannot be divorced from all films and restricted to the social activity, since all films are not treated in the same way.

It is important to note that parental regulation of *The Exorcist* was not a particularly confrontational process. In the case of participant #587, he went to great lengths to record the film off television onto VHS and spent a fortnight watching it in small chunks after bedtime with headphones, watching as much as he could get away with at a time without being caught. Triumphant, he eventually told his dad he had seen the film and the convoluted means by which he had been able to accomplish it. His dad offered no punishment, despite having previously banned the film from their home in strong terms. He was simply perplexed by the great lengths to which his son had gone to watch the film. Few strict punishments are discussed by participants; the worst, suffered by Kirsty (interview, UK), was having the television removed from her bedroom for a week. Parents do not always take regulation entirely seriously. They do not take it as seriously, for the most part, as do children in subverting it. Regulation of their children's viewing is but one part of everyday parental duties which include a hundred other activities. Save a stern reprimand here and there, consequences for children subverting regulation were mild. Parents recall their children's actions with a sense of amused resignation. Children who were caught watching the film and punished recount the experience with similar amusement. The most important part of the story, when told by participants who overcame such parental regulation, is the inventiveness with which they skirted the rules, or their own fiercely independent attitude towards such material at a young age. Marco (UK, interview), for example, took pride that his parents had quickly resigned themselves to the fact that they had raised a 'little horror geek'.

Parental regulation is not always defined by tension and dominance and may even be desirable for the child. It was not uncommon for children to ask for parents or other relatives to be present to mitigate the expected impact of *The Exorcist*. This strategy allowed a child to watch *The Exorcist* with a feeling of safety, a strategy Buckingham also found in his study (1996: 307). These protectors warned children and hid them when the film got scary. This timeless strategy is noted even in Sarah Smith's study of 1930s cinemagoing:

> I got a dreadful shock and looked away from the picture instantly. Mother told me she would tell me when to look again . . . From then

on, if it looked as though there would be anything frightening in the film I would tell whoever was with me to tell me when to look again. (Smith 2005: 134)

If the child became too distressed watching *The Exorcist*, this was the cue for the parent to turn the film off: 'Watched it with my mom, who made me stop watching it because I was getting freaked out' (participant #299, survey, USA). Another way of de-fanging *The Exorcist* involved a participant's mum undermining the child's sense of it being real:

> I was little and all I remember was hearing that it was a bad, bad movie. My mother told us to not be scared, that they used peas to create the vomit, and that it was all fake, there were people behind cameras. She showed us pictures of Linda Blair in a magazine too. I don't think that we were scared. We all watched horror movies all the time and my parents were very cynical about the practical effects, plot holes and implausibility of the events in movies. My mom helped by telling us things like 'When have you seen on the news of someone killed by a demon or a ghost?' (#496, survey USA)

This way of managing potential distress tallies with Buckingham's findings on children's coping strategies, of 'challenging the text's reality status' (1996: 307). Parental supervision, regardless of the approach, was useful and wanted by the child in these circumstances.

Some participants whose viewing practices were not regulated, or who were granted permission to watch *The Exorcist*, recall with regret that they were allowed to watch the film at a young age:

> I first watched it with my mum and dad probably around 1982. To be honest, I reckon they should've shown more caution as I was already a nervous type after they let me stay up late and watch the Saturday night horror double bills on BBC2. So, yes, *The Exorcist* did as I thought it would do and scared the living Hell out of me and I didn't sleep properly at night for the following six months. But I loved the film . . . although I did show caution and didn't re-watch it straight away even though it was there on the shelf. (Participant #615, survey, UK)

There are many examples of participants watching the film as children and experiencing negative effects, such as nightmares, which explains this wish for protection where it is found. Occasionally, the parents are blamed:

> My dad took my sisters and me to see it in a movie theater in the San Fernando Valley. I was eight (thanks, dad), didn't know anything about

it beforehand. It was unbelievably scary. I had nightmares about it for weeks. My mom had the book and I hid it in the bookshelf because even the cover scared me. (Participant #236, USA)

Whereas in these instances parental presence seems ineffective to keep the child free from distress, other parents were more active in real-time regulation. In the instances quoted above, parents chose for the children and there was no stage of the child requesting access. They are in this way a separate proposition from such instances where approval has been asked for and granted on the condition of an adult being present, but the process is the same as parents try to mitigate the damage. Parents' wishes and tastes trump the child's tastes or preparedness in these examples and, as with regulation, the choice is taken out of their hands.

Outcomes

The following outcomes of parental regulation were the most common or important in this study:

1. Both parents banned the child from watching *The Exorcist* and this was obeyed.
2. Both parents banned the film and the child disobeyed.
3. One parent banned the child from seeing the film and this was obeyed.
4. One parent banned the child from seeing the film and this was disobeyed and facilitated by the other parent who swore the child to secrecy.
5. Another party (another relative, a friend's parents or another direct regulator) banned the film and this was obeyed, frequently due to the rule being tied to the place where the viewing was taking place (for example, a friend's house, a classroom).
6. The child was banned from watching *The Exorcist* and obeyed until leaving the family home as an adult.

The first category is not covered in this study as having seen the film was a prerequisite for taking part in this research.

Parental regulation often caused changes in the text itself, as when watching a poor-quality bootleg VHS in secret, but, more importantly, the process of viewing was often interrupted or distorted. These interruptions and distortions ranged from having to watch the film piecemeal to avoid detection (participant #587, UK) to being told by parents to look away for all of the 'good bits' (Courtney, interview, UK). Nothing hinders the interpretation of a film more than the removal of certain elements or moments. Viewings of the film discussed in this chapter were changed by parental intervention as effectively, if not more so, than when the film was censored for television, an action which directly changed the material nature of the film. Elements and moments of *The Exorcist* were denied to children. The experience of watching the film was fragmented either due to parental intervention during the viewing or, more frequently, because of a secret attempt to skirt around a parental ban. The following participants were denied the full experience in different ways:

> My parents went to see it at a drive-in, certain I would be fast asleep in the rear of the family wagon. I faked it and only LISTENED to the film . . . and THAT VOICE. Scared the hell outta me. (Participant #183, survey, USA)

> The cable company gave us a trial for Showtime/AMC, and I watched the film in the basement late at night with the volume low so my parents wouldn't hear. I remember being confused (because I couldn't hear the dialogue), but did enjoy the movie well enough. It wasn't particularly terrifying for me (again, the volume was too low), but I could still understand why it was so well-regarded in its genre. (Participant #457, survey, USA)

> I peeked into my sister's room who was watching it and I caught glimpses and scenes, but she wouldn't allow me to watch. I recall not being allowed to watch it on multiple occasions and it being so taboo appealed to me even more. (Participant #36, survey, Japan)

The first participant (who was three years old at the time) was denied the visuals as he pretended to be asleep; the second was denied sound due to watching surreptitiously; and the third could only experience the film in brief snippets before being ordered out of the room. It is crucial when discussing censored films (institutionally censored or otherwise) to place these viewings in the real world and to note the consequences of such censorship on the material experience.

The clearest change in meaning for children who were denied the entire experience was the decontextualisation of the film's elements. For those for whom *The Exorcist* remained incomplete, merely a series of terrifying sounds or flashes of disturbing images taken out of context, the film remained with them in this state for many years. The sense of the story – which has a happy ending for Regan – is lost when the child is permitted only glimpses at the film. (For participant #457 above, the lack of understanding due to the unintelligible sound removed any sense of stakes from the film and had the opposite effect.) It was only later – much later for some – that the whole picture of *The Exorcist* was available, and the isolated images from the earlier experiences could be re-confronted and contextualised within the story and potentially, though not always, made safe. Caitlyn (interview, UK) described her first encounter with a fragment of the film, stating, 'I think what made it so scary was the lack of context because I'd just happened upon that scene, rather than watching the whole thing.' The lack of context defines her haunting encounter with a film she later came to love and rewatch many times. Her confusion was part of what she found scary, which is consistent in such experiences when the participant was at a young age. Participant #606 (survey, Germany) and Holly (focus group 2, UK) both experienced the film first in fragments, the former being still unable to face the film again. Holly, like Caitlyn, eventually worked this experience into a narrative of fandom, but it is clear that acts of parental regulation which forced children into fragmentary viewings had the potential to greatly change the experience in this way. Fragmentary viewing does not simply present a text in pieces, with these pieces eventually making up the same whole as they would have were the film watched in one sitting; isolated images and sounds, especially in the case of *The Exorcist*, can take on more power *because* of their fragmentation.

The Meaning of Censorship

The directness of the relationship between the regulator and the regulatee decides the extent to which the act of regulation affects meaning. This study found that regulation from family members, friends, schoolteachers and others directly in one's life means a great deal more to audiences than regulation from the MPAA, the BBFC, the government and other national organisations. Even for adult horror fans with strong anti-censorship attitudes, talk of censorship was always discussed within the framework of parental relationships (for example, in participants' talk of their parents' disapproval of their watching banned films).

The directness of a relationship between a regulator and a regulatee is measured through how much *in-person* contact the regulatee has with their regulator. The more direct the relationship between the regulator and the regulatee, the more action needs to be taken for the latter to access the film. One does not need to try hard to circumvent the MPAA or BBFC and, as stated, such organisations are only afforded power by *direct* regulators. Parental regulation is the most difficult to circumvent and runs the risk of disapproval and punishment that does not come from disobeying a national censor board.

The more actions required to circumvent the regulation, the more meaningful the effect upon interpretation. As a child living with one's parents, the regulatee must go to greater lengths to watch *The Exorcist* than must an adult watching a banned film in his or her own home. Actions taken, such as recording the film in secret off television or watching with the sound low so as to not be heard, add to the film experience for the former. The latter may only have the spectre of his or her parents' potential disapproval hanging over his or her head, which changes the experience but not in as direct a way. The amount of initial resistance from the regulator is what prompts action and creates meaning for the regulatee.

The 'creation of meaning' refers to added interpretations of *the film itself* and *the act of watching the film* that would otherwise not exist. For example, a child threatened with punishment for watching *The Exorcist* has an added element of danger, adding meanings related to risk and rebellion. Watching *The Exorcist* against the wishes of one's parents, for the regulatee, says something about one's character. It adds a meaning of 'I am a person who goes against my parents' wishes.' The adult watching *The Exorcist* in his or her own home against his or her parents' preferences may have the added meaning of 'I like different films to my parents' or, more broadly, 'I am not like my parents.' Such sentiments, and such identity work, which are a crucial part of identity formation in children's teenage years, contributed greatly to participants' memories here.

Participants positioned themselves in opposition to or in accordance with other identities, for example, 'I am not like my parents', 'I am like my brother', 'I am not like religious people.' There was an element of performance in this, the pull towards certain people and the push away from others, both for their own benefit and for the benefit of myself as the researcher and near-stranger. Interactions between myself and interviewees were, in essence, *introductions*, and participants' recollections are to be treated as such. Participants presented a version of themselves for the purposes of the interview in the same way Kuhn (2002: 9) discusses how memory texts are performed. This is not a false version; it is merely the most relevant version for the purposes of the interview.

Where parental or other direct relationships do not produce resistance, it is in the interest of the regulatee, in positioning themselves, to *construct* resistance using a hypothetical group. This resistance is based on experiences with materials such as newspaper coverage of groups' disapproval. The condemnation of *The Exorcist* by religious figures such as the Nationwide Festival of Light, Pastor Billy Graham, and other clergymen served well here as fuel for the fire. Resistance does not require such materials, of course, as they can be based on lived experience or prejudice. For example, negative experiences growing up in a religious household, their own irreligious beliefs, or unfavourable views of organised religion underpin some participants' statements in which they use religious others to provide resistance.

A controversial or censored film produces a desire to create a 'figure of the censor' in this way. Martin Barker discusses in his work on censorship how regulation is justified by censors and commentators by the creation of a hypothetical worst-case-scenario spectator who may be influenced or damaged by violent media, a 'figure of the audience' (2016: 123). It is clear from this study the reverse is also true: audiences of violent media create a 'figure of the censor', a hypothetical censor who disapproves of the film and their viewing of it. This makes an everyday film experience into raw materials for identity work, for positioning oneself. It fosters a feeling of rebellion against imagined oppressors, which can also add to the enjoyment of the film. Whereas 'figures of the audience' are based on presumed responses to violent media, 'figures of the censors' are based on hypothetical disapproval of the person's act of viewing (and enjoying) violent media.

An instance of censorship provides a platform for those who are denied access to construct for themselves certain identities. In childhood, instances of censorship or direct parental regulation provide a space for children to set themselves apart from their parents and develop identities of their own. The fact that the average age of participants watching *The Exorcist* for the first time across the board, through all periods and in all countries, settles at thirteen years old is no coincidence, since this is the age at which children begin to want to identify themselves as separate from their parents. In Erik Erikson's (1965) psychosocial model of identity development, it is between twelve and eighteen when children begin to seek independence from their parents and form an identity of their own. Resisting acts of parental regulation fuels this journey, as does railing against imagined others to better construct one's own identity. There is also the appeal, for children, of testing parental boundaries. Hill (1997: 107) discusses how the appeal of violent films can come from a desire to test social and personal thresholds; similarly, the act of watching the film tests the boundaries of the parent–child dynamic for those younger children not yet ready to break away and form their separate identity.

Circumvention of indirect regulation from imagined others is a poor substitute for circumventing regulation from more direct relationships, however. Where regulatees can position themselves as going against the wishes of a parent or other more personal authority figure, this takes precedence in the telling over the circumvention of any laws. Marco (interview, UK) talks of how his brother took horror magazines to school, for example, and a girl called him 'the son of Satan'. This is worth more to Marco in identity construction – he is demonstrating an affinity with his brother and therefore any identity work for his brother reflects back on himself – than is simply watching a film the BBFC had banned. Circumventing censorship functions as a way of constructing or maintaining facets of an identity in this way. Circumventing censorship when assisted by another person can produce an ally, a shared identity, and build relationships. This perhaps drives those situations when one parent secretly goes against the wishes of the other to allow the child to watch the censored text; they are forming a secret alliance.

The findings of this study complement well the findings of my previous study into audiences' censorship discourses (Smith 2018, 2019b), showing a range of subject positions adopted with corresponding motivations linked to positive identity formations. Participants here, through stories of being regulated in their childhood viewing, construct a version of themselves and a version of their past that is pleasurable. It is often presented as a formative experience, either through its extreme nature, as in stories of being traumatised by *The Exorcist*, or through it being part of an ongoing routine, such as parental regulation of viewing, that presents a snapshot of their childhood as a whole.

Identity work is not restricted to those children whose viewing was regulated. The act of parental regulation is also meaningful for the regulator in much the same way. This is particularly true of cases where participants were stopped from seeing *The Exorcist* due to a parent's bad experience with the film in his or her own childhood. Kate Egan (2020) discusses how, for Monty Python fans, sharing their love of comedy with their children allows them to discuss their past, to situate themselves in the time when the shows and films were originally produced. Stopping their children from seeing *The Exorcist* allowed some regulators to discuss their own childhood experiences, to recalibrate themselves for their children as someone who was once a child themselves. Talk of hardships such as watching *The Exorcist* in the cinema or being banned from it due to their own religious upbringing allowed a space for parents to share in the pains of being a child, fostering understanding between the two. While children who circumvent regulation often seek to distinguish themselves apart from their parents, those same parents who wish to regulate their viewing are often seeking to close the gap. Parents who assist their nervous children by actively supervising their viewings are also, through their protection, fostering trust and positioning themselves as the protector. Whether confrontational in nature or supportive, acts of regulation and censorship speak of the identity of the regulator and regulatee. Both may be driven by a parent's desire for a more positive relationship with their children.

There is a drive towards maintaining a positive self-image in the recollection of these often-treasured memories, and it is the self-image which predominates rather than discussion of the film itself. For many participants in this study, *The Exorcist* was an important milestone in their development as film fans and often as independent people apart from their parents. It was sometimes used to describe a child who was not ready to leave the nest, too, in cases where parents helped them to negotiate the troublesome terrain of the film's horrors. A point worth reiterating concerning regulation is that it is not necessarily a source of enmity. There can even be the creation of support structures where the distaste towards horror for the parent or child is managed by the other.

The design of this study, focused on a single film rather than a given time period, resulted in a stable of participants with a wide range of ages. No participants were under the age of twenty; many were over fifty. Interesting in the recollections of parental regulation, particularly, was how participants described their own parenting strategies, either real or hypothetical. The older participants, many of whom had since lost their parents, sought to bring themselves closer to them through expressing amused disapproval of their own actions as children. Younger participants did the same and, when discussing their experiences, would offer hypothetical future scenarios in which they themselves would keep *The Exorcist* away from their children. Where acts of rebellion and illicit viewings of *The Exorcist* against their parents' wishes are, at the time, thought of as acts of separation, there are, in the remembering, steps taken towards reconciliation.

Conclusion

This study of parental regulation has revealed a new way of thinking about the impact of censorship and testifies to the importance of studying cinema memory of individual films. *The Exorcist* was the exception to the rule, and as such it functions to shed light and shade on stories of more routine film experiences. The use of a single film as the organising principle of this study also meant it could engage with people at different points in their lives. Strategies of remembering tied to family relationships here made attempts at reconciliation with parents for both the young and old, but not in the same way. Studying a single film allows those researching past screen audiences to go beyond one fixed age group and examine the differences and similarities in people's relationships with films, and one another, throughout the course of their lives.

Strategies and outcomes of regulation cannot help but produce meanings because they are closely entwined with the meanings of the relationships of the people involved. Even the most important aspect of one's study is but a fraction of a fraction of a participant's life. Audience studies, as a field, would do well in a project of discarding grand, decades-old theories and moral panics if its practitioners would bear in mind the complexity of the lives of their participants, perhaps by recalling the famous marketing slogan of Wes Craven's *Last House on the Left* (1972): '. . . keep repeating, it's only a movie . . . only a movie . . . only a movie'. *The Exorcist* did not define the relationships between parent and child; no film can. Instead, the experience of watching *The Exorcist* was defined by these relationships.

Bibliography

Allen, Robert (1990) 'From Exhibition to Reception: Reflections on the Audience in Film History', *Screen* 31(4), 347–56.

Anon. (1974) '*Exorcist* Nightmare Theory in Rating's Death Fall', *The Times*, 18 May.

Barker, Martin (2005) 'Loving and Hating *Straw Dogs*: The Meanings of Audience Responses to a Controversial Film', *Participations* 2(2). <https://www.participations.org/volume%202/issue%202/2_02_barker.htm> (last accessed 20 May 2021).

Barker, Martin (2006) '"I Have Seen the Future and it is Not Here Yet" or, on being Ambitious for Audience Research', *The Communication Review* 9(2), 123–41.

Barker, Martin (2016) 'Knowledge-U-Like: The British Board of Film Classification and its Research', *Journal of British Cinema and Television* 13(1), 121–40.

Barker, Martin, Jane Arthurs and Ramaswami Harindranath (2001) *The Crash Controversy: Censorship Campaigns and Film Reception*. London: Wallflower Press.

Barker, Martin, Kate Egan, Tom Phillips and Sarah Ralph (2016) *Alien Audiences: Remembering and Evaluating a Classic Movie*. Basingstoke: Palgrave Macmillan.

Barker, Martin, Ernest Mathijs and Alberto Trobia (2008) 'Our Methodological Challenges and Solutions', in Martin Barker and Ernest Mathijs (eds), *Watching The Lord of the Rings: Tolkien's World Audiences*. New York: Peter Lang, pp. 213–40.

Buckingham, David (1993) *Children Talking Television: The Making of Television Literacy*. London and Washington DC: The Falmer Press.

Buckingham, David (1996) *Moving Images: Understanding Children's Emotional Responses to Television*. Manchester: Manchester University Press.

Charmaz, Kathy (2014) *Constructing Grounded Theory*, 2nd end. London: SAGE.

Egan, Kate (2007) *Trash or Treasure?: Censorship and the Changing Meanings of the Video Nasties*. Manchester: Manchester University Press.

Egan, Kate (2020) 'Memories of Connecting: Fathers, Daughters and Intergenerational Monty Python Fandom', in Kate Egan and Jeffrey Weinstock (eds), *And Now for Something Completely Different: Critical Approaches to Monty Python*. Edinburgh: Edinburgh University Press, pp. 207–25.

Erikson, Erik (1965) *Childhood and Society*. Harmondsworth: Penguin and Hogarth Press.

Fish, Stanley (1980) *Is There a Text in This Class? The Authority of Interpretive Communities*. Cambridge, MA: Harvard University Press.

Gray, Jonathan (2003) 'New Audiences, New Textualities: Anti-fans and Non-fans', *International Journal of Cultural Studies* 6(1), 64–81.

Hill, Annette (1997) *Shocking Entertainment: Viewer Responses to Violent Movies*. Luton: University of Luton Press.

Hirsjärvi, Irma, Urpo Kovala and Maria Ruotsalainen (2016) 'Patterns of Reception in Denmark, Finland, and Sweden: In Search of Interpretive Communities', *Participations* 13(2), 263–88.

Jones, Bethan (2015) 'Anti-fan Activism as a Response to MTV's *The Valleys*', *Transformative Works and Cultures*, 19. <http://journal.transformativeworks.org/index.php/twc/article/view/585/486> (last accessed 20 May 2021).

Klemesrud, Judy (1974) 'They Wait Hours – to be Shocked', *The New York Times*, 27 January.

Kuhn, Annette (1988) *Cinema, Censorship, and Sexuality, 1909–1925*. London and New York: Routledge.

Kuhn, Annette (2002) *An Everyday Magic: Cinema and Cultural Memory*. London: I. B. Tauris.

Kuhn, Annette (2011) 'What to Do with Cinema Memory?', in Richard Maltby, Daniel Biltereyst and Philippe Meers (eds), *Explorations in New Cinema History: Approaches and Case Studies*. Malden, MA: Wiley-Blackwell, pp. 85–98.

Kuhn, Annette, Daniel Biltereyst and Philippe Meers (2017) 'Memories of Cinemagoing and Film Experience: An Introduction', *Memory Studies* 10(1), 3–16.

Pett, Emma (2017) 'Transnational Cult Paratexts: Exploring Audience Readings of Tartan's Asia Extreme Brand', *Transnational Cinema* 8(1), 35–48.

Smith, Martin Ian (2018) 'Serb Your Enthusiasm: Anti-fandom and *A Serbian Film*', *Participations* 15(2), 115–34.

Smith, Martin Ian (2019a) 'Researching Memories of *The Exorcist*: An Introduction to Grounded Audience Studies', *Participations* 16(1), 844–64.

Smith, Martin Ian (2019b) 'Shock Value: Audiences on the Censorship of *A Serbian Film*', *Journal of British Cinema and Television* 16(2), 191–212.

Smith, Sarah J. (2005) *Children, Cinema and Censorship: From Dracula to Dead End Kids*. London: I. B. Tauris.

Stokes, Melvyn and Matthew Jones (2017) 'Windows on the World: Memories of European Cinema in 1960s Britain', *Memory Studies* 10(1), 78–90.

Taylor, Helen (1989) *Scarlett's Women:* Gone with the Wind *and Its Female Fans*. New Brunswick, NJ: Rutgers University Press.

Trevari Gennari, Daniela and Silvia Dibeltulo (2017) '"It existed indeed . . . it was all over the papers": Memories of Film Censorship in 1950s Italy', *Participations* 14(1), 235–48.

Veenstra, Aleit, Annemarie Kersten, Tonny Krijnen, Daniel Biltereyst and Philippe Meers (2016) 'Understanding *The Hobbit*: The Cross-National and Cross-Linguistic Reception of a Global Media Product in Belgium, France, and the Netherlands', *Participations* 13(2), 496–518.

Weir, Kenneth and Stephen Dunne (2014) 'The Connoisseurship of the Condemned: *A Serbian Film*, *The Human Centipede II* and the Appreciation of the Abhorrent', *Participations* 11(2), 78–99.

12. CHILDHOOD MEMORIES OF HORROR FILMS IN THE HOME: QUESTIONS, PATTERNS AND CONTEXTS

Kate Egan

Drawing on and surveying existing scholarship on audiences' past encounters with horror cinema (Cherry 2002; Kuhn 2002; Hills 2005; Barker et al. 2016; Smith 2019), as well as my ongoing research findings on memories of encounters with horror films on video and television, this chapter identifies key questions that, arguably, should continue to drive and motivate this area of historical audience research. With a particular focus on the 'non-theatrical modes of film distribution and exhibition' (Kuhn et al. 2017: 7) that have dominated film consumption cultures since the 1970s, the chapter considers the important roles played by past technologies, families, domestic spaces and sensory experiences in respondent memories of horror films in the childhood domestic context and, consequently, the continued meanings and significance of these memories in the present day.

AUDIENCES FOR HORROR AND THE CHILDHOOD EXPERIENCE

The existing work on childhood memories of horror cinema has noted the strikingly young ages at which respondents remember first encountering horror films. In *Alien Audiences* (2016), the book based on the 2012–15 'Remembering *Alien*' international audience project, Barker, Egan, Phillips and Ralph acknowledge the early age at which many questionnaire respondents state that they had first encountered *Alien* (1979), with many first viewing the film at age seven or even younger. Prior to this, in 2011, during my research for the

Cultographies volume on Sam Raimi's *The Evil Dead* (1981), I uncovered numerous reminiscences online from fans who had first encountered the film at some point in the 1980s when the film was available on home video and these fans were young children (the age range cited is generally between ten and fourteen, although a couple of fans stated they were only five or six years old). More recently, Martin Ian Smith, in his doctoral thesis, 'Remembering "the scariest movie of all time": A Grounded Audience Study of *The Exorcist*', considers 'how audiences have engaged with and now remember' (2019: 5) *The Exorcist* (1973) through memories gathered from 746 survey respondents and thirty-two interviewees. Crucially, and as illustrated in Smith's chapter in this volume, the memories he gathered once again acknowledged the young age at which many participants had first seen *The Exorcist*, and the 'importance of the home as a venue for film-watching' (2019: 173) from the home video era and onwards.

Indeed, and as Smith argues, this venue and its significance has been underexplored in work on cinema memories within the New Cinema History tradition. This tradition of scholarship – much of which is represented through the History of Moviegoing, Exhibition and Reception Network (HoMER) – is continually producing groundbreaking methodological models and concepts for studying and researching the history of moviegoing. However, as Smith rightly notes, this work has primarily focused to date upon memories of cinemagoing up to 1960 – the decades, as Kuhn, Biltereyst and Meers put it in the introduction to a special issue of *Memory Studies*, 'of the twentieth century before the arrival of the multiplex, home cinema and other changes in modes of film exhibition and consumption when going to the cinema was an essential leisure-time activity for millions everywhere' (2017: 7). Towards the end of this introduction, Kuhn et al. note that

> people's earliest memories of film will in future be associated first and foremost with consumption via television, downloads and portable devices: 'digital natives' typically consume large quantities of films in domestic or other private contexts before ever setting foot inside a cinema. The complexities of the contemporary cinema and media landscape, in which the cinema memories of the millennial generation will be forged, make future cinema memory work ever more fascinating, demanding constant rethinking and re-evaluation of research resources and strategies. (Kuhn et al. 2017: 11)

While this acknowledgement of the need to consider the importance of the domestic context within cinema memory studies is very welcome, what is elided here – in their focus on contemporary digital consumption – is the extent to which the formative experiences of the generations (born in the 1970s, 1980s and 1990s) who experienced a substantial shift from public to private consumption of the cinema within their everyday lives, due to analogue technologies such as the VCR and portable television set, have yet to be foregrounded and considered (in terms of the conceptual and methodological implications for cinema memory research) as fully as they could be. With this in mind, bringing the viewing venue of the home to the centre of investigation in this chapter on childhood memories of horror allows for further consideration, in particular, of the experience of being scared in the domestic context, and the roles this specific circumstance might play in home cinema audiences' memories of their first encounters with horror cinema.

However, it is important to note here that the notion of being scared by horror (and its relation to the life histories of horror fans and audiences) has been discussed in conflicting ways in existing scholarship on audiences' past encounters with horror cinema. In 2002, Annette Kuhn devoted a chapter in her groundbreaking study of the memories of 1930s British cinemagoers, *An Everyday Magic*, to an illuminating analysis of these cinemagoers' childhood memories of watching horror and being frightened (in a pleasurable way) at the pictures. Strikingly, Kuhn here noted, in her discursive analysis, that the 'primacy of anecdotal discourse' in these memories was 'in marked contrast to informants' memory-talk in general' (2002: 76). As she outlines:

> Memory-talk about frightening films . . . embodies a highly distinctive mix of contents and discursive registers, typically taking the form of strong anecdotal accounts of isolated scenes or images in films and of narrators' responses to these. This is in marked contrast with cinema memory in general, in which such vividly detailed anecdotes are most unusual, and it suggests there is something culturally distinctive about the 'distress and delight' of cinema terrors. It certainly suggests that the fear element has a particularly strong purchase in the individual psyche and the collective imagination. (Kuhn 2002: 80)

In 1996, David Buckingham talked to children about their emotional responses to viewing horror films as part of his wider project/book *Moving Images: Understanding Children's Emotional Responses to Television*. While these were contemporary responses from children at the time the research took place (rather than adult memories of past childhood responses), this research uncovered some key aspects of childhood viewing habits relating to horror media, including the notion of being scared by horror as a frequently pleasurable experience. In 2011, I noted, in my analysis of the aforementioned online fan reminiscences of first encounters with *The Evil Dead*, that the film had stood out for these fans because it had 'scared the hell' out of them (cited in Egan 2011: 45) and, for many, had led to nightmares and sleepless nights. Furthermore, many of these fans also noted that this fear and fright had never gone away and that the film continued to scare them when they watched it in the present day.

These findings are in marked contrast to Matt Hills's illuminating analysis of horror fan practices in his 2005 book *The Pleasures of Horror*, where he focuses on the dominant discourses in published or online fan discussions of the pleasures of watching horror, including fan reflections on their first encounters with horror. Here, in accounts which include journalist and well-known horror fan Mark Kermode's overview of his own history of horror fandom, Hills notes that there is a consistent discursive 'privileging' of 'knowledge over affect', with horror fans online presenting themselves as 'unafraid' and 'master[ing] their beloved horror texts through repeated viewing and aesthetic study' and accumulation of genre knowledge (ibid.: 75). As Hills argues, for fans like Kermode, 'horror fans are divided from non-fans, since the latter group lack detailed information about any horror film they see, and are simply "scared by it, then wander . . . out of the cinema and back into the mundanity of their everyday lives"' (Kermode 2001, cited in Hills 2005: 74; see also Jancovich 2000 for a similar discursive analysis of these kinds of horror fan distinctions online). Furthermore, for Hills, such fans also ward off 'the culturally feminizing spectre of horror as fear provoking' (2005: 77) by presenting their initial childhood encounters with horror as initiating an intense, romantic fascination with horror, rather than predominantly inducing fear. For him, this 'micro-narrative' of romantic intensity is then 'fixed', by these fans, 'as a childhood experience' distinct from the 'tutored', 'cool knowledgeability' of the adult horror fan (ibid.: 78, 83, 77–8).

These fan accounts thus present a picture of the 'real' or 'true' horror fan whose responses to horror (and the pleasures they find in horror) are at odds with the notion of pleasurable scares and their impact, as recounted and explored in Kuhn's, Buckingham's and my own previous research on horror audiences. Indeed, and as illustrated in Kermode's comment about non-fans who are scared by a horror film and then 'wander . . . out of the cinema and back into the mundanity of their everyday lives', it is noteworthy that this distinction is compounded not only by the fact that 'the act of being scared is [here] predominantly located on the side of non-fandom (or casual horror film viewing)' but also that, for non-fans, their affective responses to horror are presented as 'passing scares' that do not have a lasting effect or stay with these audiences in any way (Hills 2005: 74; Kermode 2001, cited in Hills 2005: 75). There are two key factors that, arguably, inform this disparity. Firstly, there is the wider issue of shifting and changing culturally informed distinctions between horror fans and non-horror fans. Hills acknowledges clearly in his work that the written fan accounts and online fan postings that he analyses need to be approached 'as a specific textual production of fan identity, one that is aimed at a readership assumed to be made up of other horror fans' and which, with the marked emphasis on fan knowledge and connoisseurship, are clearly informed by the need to 'ward[. . .] off the taint of "pathologized" horror fandom' (2005: 78) that might associate them with the passive, vulnerable or suspect image of the horror audience frequently evoked in public moral panics around horror media such as, in particular, the 'video nasties' controversies of the early 1980s and 1990s (see Barker 1984; Petley 2001; Egan 2007). As Hill argues, this clearly informs many of the distinctions being made in these fan accounts in the early to mid-2000s. Indeed, this argument is strengthened by the fact that Kermode's piece was written for Barker and Petley's landmark book, *Ill Effects*, which is focused on the scholarly critique of media moral panics and the 'effects' logic, and attendant conceptions of the corrupted or vulnerable media audience which sustains them. Consequently, Hills is primarily interested, in his analysis, in the performativity of such accounts and their discursive value for these fans, a performativity which often excludes or omits the experiences of other kinds of horror fans. This includes fans who do not consistently participate in online communities focused around horror and/or, as Brigid Cherry's research has illustrated, female audiences who have watched and loved horror since childhood and consider themselves horror fans but who have historically been low participators in what she terms 'traditionally organized fandom' (2002: 42).

Secondly, Hills's valuable acknowledgement of the agendas that shape the life narratives recounted by horror fans online also raises the question of how other methods of generating and gathering audience memories of horror might impact on these recounted narratives, including online quali-quantitative questionnaires (as employed in the 'Remembering *Alien*' project) or face-to-face interviews or focus groups (as employed in Kuhn's, Buckingham's and Smith's research). Both Kuhn and Daniela Treveri Gennari et al. have centrally addressed the important role played by interaction in these latter forms of memory gathering, where the production of memory stories about the respondents' past film consumption is 'a dialogic process' with 'the researcher' acting 'as midwife to the informant's stories' (Kuhn 2002: 8). In acknowledging that *all* audience talk (whether online, in written and published form, in response to a quali-quantitative questionnaire, or produced during an interview or focus group) is constructed and performed within a particular social situation, a key question I therefore wish to consider, for the remainder of the chapter, is how horror fans might articulate and outline their childhood memories of horror fandom in an alternative context from the online fan forums explored by Hills – namely, within a face-to-face, semi-structured interview conducted by one male and one female researcher.

These two issues centrally informed the planning of a wider, ongoing practice-based project that I have been conducting, since March 2019, with my co-researcher, Jamie Terrill. The primary aim of this project was to make a film, *Horror Film Events and Their Audiences*, about audience practices at horror film events (particularly in relation to gender and generation), with the aim that the finished film would function as a valuable educational resource for universities teaching horror cinema, genre cinema and media audiences. To date and prior to the 2020 and 2021 periods of Covid-19 lockdown in the UK, the project has focused on one particular case study, Dirt in the Gate Movies, held regularly at the Shelley Theatre, Bournemouth. Dirt in the Gate Movies is run by the husband and wife team Darren and Ruby Payne, and specialises in 35mm film exhibition. Their first screening of *Re-Animator* (1985) in April 2015 was, at that point, a one-off to raise funds for a local charity at the then newly reopened and partially restored Shelley Theatre (which was originally built in 1866 as a private theatre belonging to Sir Percy Florence Shelley, son of the poet Percy Bysshe Shelley and novelist Mary Shelley). However, Darren and Ruby were so bowled over by the fact that the event sold out, and encouraged by the enthusiasm and feedback of the audience at the event, that they soon moved on to host regular 35mm screenings at the theatre, installing brand new 35mm projectors from Italy and operating under the banner of Dirt in the Gate Movies. Up until March 2020, Dirt in the Gate had held over sixty individual film screenings including three popular annual Grindfest festivals (running over a day or more) in September 2017, 2018 and 2019.

While Dirt in the Gate's primary aim has been to champion 35mm and keep it in the public eye, the majority of their screenings have been horror films, predominantly from the 1970s and 1980s. This is firstly because, as Darren and Ruby noted in an interview for our film project, Darren – who has worked as a film projectionist for many years – is a long-term horror film fan who was brought up on horror from the age of five or six when he used to lace up his father's 8mm projector with classic horror films like *Bride of Frankenstein* (1935). And, secondly and crucially, because, from the first screening of *Re-Animator* onwards, Darren and Ruby registered that the horror films they showed (as opposed to the romantic comedies, musicals and dramas they have also screened) seemed to be what their most loyal audiences wanted, with Ruby noting that their repeat attendees come back primarily for the horror films and are far more interactive and communal than the audiences that have attended their non-horror film screenings. Crucially, Ruby, who has consistently talked and interacted with these attendees during these screenings, also noted that those who come regularly had given her the impression that the screened horror films 'were the films they saw growing up as children and teenagers' and that it seemed 'like there's a nostalgic element for a lot of older audiences' (Darren and Ruby Payne, Interview, 16/3/19). Further to this, Darren and Ruby both noted in this initial interview that, particularly compared with much larger horror-related events, the gender make-up of the audience was much more balanced, and it became clear, as we conducted further research, that these events were seen, by many regular attendees, as being much easier to attend for local people with children or work responsibilities than London-based horror events like Frightfest. Indeed, this is the primary reason why we ultimately chose to focus, in depth, on the Dirt in the Gate events as the first case study for our wider film project, as, informed by our engagement with scholarship on horror audiences to date, we were particularly concerned, through our project, to explore and research potentially more hidden, less publicly visible kinds of horror audiences than the kinds associated with what Cherry terms 'traditionally organized fandom'.

Informed by these concerns, as well as the key observations made about regular attendees and their childhood horror consumption in our initial project interview with Darren and Ruby, we constructed the following schedule for our interviews with regular Dirt in the Gate audience members, with Question 3 included in order to purposefully assess the importance of being scared to their engagement with horror:

1. How long have you been attending the Dirt in the Gate events?
    i. How did you hear about them?
    ii. What attracted you to them?
2. Many of the events focus on horror films. To what extent was that part of the appeal of the screenings for you?
    i. Why is horror particularly appealing to you?
    ii. Are there specific films that represent that appeal for you, particularly well?
3. Do horror films scare you? Do you remember being scared by particular horror films at any point?
4. What is the earliest horror film that you can remember watching?
5. Who do you tend to watch horror films with, now or in the past?
    i. Are there any horror films that you tend to watch repeatedly, or that you've watched a lot?
6. Have there been particular Dirt in the Gate screenings that you've particularly enjoyed, or that were particularly memorable?
7. It's often assumed that horror fans tend to be male. What are your views on this argument?
    i. In your experience, is this reflected in the audience for the Dirt in the Gate screenings?
8. What are your views, generally, on horror film culture in the UK? Do you ever attend other horror film events or festivals?
    i. How do they compare to Dirt in the Gate?

Employing this schedule as a guide, to ensure consistency across our semi-structured interviews, we have, to date, conducted filmed interviews (of approximately twenty minutes in duration) with twelve regular Dirt in the Gate attendees, in a private room in the Shelley Theatre before and after Dirt in the Gate film screenings in March, April and September 2019. Disappointingly, and despite our consistent, active encouragement of female attendees to come forward and take part and the fact that the balance between genders was strikingly evident at each Dirt in the Gate event we attended, the interviews so far have predominantly been with male attendees (ten men and two women) but we will continue to proactively encourage more female regulars to participate when we can safely return to the Shelley Theatre to conduct further research in the near future. Ten of these interviewees were aged between 40 and 55, while two (Alice and Harry) were in their twenties but all twelve outlined, in the interview context, the ways in which the horror focus of these screenings related to their engagement with and consumption of horror in the domestic context during their childhood.[1] The next section of the chapter will therefore map out some of the key trends I have identified across the Dirt in the Gate interviews that we have conducted to date, in order to consider how they might relate to, build on or challenge existing scholarship on horror audiences and their childhood memories of horror. Towards the end of the chapter, I will also illustrate how some of these findings correlate with memories recounted by respondents to the 'Remembering *Alien*' project questionnaire.

Childhood Memories of Horror at Dirt in the Gate

Chiming with the arguments of Barker et al., members of the family were seen to play key roles in many of these memories of early encounters with horror. This is evident, for instance, in the responses below:

> IRIS: My mum really used to like horror, she'd get really twitchy and stuff . . . as a family we made a bit of an event around horror films when they were on TV . . . I saw with my mum a pirate copy of *Evil Dead* in one of her friend's caravans in the middle of a wood. It was kind of a big event. (Interview, 13/4/19)

> NIGEL: We lived in a block of flats, and one of the guys who lived in one of the other flats gave my dad a bunch of videos to watch and they were mostly horror films – *House* was one, *Fright Night*, *The Blob*, *Aliens*, *Return of the Living Dead*. There were loads of them and I sort of made my way through them, I was probably around eight or nine. (Interview, 20/9/19)

> MIKE: The first horror film I remember watching was *Killer Clowns from Outer Space*. My Uncle Gary is a very bad influence on me. I was probably about five, six and he was like 'let's watch this' and I remember my mum going 'what are you watching', 'oh it's a film about clowns', and my mum was like 'that's a horror film, you can't watch that' and then she watched it and she was laughing. It's just a really weird film. (Interview, 21/9/19)

As Barker et al. acknowledge in *Alien Audiences*, a key role of family members in such childhood memories is as gatekeepers enabling access to these films, considering that many respondents were significantly underage at the time. However, as indicated by the quotations from Iris's and Mike's interviews above, family members can also function in these memories as fellow travellers rather than gatekeepers, experiencing these films alongside their children rather than just introducing them to these films or enabling access to them. With this in mind, also of note is how performative Mike's memory of this event is (in recounting what his mother said in reaction, as she discovered him watching the film). This chimes with our findings in *Alien Audiences* where these 'performative memories' often suggested the intensified significance of these memories because of the fact that they involved family members (Barker et al. 2016: 73).

In *Alien Audiences*, we related this observation, about intensified family memories, to David B. Pillemer's summarisation of the oft-employed concept, within memory studies, of a 'personal event memory' which, for him, has the following features:

> (1) it is a memory of 'a *specific* event that took place at a particular time and place'; (2) the person can provide a '*detailed* account of the rememberer's *own personal circumstances* at the time of the event'; (3) the memory has '*sensory images*, including visual, auditory, olfactory images or bodily sensations, that contribute to the feeling of "reexperiencing" or "reliving"' the event; (4) 'memory details and sensory images correspond to a particular *moment* or moments of phenomenal experience'. (Pillemer, cited in Staiger 2005: 188, italics in original)

As Janet Staiger notes, in her overview of work on personal event memories, if the event remembered 'provoked an emotional reaction, that also increases its impact' (2005: 189), which chimes with Kuhn's earlier-cited argument about the 'vividly detailed anecdotes' that, in her research, characterised '[m]emory-talk about frightening films'.

The utility and applicability of the concept of personal event memories, when analysing memories of childhood encounters with horror films, should be evident from Pillemer's summary. However, while Barker, Phillips, Ralph and I explored this applicability in our *Alien Audiences* book, we there primarily related this conception of the sensory nature of personal event memories to audience memories which recalled the sensory aspects of *Alien*, the film under discussion (its memorable sights, sounds, etc.). I would argue that this conception of the sensory aspect of personal event memories is also applicable to memories associated with feeling scared, either during the viewing of the film or afterwards, particularly at night in bed, where, as David Buckingham notes, 'the coping strategies that are available at the point of viewing no longer apply in the darkness and isolation of one's bedroom' (1996: 105). This focus on post-viewing reactions is evident in these memories from Dirt in the Gate interviewees:

> MATT: I went round a friend's house and watched it because I wasn't allowed to watch it. I was quite young and I think it was *Blood on Satan's Claw* and that was kind of quite creepy and I found that genuinely scary to the point where I got up in the night and wanted to go to the loo but I couldn't because I was too scared to go out of the room . . . it had that effect, of thinking what's out there . . . I would have been ten or eleven something like that . . . I suppose that kind of hooked me in. (Interview, 21/9/19)

> HARRY: The earliest film I remember watching was probably *Halloween Resurrection*. It was being screened on TV. I wasn't really big into horror when I was a kid so I just sat down and watched it. My mum said you can watch it with me but, if you have nightmares, that's your own fault, you take responsibility for it. So me being a kid, I thought it's not going to scare me. Looking back on it now, it's not a very good film, one of the weaker *Halloween* sequels. But at the time I was terrified. I had to go to sleep with the night light on. I had my mum take me in and show me that everything was OK. What an experience. (Interview, 20/9/19)

In *An Everyday Magic*, Kuhn notes that some of the respondents' memories of being frightened by horror films were 'so uncommonly vivid and detailed' that it sometimes seemed 'as if, in the process of narrating them', respondents were 'accessing the "child's voice" within themselves and reliving the experience of being scared out of their wits' (2002: 66–7). While Matt's and Harry's memories above illustrate that they are recounting their feelings of terror or fear in the past rather than present tense (and are thus not accessing 'the child's voice' in the way Kuhn describes), they still here give a detailed account of the personal circumstances that led up to this moment of fear and convey the intensity of this phenomenal experience (note, for instance, Matt's comment that 'I found that genuinely scary to the point where I got up in the night . . .'). Furthermore, through the employment of the past tense when recalling this experience, they are able to recount it vividly but also reflect on its autobiographical significance from the present day – evident in their comments 'I suppose that kind of hooked me in' and 'what an experience', which convey the, at least in retrospect, pleasurable aspects of these seemingly traumatising experiences.

In terms of '"reexperiencing" or "reliving"' this 'personal event memory', and nostalgically reflecting on it, three of the Dirt in the Gate interviewees also outlined how that initial experience of being scared had fixed itself to these films in their subsequent viewings of them or, in the last case, to their subsequent encounters with horror films more broadly. As they note:

> NATHAN: Even though I'm older, when I watch *Gremlins*, there's still this little thing . . . I'm not scared but I remember how scared I felt when I was six so that was one of the first . . . You get shocked and you get unsettled. I don't think I've been properly scared by a horror film since . . . maybe when I saw *The Ring* was the last time I was actually scared by a horror film. It's the weird thing about horror, that the scare is somehow enjoyable, you like being scared by it . . . It was quite nice watching *Alien* with my nephew because there's a few moments that still make me jump even now and it was kind of fun watching my nephew jumping during it and scared during it. Being scared when you're in a moment of safety. (Interview, 21/9/19)

> KARL: Certain films I like I'll keep upgrading them. *Halloween* is an example. I brought it on VHS, DVD, Blu-ray, 4K . . . there's got to be a sense of nostalgia there. I think that's what I'm holding on to some degree . . . I remember where I was when I saw it and I remember how I felt when I was watching it and even now I'm feeling a bit goosey because I've got that association. I could watch it here, I could probably watch it in some church town hall, I'd still feel the same and that's because it's the power of that film, it's triggering these reflexes, these memories in me. (Interview, 20/9/19)

> HARRY: Part of the appeal is chasing the scare because generally it's only about one out of a hundred horror films that will scare me but it's finding that one in a million that is able to affect you on a deeper level. Where you have to go to bed with the lights turned on in the next room. I love when a film can make me feel something. You might think about and appreciate what it's trying to say but when you're affected on a deeper level . . . it's always chasing the next one. (Interview, 20/9/19)

What is evident in all these examples, then, is the way in which these scares (what they felt like and the consequences of them, e.g. nightmares, sleepless nights, leaving the light on, making them feel something) are returned to and nostalgically reflected upon when these interviewees recall their viewing history with a particular film or their history of viewing horror in general. What is evident in Nathan's and Karl's accounts, in particular, are the ways in which the films under discussion – *Gremlins* (1984) in Nathan's case and *Halloween* (1978) in Karl's – are presented as what Barbara Klinger has termed, in her work on repeat viewing, 'autobiographical landmarks that represent points of orientation to the past as well as to the present' (2006: 174–5). So, while Nathan might not feel as scared when he re-watches *Gremlins* as an adult, the memory of how scared he felt when he watched the film as a six-year-old is still drawn and reflected upon and informs his response to the film on each viewing, making his orientation to the film, in Klinger's terms, 'highly personalized' (ibid.: 174) and informed by what Harrington and Bielby (2010) term 'autobiographical reasoning'. For Harrington and Bielby, 'autobiographical reasoning' conveys 'continuity in the self over time', and 'personality coherence from infancy to adulthood' (ibid.), and I would argue that this is clearly evident in all three accounts above. From Nathan's invoking, on repeat views, of the sensory experience of first watching *Gremlins* as a six-year-old on repeat views, to Karl's statement that *Halloween* always triggers memories of first watching it whenever and wherever he views the film, to Harry's identification of his early experiences of 'feel[ing] something' when watching horror films as a qualitative measure for his ongoing encounters with the genre and the continued appeal of such encounters. Indeed, such past- and present-facing accounts are very much at odds with the online horror fans discussed by Hills who were seen to enact a 'discursive distancination' (2005: 77) from their initial childhood encounters with horror, in order to foreground their primary identity as knowledgeable, literate adult fans.

Also referred to in two of the Dirt in the Gate interviews was a key aspect of encountering horror as a child in the domestic sphere, which is also explored in relation to *The Exorcist* in Martin Ian Smith's chapter in this volume – memories of partial viewings of a particular horror film, either because the child only heard the film and did not see it (or vice versa), or because they only managed to watch parts of the film due to being too scared to watch the whole thing. As these interviewees note:

> NIGEL: *The Shining* was one, it went on for five minutes and then had to go off, it was awful. So a lot of these films I only watched bits of. (Interview, 20/9/19)

> NATHAN: I remember when I was probably about ten or eleven, my sister was watching *Alien* and I think it was on after my bedtime anyway

but I crept down after they thought I'd gone to bed and I was listening outside the door and just hearing the sound of it. I remember at the time thinking this sounds like the absolute scariest film ever. (Interview, 21/9/19)

As Martin Ian Smith astutely argues, this illustrates 'the malleability of the home as a viewing environment' (2019: 140), in that, unlike with cinema viewing, horror films screened on television or played on the VCR could be turned off when they got too much for the child viewer, or could at least be partially consumed (even if only heard, not watched) by those children indulging in what was termed, in the *Alien Audiences* book, 'sneaky viewing', that is, viewing of horror films which has not been sanctioned by the child's parents (Barker et al. 2016: 67).

Returning to the 'Remembering *Alien*' project dataset, and in particular to our respondents' memories of their first encounters with *Alien*, revealed to me that these partial, bitty screenings of horror films were more common than was perhaps fully acknowledged in our 2016 book, and that they often occurred within what I would term temporal and/or spatial 'access points'. As illustrated in the case of Nathan's memory, one of these temporal 'access points' was broadly after they were supposed to be in bed, when they could engage in sneaky (albeit partial) viewings of horror films by listening outside the living room door – an experience which, in Nathan's account, clearly enhanced significantly the impact of his first encounter with *Alien*. Another spatial and temporal access point was referred to consistently across a number of audience responses from our 'Remembering *Alien*' project dataset, including in the following examples:

> I first saw it (or most of it) on TV, the first UK showing, late night ITV. I was alone, in my bedroom, watching it on a black and white portable. It was terrifying, and I don't think I saw much of the last half, just heard it all from under the bed covers. [36–45, Male]

> I remember watching it on Channel Four in about 1995 (I was 12 or 13ish). It was well past my bed time and I had to be really close to the TV in my bedroom because I had to keep the volume right down. This wasn't really an issue as I had it muted most of the time anyway. I remember absolute terror when the Chest Buster appeared and had to change channel for about five minutes. But, curiosity got the better of me and I eventually turned back to watch the rest. [26–35, Male]

> Watching it when I was about 12 after I got a TV in my room for the first time. I was not supposed to be watching it and had to keep the volume down and listen for my parents in case they busted me, this only added to

the tension. It was on quite late and although the screen was quite small (14″) I had to sit quite close in case I had to turn it off quickly (in case of an imminent parent bust) . . . Having no clue what was going to happen combined with the small and rubbish screen, low volume and the danger of a parental 'bust' made for a quite terrifying experience. [26–35, Male]

What these memories illustrate is not only the ways in which, as Martin Ian Smith notes, memories of early domestic consumption of horror tend to be shaped by 'the people and practices within' the home (2019: 174), but also the distinct spaces of the home (particularly, as in these examples, childhood and teenage bedrooms), as well as the past technologies within these remembered spaces – including the era-specific technology of the portable bedroom-based television set, whose role in memories of film consumption from the pre-millennial era deserves further research and exploration. Mirroring Nathan's reminiscence of sneaky viewing from his Dirt in the Gate interview, the novel aspects of the viewing experiences recounted above – hearing the film from under the bed covers, watching at close proximity to the TV set, watching the film at low volume or on mute, being poised to change channel – all appear key to the memorability of the experience. This illustrates clearly how what David Buckingham has termed the 'coping strategies' that young viewers employ when watching horror and/or the strategies they employ to engage in 'sneaky viewing', all feed – alongside the involvement of family members and the centrality of sensory/phenomenal experiences within the memory – into the 'strong purchase' (Kuhn 2002: 80) childhood memories of horror have for many audiences who continue to gain pleasure from horror into their adulthood.

Conclusion

In his 2000 article on horror, cultural distinctions and online fandom, Mark Jancovich argued that:

> within certain circles, the very value of watching these films, or at least the value of saying certain things about that viewing experience, is to assert that they do not frighten but only amuse . . . within certain contexts, it would be inappropriate (other than in exceptional circumstances) to admit to being frightened by horror films. (Jancovich 2000: 32)

While extremely important to understandings of horror fan cultures, this dominant conception within, as Jancovich puts it, 'certain circles' and fan 'contexts', of horror fans as primarily distinguished from non-fans by their knowledge and aesthetic appreciation, at the expense of their history of affective experiences of horror, continues to dominate scholarly discussion of horror fandom (see, for instance, the arguments on conceptions of horror fandom in Church 2021). In his 1996 book, Buckingham called for further 'consideration of the *pleasures* that must largely explain why viewers choose to watch horror' (1996: 97, italics in original). This chapter has put forward the argument that, while online investigations of horror fandom have enormous value (and, indeed, I have conducted a number of such investigations myself), confining analysis to just these sites and contexts may limit what can be explored in response to Buckingham's call. With this in mind, the initiation and analysis of reminiscence from horror audiences through quali-quantitative questionnaires, interviews or focus groups may enable other aspects of audience engagement with horror (particularly their history of affective responses to horror and their changing significance and meaning) to be discussed and explored. The emergent patterns from the initial interviews from the 'Horror Film Events and Their Audiences' project – and their consistent occurrence in the datasets of other complementary projects such as 'Remembering *Alien*' and 'Remembering "the scariest movie of all time"' – suggest there is still much to be learned about how the formative experience of being scared in the home might inform the life histories of a wider range of horror film audiences, and their continued investment and emotional engagement in this perennially popular genre.

Note

1. All Dirt in the Gate Interviewees have been anonymised, aside from the Dirt in the Gate Movies organisers, Darren and Ruby Payne.

Bibliography

Barker, Martin (1984) 'Nasty Politics or Video Nasties?', in Martin Barker (ed.), *The Video Nasties: Freedom and Censorship in the Media*. London: Pluto Press, pp. 7–38.
Barker, Martin, Kate Egan, Tom Phillips and Sarah Ralph (2016) *Alien Audiences: Remembering and Evaluating a Classic Movie*. Basingstoke: Palgrave Macmillan.
Buckingham, David (1996) *Moving Images: Understanding Children's Emotional Responses to Television*. Manchester: Manchester University Press.
Cherry, Brigid (2002) 'Screaming for Release: Femininity and Horror Film Fandom in Britain', in Steve Chibnall and Julian Petley (eds), *British Horror Cinema*. London: Routledge, pp. 42–57.
Church, David (2021) *Post-Horror: Art, Genre, and Cultural Elevation*. Edinburgh: Edinburgh University Press.
Egan, Kate (2007) *Trash or Treasure?: Censorship and the Changing Meanings of the Video Nasties*. Manchester: Manchester University Press.
Egan, Kate (2011) *The Evil Dead*. New York: Columbia University Press.

Harrington, C. Lee and Denise D. Bielby (2010) 'Autobiographical Reasoning in Long-Term Fandom', *Transformative Works and Cultures* 5. <http://dx.doi.org/10.3983/twc.2010.0209> (last accessed 20 May 2021).

Hills, Matt (2005) *The Pleasures of Horror*. London: Continuum.

Jancovich, Mark (2000) '"A Real Shocker": Authenticity, Genre and the Struggle for Distinction', *Continuum: Journal of Media and Cultural Studies* 14(1), 23–35.

Kermode, Mark (2001) 'I Was a Teenage Horror Fan: Or, "How I Learned to Stop Worrying and Love Linda Blair"', in Martin Barker and Julian Petley (eds), *Ill Effects: The Media/Violence Debate*, 2nd edn. London: Routledge, pp. 126–34.

Klinger, Barbara (2006) *Beyond the Multiplex: Cinema, New Technologies, and the Home*. Berkeley: University of California Press.

Kuhn, Annette (2002) *An Everyday Magic: Cinema and Cultural Memory*. London: I. B. Tauris.

Kuhn, Annette, Daniel Biltereyst and Philippe Meers (2017) 'Memories of Cinemagoing and Film Experience: An Introduction', *Memory Studies* 10(1), 3–16.

Petley, Julian (2001) 'Us and Them', in Martin Barker and Julian Petley (eds), *Ill Effects: The Media/Violence Debate*, 2nd edn. London: Routledge, pp. 170–85.

Smith, Martin Ian (2019) 'Remembering "the scariest movie of all time": A Grounded Audience Study of *The Exorcist*'. Doctoral thesis, Northumbria University.

Staiger, Janet (2005) *Media Reception Studies*. New York: New York University Press.

Treveri Gennari, Daniela, Catherine O'Rawe, Danielle Hipkins, Silvia Dibeltulo and Sarah Culhane (2020) *Italian Cinema Audiences: Histories and Memories of Cinema-Going in Post-war Italy*. New York: Bloomsbury.

INDEX

Note: *italic* page numbers indicate figures; n indicates note

After Office Hours, 161
Ahmed, Aisha, 176–7
Alf's Button, 138
Alien, 203, 212, 233, 234–6
   'Remembering *Alien*' project, 227, 230, 235, 237
Allen, Robert, 1, 203
Altenloh, Emilie, 20
Amelan, Tessa, 40
Anderson, Benedict, 88
Andreotti, Giulio, 200n11
Antonello, Daniela, 192
archives
   Brazil: German immigrants, 87
   Cohen, John, 179
   digital, 3
   Harry Sanders Archive, Bradford, 146–8, 163–4; diaries, 149, 150, 153–4, 156, 158, 161; ledgers, 125, 127; letter, 149, *150*; notebook designs, 155, *155*; playbill, *159*; programme design, *152*; promotional 'wheeze', *153*
   Italy, 186–8, 189
   primary source documents, 7
Argentina *see* Buenos Aires
Arts and Humanities Research Council (AHRC), 2
As You Like It, 135
audience studies, 18–22
   grounded, 204–5
   and participants, 220
   sources, 19–20, 28–30
audiences, 23
   behaviour, 129, 162
   and censorship, 205–6
   child, 20–1, 22, 98, 130, 132, 175–6, 192–3, 195–6, 206; parental regulation, 11, 207–8, 209–16, 218–20, 231, 235
   and cult films, 206–7
   and emotions, 102, 103–4, 105, 162
   enjoyment of, 140

239

audiences (*cont.*)
  and films, 203–4; horror, 229–36
  and gender, 125
  photographs of, 29
  reactions to violence, 206, 217–18
  sociology and, 2
  television, Italy *see under* television
auditoria
  comfort of, 162
  as emotional spaces, 105–7
Aveyard, Karina, 6

Barker, Martin, 204, 206, 211–12, 217–18
Barker, Martin and Petley, Julian (eds): *Ill Effects*, 227
Barker, Martin et al.: *Alien Audiences*, 223, 231, 232, 235
Bartholomew, Freddie, 160
Battle of the Somme, The, 141n5
Bauer, Ela, 69
Bedales School: *Sixth Form Opinion* (magazine), 168
Belgium
  Never Trust a Woman in, 23, 26, 27
  Wets 1920 enquiry, 21
Bernstein, Sidney, 134, 137
Beyfuß, Edgar, 89
Bielby, Denise D., 234
Big Cage, The, 136–7
'Big Society', 53, 58
Biltereyst, Daniel, 2, 5; *see also* Kuhn, Annette et al.
Birmingham: Cinephone, 175
Birmingham Centre for Contemporary Cultural Studies, 34, 35
Birmingham Evening Mail, 176
Birmingham Post, 175
Black Torment, The, 178
Blackburn, 141n14
Blank, Thais, 97
Blood on Satan's Claw, 232

Blu-ray, 51
Blue Moon, 135
Bolton: Beehive Picture House, 130–1, 138, 150, 152
Bourdon, Jérôme, 19, 20, 190
Bournemouth *see* Dirt in the Gate Movies
Brazil
  Brazilian Society of Film and Audiovisual Studies (Sociedade Brasileira de Estudos de Cinema e Audiovisual) (SOCINE), 99n2
  Faulhaber Foundation (Faulhaber Stiftung), 98
  German-Brazilian Cultural Film Service (Deutsch-Brasilianischer Kulturfilmdienst (DKD), 89, 90, 93, 98
  German Cultural Films, 7, 86–99; audiences, 88–9, 96–7; screenings, 89–94
  German cultural propaganda, 94–8
  immigrants, 98–9; archive, 87; German, 86, 88, 93–4
  National Association of German-Brazilian Teachers (L.D.L.), 90–3, 94, 95, 98; exhibition (1936), 92
  Nazism, 93–4, 97–8
  and the transnational, 86, 88–9
  travelling cinemas, 98
  voluntary associations, 87–8
  see also Rio de Janeiro; São Paulo
Brief Encounter, 115
Bristol: King's cinema, 125, 131, 150–1, 158, 159, 161
Bristol Times and Reporter, The, 159
British Board of Film Censors (BBFC) (later Classification (BBFC)), 127, 128, 167, 170, 171, 205, 208–9

British Federation of Film Societies
(BFFS) (later Cinema For All)
and Community Cinemas, 51
*Forming and Running a Film
Society* guides, 55
mission statement, 53
records, 54
British Film Institute (BFI):
Neighbourhood Cinema scheme,
58
British Medical Association, 168,
172
Brothers Under the Skin, 152
Buckingham, David, 206, 207, 211,
213, 225, 232, 236
Buenos Aires: German Cultural Films,
76
Burgin, Victor, 39, 40–1
Burke, Peter, 104–5
Burton, Alan, 124, 126, 137,
139

Cambrian News, 157–8
Camille, 150–1
Camus, Albert, 17–18
Canton Girl, 158
Carreras, Ernesto, 150
Carreras, James, 150
Casetti, Francesco, 186
Cat and the Canary, The, 160–1
Cattini, Irene, 192, 194
censorship, 10–11, 179, 205–7
and anti-fandom, 210
and audiences, 205–6
Exorcist, The, 10, 205, 206,
207, 215
Italy, 200n11, 206
local, 128–9
meaning of, 216–20
motives for, 209–10
'New Wave' films, 141n13
and parental regulation, 207–8,
209–16

Poland, 70
regulators *see* British Board of Film
Censors; United States: Motion
Picture Association of America
young people and, 129, 211
see also morality
Chapman, James, 1
Cheetham, Arthur, 148
Cherry, Brigid, 227
Chibnall, Steve, 124, 126, 137, 139
Chickering, Roger, 88
child actors, 171; *see also*
Bartholomew, Freddie
children
as audiences, 20–1, 22, 98, 130,
132, 175–6, 192–3, 195–6
clubs for, 130, 160
emotional development, 174
identity development, 218–19
memories of cinemagoing, 44,
141n14
memories of films, 41–2, 43
memories of horror films, 223–37;
The Exorcist, 206, 207–8, 218,
219, 223
and parental regulation, 11, 207–8,
209–16, 218–20, 231, 235
and sexuality, 168–9
Children's Film Foundation (CFF),
160
Chile: German Cultural Films, 76
cinema/cinemas
Asian, 206
and choice, 126–7
Community, 6, 49–59; first- and
second-wave compared, 52, 55;
and social inclusion, 52–3, 57;
volunteers, 52, 53, 56–8; *see also*
film societies
and education, 132, 133
and exploitation, 9, 178–9
emotion in, 114–16; gendered,
111–14

INDEX

cinema/cinemas (*cont.*)
  and film, 17
  grassroots, 54
  models, 27–8
  multiscreen, 162
  music in, 159–60
  national, 88–9, 99
  neighbourhood, 58
  New Cinema History, 19, 69, 103, 124, 203–4, 224
  and respectability, 127–8
  societal role, 18
  Sunday opening, 154–5
  'super', 151
  ticket prices, 157
  travelling, 76, 98
  see also film
Cinema, The (magazine), 137, 138, 151
cinema clubs
  adult, 167
  junior, 130
  see also film societies
'Cinema Culture in 1930s Britain' study (CCINTB), 2, 3, 5, 34, 35, 38, 40, 42, 43, 44
Cinema For All, 53, 58; *see also* British Federation of Film Societies
Cinema Management (journal), 126–7, 129
cinema managers
  and audience morality, 129–30
  and censorship, 128–9
  and charitable fundraising, 130–1
  and choice of films, 132, 133–4
  lives, 157
  marketing strategies, 8–9
  publicity campaigns, 123–4, 126–7, 132–3, 135–41
  role, 124–5
  see also Sanders, Harry

cinemagoing
  experience of, 22–8
  memories of, 35–9, 46, 141n14, 224; children, 44, 141n14
  see also filmgoing
Cinematograph Exhibitors' Association, 131
Cleland, Sir Charles, 133
Cockshott, Gerald, 55
Cohen, John, 176, 179
Cohen, Stanley, 2
Compton-Cameo, 168
Compton Film Distributors, 168
Compton Films, 167, 179
Compton-Tekli, 168, 170–1
conferences
  Aberystwyth University: Researching Past Cinema Audiences conference, 2018, 4
  Glasgow: Screen Studies Conference, 1996, 36–7
Cook, Hera, 113
Crash, 206
Cressey, Paul, 21, 22–3, 27
critics, 162
Czar of Broadway, 158

DVDs, 51
Daily Cinema (trade paper), 178
Daily Mail, 206
Daily Mirror, 168
Damaged Goods, 132–3
Davies, Terence, 43
de Certeau, Michel, 57
De Rita, Lidia, 186
Dead of Night, 161
deCordova, Richard, 20
Degl'Innocenti, Massimo, 193
Deutsch, Oscar, 131
Devil Dogs of the Air, 137
Dibeltulo, Silvia, 206
Dirt in the Gate Movies, 11, 228–31, 232

Dixon, Thomas, 115

Eco, Umberto, 187–8
Economic and Social Research Council (ESRC), 2
Egan, Kate, 11, 207, 212, 219, 223–4, 227–8; *see also* Barker, Martin et al.
Eley, Geoff, 87–8
Elsaesser, Thomas, 1
emotions
  audiences, 102–4, 105–16, 162
  development of, 174
  expression of, 105, 114
  and history, 104–6
  regimes and refuges, 115
Erikson, Erik, 218
Evil Dead, The, 224, 225–6, 230
Exorcist, The, 203–4
  censorship of, 10, 205, 206, 207, 215
  children's memories of, 206, 207–8, 218, 219, 223
  grounded audience studies of, 204
  parental regulation of, 207–8, 210–16, 218, 219–20
  reactions to, 204, 224, 234

fans
  cult films, 206–7
  horror films, 224, 225–7, 228, 236–7
Farmer, Richard, 139, 141n9
Faust, 151
Fields, Gracie, 159–60
film and films
  animation, German, 96, 97
  arthouse, 166–7
  audiences and, 17, 203–4; and memory, 39–44
  certification of, 167, 172, 174, 178
  and cinema, 17
  cult, 206–7
  educational, 132, 133, 167
  exhibition of, 124
  German language: Brazil *see under* Brazil; Chile, 76; *see also Man's Heart, A; Never Trust a Woman*
  home viewing of, 9–11; *see also* television, Italian
  horror: children and, 209–10; fans, 224, 225–7, 228, 236–7; home viewing of, 11, 211–13, 214, 215, 216–17, 223–4, 230–6; 'Horror Film Events and Their Audiences' project, 227–8, 236–7
  Jewish, 68, 70
  marketing strategies *see* cinema managers: publicity campaigns
  New Film History, 1–2, 5
  'New Wave', 140
  nudist, 167, 168
  open-air screenings of, 28
  popularity statistics, 134–5
  promotion of, 123–4; *see also* cinema managers: publicity campaigns
  silent, 162
  technologies, 51
  see also cinema
film distributors, 168
film societies, 51, 52
  audiences, 55
  directions for running, 55–6
  goals, 52–3, 55–6
  Grantham: King's School Film Society, 163
  see also British Federation of Film Societies; cinema clubs; Cinema For All
Film Weekly (magazine), 134–5
Film4, 51
filmgoing, 36; *see also* cinemagoing
Finegold, Leonard, 43
Fireman, The, 150

INDEX

Fish, Stanley, 204–5
Fisher, Robert, 149
Five of a Kind, 161
For Heaven's Sake, 158
Ford, Derek, 169
Ford, Donald, 169
Four Sons, The, 42
Francis, Martin, 112
Fraser, Nancy, 87
Freud, Sigmund, 40
Friday the 13th, 210
Fuhrmann, Wolfgang, 7
Fuller-Seeley, Kathryn H., 124

GIS (geographic information system), 7, 69–70; *see also* QGIS
Galewski, Józef, 70–1
Gardner, Caron, 178
Garofalo, Damiano, 10
gender
  and audiences, 125, 152–3, 230
  and emotion, 111–14
  and television, 188–9, 190, 198
  see also men; women
geographic information systems
  see GIS; QGIS
German language films
  Brazil *see under* Brazil
  Chile, 76
  see also Man's Heart, A; Never Trust a Woman; Tag von Potsdam, Der
Germany
  audience analysis, 20
  cultural propaganda, 94–5
  German Association for Image Use (Deutsche Bildspielbund), 89–90
  Illustrierte Film-Kurier (magazine), 24
  newsreels, 97
  voluntary associations, 88
Gertz, René, 93
Glancy, Mark, 1
Gomery, Douglas, 1

Gone With the Wind, 203
Gould, Sir Ronald, 172
Granada cinema chain, 134, 157, 158; *see also under* Grantham
Granada Newsletter, 158, 163
Grantham
  King's School Film Society, 163
  State (later Granada) cinema, 125, 153–4, 156, 163; café, 159; charitable fundraising, 131; children's club, 130; musical entertainment, 159–60; promotional material, 158–9, *159*; publicity campaigns, 124, 158, 161; ticket prices, 157
Gray, Jonathan, 187
Great Dictator, The, 163
Greatest Show on Earth, The, 123–4
Green, Pamela, 168
Gremlins, 233, 234
Guba, Egon G., 56
Gurney, Peter, 116n4

Habermas, Jürgen, 87
Halloween, 233, 234
Halloween 4, 209
Halloween Resurrection, 232
Hamilton, Carrie, 106–7
Hammer films, 150
Harcourt, Harry, 130
Harper, Sue, 1, 148
Harrington, C. Lee, 234
Harrisson, Tom, 103
Hartford-Davis, Robert, 168, 170, 173, 174
Hendrykowska, Małgorzata, 71–5
Henry V, 132
Higson, Andrew, 88–9
Hilbury, F., 136–7
Hill, Annette, 206, 218
Hills, Matt, 226–7, 234
Hindenburg, Paul von, 94
Hinton, James, 103

Historical Journal of Film, Radio and Television, 148
History of Moviegoing, Exhibition and Reception Network (HoMER), 69, 124, 224
Hitler, Adolf, 94
Hochman, Aleksander, 71
HoMER *see* History of Moviegoing, Exhibition and Reception Network
Hungry for Love (Adua e la compagne), 167

imagination, 20, 25
 collective, 225
 imagined communities, 88–9, 97, 98
 Magritte and, 29–30
 and memory, 37–8
 power of, 29
 and social behaviour, 22, 23, 27, 30
 sources of, 28–30
internet, 51
interviews
 as a research source, 19
 responses to, 217
Isle of Levant, 179n1
Italian language films, 167
Italy
 archives, 186–8, 189; diaries, 191–4
 censorship, 200n11, 206
 'CineRicordi', 3
 Corriere d'Informazione (newspaper), 191
 Famiglia Cristiana (magazine), 195–6, 200
 RAI, 186, 187–8, 189, 191, 196
 radio, 196, 197
 television: audiences, 10, 185–200; ownership, 190–1; programmes, 191, 192–3
 Vie Nuove (magazine), 195, 196–7, 200

Jacey group, 175
Jailbirds, 161
James, Robert, 8–9, 148–9
James, William, 114
Jancovich, Mark, 236
Jasielski, Aleksander, 71
Jewish films, 66, 68, 70, 80
Jewish studies, 68, 69, 70
Jews, Polish
 as audiences, 68–9, 72, 75, 80, 81
 and film making, 66, 68, 70–1
 Warsaw, 71–2, 74–5, 76, 78–80
 see also Yiddish language
Jones, James, 7–8
Jones, Janie, 1814n34

Kermode, Mark, 226, 227
Kid, The, 43, 149
Killer Clowns from Outer Space, 231
Kimberly, Lord, 170–1
Kinematograph Weekly (Kine Weekly), 123, 130, 132–3, 135, 136, 139, 158
King Kong, 43
Kletonic, Jeffrey, 69
Klinger, Barbara, 6, 30, 148, 234
Klinger, Michael, 167, 168, 170, 174, 177, 179
Kosche, Walther, 90–1
Krzemiński, Antoni, 71
Kuhn, Annette
 on censorship, 205, 206, 208
 on cinema as a public space, 106
 on cinema experience, 105, 227
 and 'cinema memory' studies, 203
 on horror film viewing, 225, 232
 see also 'Cinema Culture in 1930s Britain' study
Kuhn, Annette et al., 55

Labour Party, 52
Lanaro, Silvio, 199
Last House on the Left, 220

Lee, Hermione, 147, 148
Leeds: Odeon cinema, 133
Lejman, Szymon, 80
Letter, The, 152–3, *153*
life stories, 190, 199
life-writing, 147, 148
Lilienfeld, Maurycy, 80
Lincoln, Yvonna S., 56
Łódź, 68
London
    Balham Picture House, 137, 150, 158
    Cinephone, Oxford Street, 176–7, *176*
    Compton Cinema Club, 167
    Lido, Islington, 151, *152*, 153, 160, 161, 162–3
London Gazette, 164n2
London in the Raw, 177, 178
Lotz, Amanda, 187
Love Burglar, 158
Love in Our Time, 179
Love on the Dole, 162

MacDonald, Norman, 43
MacDonald, Richard, 54
Mademoiselle Strip-tease, 167
Madge, Charles, 103
magazines
    as a research source, 19, 194–8
    women's, 188
Magritte, René, 29–30
Malaspina, Luciano, 196
Maltby, Richard, 1, 103
Man's Heart, A, 135
mapping *see* GIS; QGIS
Martine, Gaynor, 171, 180n21
Mass Observation, 7–8, 102–16
    and history of emotions, 103–6
    purpose, 103
    research methods, 103–4, 105–6, 115
    volunteers, 103

Massani, Giampaolo, 192–3
Massey, Doreen, 69–70
Mayer, Jacob-Peter, 21
Mazdon, Lucy, 166
Meers, Philippe *see* Kuhn, Annette et al.
memories
    of cinemagoing, 3, 35–9, 46, 224; children, 44, 141n14
    cultural, 10, 34
    horror films, 11
    implanted, 43
    reclamation of, 106–7
    repetitive, 45
    and research, 179
    and television, 189, 192–3
    topographical, 37–8
memory studies, 203
    and experience of film, 224–5
    and grounded audience studies, 205
    personal event memories, 231–2, 233
Memory Studies (journal), 224
memory texts, 41
men
    and censorship, 212
    and emotions, 112–13
    and television, 189
Men Like These (*Trapped in a Submarine*), 137
Metropolis, 158
Mexico: open-air screenings, 28
Miller, Glenn, 159
Mitchell, Marion, 177
Mitchell, Valerie, 177
Mitchum, Robert, 177
Molisak, Alina, 70
Montaldi, Danilo, 199
Monthly Pictorial, The, 123
Monty Python, 212, 219
Moores, Shaun, 189

morality, 132, 140
  British Medical Association and, 168
  campaigns, 127–8
  Italian television, 195–6
  National Council of Public Morals, 129
  Public Morality Council, 128
  teenagers, 169, 176
  see also censorship
Mr Flotsam and Mr Jetsam, 151
Muggeridge, Malcolm, 128
Müller, Karl Otto, 88, 91
Mummy, The, 41, 42
Münsterberg, Hugo, 20
Murders in the Rue Morgue, 161
My Fatherland, Minha patria, 95–6
Mystery of the Wax Museum, The, 161

Naked – As Nature Intended, 168
Nanook of the North, 160
National Council for the Unmarried Mother and Child, 172
National Union of Teachers, 172
Nazario, Luiz, 93
Nazism, 93–4, 97–8
Neely, Sarah, 3
Netherlands *see Never Trust a Woman*
Never Trust a Woman (*Ich glaub' nie mehr an eine Frau*), 5, 23–7, 25; Amsterdam: Tuschinski film theatre advertising, 26; *Illustrierte Film-Kurier* cover, *24*; promotional newsreel, 24, 25, 29
No Orchids for Miss Blandish, 128

Odeon cinema chain, 131, 133, 153
oral histories, 55
  and emotions, 106–7
  as a research source, 19, 28–9, 45
  and television, 189–91
O'Regan, Tom, 51

Paradise for Two, 137
Participations (journal), 4
Payne, Darren, 228
Payne, Ruby, 228
Payne Fund, 21, 22
Pember, W. L., 157
Penati, Cecilia, 10, 189–90
Penrhyndeudraeth, 149, 156
Peterborough
  City Picture House, 136, 137
  Princes Theatre, 134
Petley, Julian, 227
Pett, Emma, 206–7
Phillips, Tom *see* Barker, Martin et al.
Pictures and the Picturegoer (magazine), 131, 134
Pillemer, David B., 231
playbills, 158–9, *159*, 162
Pleasure Girls, The, 173
Plymouth
  censorship, 132
  morality, 129
  Tivoli Picture House, 130, 132
Poland
  communist, 66, 70
  film industry, 65–81; (1908–14), 71–5; (1918–39), 75–80
  GIS mapping, 7, 69
  Jewish audiences, 68–9
  Jewish films, 68, 70
  Polish Federation of Digital Libraries (FBC), 71
  Polish language, 71, 72, 78, 80
  press, 71
  QGIS mapping, 72, 78, 81
  travelling cinemas, 76
  Yiddish language, 66, 68, 70, 72, 78, 80, 81
  see also Łódź; Warsaw
POPSTAT, 2
Portelli, Alessandro, 45

INDEX

Portsmouth
  censorship, 128–9
  cinema ledgers, 148
  Commodore cinema, 132, 137
  Gaiety Cinema, 136
  'Junior Cinema Clubs', 130
posters, 136, 139, 154, *154*, 158, 161
Potsdam Day, The see *Tag von Potsdam, Der*
Private Property, 167
Prokop-Janiec, Eugenia, 70
Pryt, Karina, 7
Public Morality Council, 128
public sphere, 72, 80, 87–8
Puwar, Nirmal, 45

QGIS (quantum geographic information system), 72, 78, 81
questionnaires, 35, 103, 134

Ralph, Sarah *see* Barker, Martin et al.
Re-Animator, 228
Reckless Lady, The, 125
Reddy, William, 104, 115
Reed, Patrick, 132–3, 137, 138–9
Reichmann, Max, *25*; *see also Never Trust a Woman*
research
  creativity in, 4–6
  ethnographic, 19, 35
  materials for, 125
  methodologies, 1–3; British Community Cinema, 54–8; Italian television, 199; Mass Observation, 103–4, 105–6, 115; Polish film, 68–71
  objects and outcomes, 6
  see also audience studies
researchers, 6, 56
revisionism, historiographical, 1, 3–4
Richards, Helen, 106, 107
Richards, Jeffrey, 2, 107
Ring, The, 151–2, *152*

Rio de Janeiro: German language films, 92, 98
Rodrigues de Moraes, Olga, 93
Rolfe, Malte, 72
Rosenwein, Barbara, 104, 114
Russia
  film production, 73
  Kine Zhurnal (journal), 74
  Sine Fono (journal), 72
Ryder, H. C., 136, 137, 138–9

Sabotage, 102
Samson of the Circus, 138, 157, 158
Sanders, Harry, 8–9, 146–64
  accolades, 158
  archive materials, 146–8, 155–61, 163–4; campaign poster, *154*; diaries, 149, 150, 153–4, 156, 158, 161; ledgers, 125, 127; letter, *150*; notebook designs, *155*; playbills, 158–9, *159*; programme design, *152*; promotional 'wheeze', *153*
  awards, 136, 151, 157
  charitable fundraising, 131
  and children's clubs, 160
  chronology, 148–59
  and film promotion, 123, 125–6, 127, 130, 134, 137, 150–2, 154–5, 158
  marketing strategies, 160–1
  memories of, 163
  philosophy of cinemagoing, 161–3
  praise for, 138
  programme magazines, 158
São Paulo
  Association of German Teachers in São Paulo (Deutscher Lehrerverein São Paulo), 89–90
  German School (Olinda School), 89, 95, 97; exhibition (1936), *92*
  Martius-Staden Institute archive, 87
Saturday Night and Sunday Morning, 141n13
Saturday Night Out, 178
Scaglioni, Massimo, 186

Schaefer, Eric, 168, 173
Scotland: Committee of Church and Nation, 128
Screen, The (journal), 126, 127, 131, 132, 133, 135
Sedgwick, John, 2
Sentimental Journey, 113
sex and sexuality
  censorship, 128; see also *Yellow Teddybears, The*
  cinema model, 28
  education, 132–3, 168, 174, 175
  sex/altruism binary, 9, 167, 174, 177, 178, 179
  women and, 116n4
Sex, Love and Marriage, 179
Shail, Robert, 8–9
Sheikh, The, 149
Shining, The, 234
Shmeruk, Chone, 70
Shoulder Arms, 138
showmen, travelling, 71, 124, 148
Sight and Sound (magazine), 156
Silber, Marcos, 70
Silence of the Lambs, 209
Silent Dust, 114
Singin' in the Rain, 43
singing, community, 130, 159
Smeaton, Helen, 42
Smith, Adam, 9
Smith, Martin Ian, 10–11, 224, 235, 236
Smith, Sarah, 207–8, 211, 212–13
Snow White, 43
Soares, Bruno Pinto, 95–6
social class
  and censorship, 129
  and cinema location, 73–4, 78, 81
  cinema's influence on, 162
  and emotions, 113, 115
  and equality, 52
  and inclusion, 53
  and Mass Observation volunteers, 103
  and oral history, 45
  and taste, 135
  and television, Italy, 191–4
Spanish Passions, 159
Stacey, Jackie, 34, 35
Staiger, Janet, 231
Stearns, Peter, 104
Steckiewicz, Martyna, 68
Street, Sarah, 6, 148
Striptease de Paris (Mademoiselle Strip-tease), 167
Study in Terror, A, 178
Summer Holiday, 161
Sweet Kitty Bellairs, 135
Szczepanik, Petr, 2

Tag von Potsdam, Der/The Potsdam Day, 94
Tales of Beatrix Potter, 163
Tartan (distributor), 206, 207
Tauber, Richard, 24, 24, 25, 26–7
taxi-dance halls, 30n4
Taylor, Helen, 34, 35
television, Italian, 10
  audiences, 185–7
  and gender, 188–9, 190, 198
  magazine readers' columns, 194–8, 199–200
  'paleo-television', 187–8, 191
  and popular culture, 188–9
  social dimension of, 194
television studies, 186
Tenser, Tony, 167, 168, 170, 176, 178, 179
Terrill, Jamie, 124, 148, 227–8
Terror of Dr. Hichcock, The, 178
Texas Chain Saw Massacre, The, 210
That Kind of Girl, 168
Thin Man, The, 161
Thissen, Judith, 50, 70
Tigon (production company), 179
Times, The, 168
Topaz Film Corporation, 178
Trade Show Critic, The (trade paper), 138, 158

Tramp, Tramp, Tramp, 136, 138, 151, 161
transnational, the, 99
  Brazil, 86, 88–9
  Warsaw, 65, 66, 67, 75–6
Trapped in a Submarine, 137
Travelling Light, 167
Treat 'Em Rough (Brothers Under the Skin), 152
Trevelyan, John, 170, 172, 173, 174, 176
Treveri Gennari, Daniela, 206, 227
True Heart Susie, 150

Union Cinemas, 153
United States
  film audience analysis, 20–1
  Motion Picture Association of America (MPAA), 205, 208–9, 210
  publicity campaigns, 124
Universal Exploiteer (trade paper), 138
Universal Pictures, 158

Vélez-Serna, María, 148
videos (VCRs), 51, 211, 235
voluntary associations, Brazil, 87–8
volunteers, Mass Observation, 103

Walkden: Palace cinema, 150
Warsaw, 65–7
  cinemas, 72–80, 81; audiences (1908–39), 76; ethnic context, 74, 75, 78, 79; location and categorisation of (1911), 72–5, 73, 77; public sphere of, 80; size, 76, 78
  film production, 66, 67, 71–5
  Jewish community, 66, 68, 71, 72, 74–5, 76, 78–80, 81
  public sphere, 72, 80
  theatres, 72
  'third space' of, 70, 72, 81

and the transnational, 65, 66, 67, 75–6
World War II, 67, 70
Way of all Flesh, The, 153
Weegee, 29
Western Evening Herald, 129
Wheatley, Catherine, 166
Whitehouse, Mary, 128
Whiteley, Annette, 171, 173, 174, 179
Why Change Your Husband, 135
Williams, Raymond, 27
women
  and censorship, 211–12
  as Community Cinema volunteers, 57
  and emotions, 112, 113–14
  as filmgoers, 34
  and horror films, 230
  and sexuality, 116n4
  and television, Italy, 188–9, 198
Woodruff, William, 141n14
World War I, Britain, 131
World War II
  Britain, 131, 139
  Poland, 7, 67, 70
Wright, Annie, 41–2

Yellow Teddybears, The, 9, 166
  certification, 172, 174
  cuts to scenes, 173–4
  premiere, 173, 176, 177
  promotional imagery, 173
  reactions to, 168–9, 172, 175–6, 178
  script, 169–70, 172
  sex/altruism binary, 174, 177, 178
  soundtrack, 173
  title, 170–1
Yiddish language, 66, 68, 70, 72, 78, 80, 81
young people: and censorship, 129, 211; *see also* children

Zimmermann, Clemens, 50

EU representative:
Easy Access System Europe
Mustamäe tee 50, 10621 Tallinn, Estonia
Gpsr.requests@easproject.com

www.ingramcontent.com/pod-product-compliance
Lightning Source LLC
Chambersburg PA
CBHW071834230426
43671CB00012B/1959